the Indianapolis 500
A COMPLETE PICTORIAL HISTORY

the Indianapolis 500

A COMPLETE PICTORIAL HISTORY

JOHN and BARBARA DEVANEY

Rand McNally & Company
Chicago • New York • San Francisco

Acknowledgments

In beginning our research for this book, our first call was to the Indianapolis Motor Speedway. The Speedway's able director of publicity, Vice President Albert S. Bloemker, was generous in providing information and access to photographs. Charlene Ellis, the enthusiastic manager of the Speedway's photo bureau, patiently directed us through thousands of old photos. We are also indebted to W. B. de Meza, director of public information for the Goodyear Tire and Rubber Company, for his assistance in obtaining art and color photos, and to the public relations staff at the Firestone Tire and Rubber Company.

Of great help in locating former "500" mechanics and drivers was Bob Laycock, executive secretary of the Indianapolis 500 Old-Timers Club. Since many former drivers and mechanics were dead, we went back to old newspapers and magazines for some interview material.

Many books on the "500" were insightful, notably *500 Miles to Go* by Al Bloemker; *Famous Indianapolis Cars and Drivers* and *The Indianapolis 500* by Brock Yates; and Lyle Engel's *Indianapolis 500: The World's Most Exciting Auto Race*.

We are indebted to the reporting of men like Bill Corum of the *New York Journal-American;* Frank Blunk and John S. Radosta of the *New York Times;* and *Sports Illustrated*'s Kenneth Rudeen, Bob Ottum, and Robert F. Jones. Also invaluable were the weekly reports on auto racing by Ray Marquette in *The Sporting News* and the *500-Mile Race Record Book,* edited by Bill Pittman and published each year by the *Indianapolis News*. We are also grateful to Pete Sansone and Marty Stern of United Press International. And last but not least our thanks to John Matthew Devaney, Jr., for checking the Top Ten statistics.

Photo Credits

Authors' Collection: 25 t., 33 t.l., 34, 36 t.r., 39, 40, 44 t., 47, 49, 53 r., 56 t., 57 b., 59, 60 t., 61, 64 t., 65, 66 b., 69 t., 71 b., 77 l., b., 86 t., 91 b., 95 b., 101 t., 104 r., 109 b., 113 t., 117 t., 118, 126, 130 b., 134, 135 b., 136, 148 b., 150, 152, 215 b., 235, 238

John and Barbara Devaney: 9 b., 278, 279, 282

Firestone News Service: 28 t., 94, 95 t.

Goodyear Tire and Rubber Company: 272–273

Indianapolis Motor Speedway: 2–3, 6–7, 8, 9 t., 10, 11, 13, 14, 15, 16, 17, 19, 20, 21, 22, 24, 25 b., 26, 28 b., 29, 30, 32, 33 t.r., b., 36 t.l., b., 37, 41, 43, 44 b., 45, 48, 51, 52, 53 l., 55, 56 b., 57 t., 60 b., 62, 64 b., 66 t., 67, 69 b., 70, 71 t., 73, 74, 75, 77 t.r., 79, 80, 82, 83, 85, 86 c., b., 87, 88, 90, 91 t., 93, 96, 97, 99, 100, 101 b., 102, 104 l., 105, 107, 108, 109 t., 110, 112, 113 b., 114, 115, 117 b., 119, 121, 122, 123, 125, 127, 129, 130 t., 131, 135 t., 137, 138, 140–141, 143, 144, 145, 149, 153, 154, 156, 157, 158, 159, 160, 162–163, 166, 167, 168, 169, 171, 172, 173, 174, 176 t., c., 177, 178, 180 t., 181, 182–183, 186, 187, 189, 190, 191, 194, 195, 196, 198, 199, 202, 206–207, 208, 209, 210, 212, 213, 215 t., 216, 217, 220, 221 b., 222, 223, 224, 226–227, 230, 231, 232 t., 234, 239, 242, 243, 245, 247, 250, 251, 254, 255, 257 t., 259, 261, 262, 264, 265, 266, 267, 269, 270, 274, 275, 277, 280, 281

United Press International: 132, 147, 148 t., 165, 176 b., 180 b., 184, 193, 200, 203, 205, 219, 221 t., 229, 232 b., 237, 240, 246, 248, 252, 257 b., 260, 271

Copyright © 1976 by Rand McNally & Company
All rights reserved
Printed in the United States of America
by Rand McNally & Company

ISBN 0-528-81844-9

First printing, 1976

Library of Congress Cataloging in Publication Data

Devaney, John.
  The Indianapolis 500.

  Includes index. 1. Indianapolis Speedway Race. 2. Automobile racing—Biography. I. Devaney, Barbara, joint author. II. Title. GV1033.5.I55D47 796.7'2'0680977252   76-23129   ISBN 0-528-81844-9

For Pauline and Neko,
Teeny and Marty

"The Greatest Automobile Race Ever"

"We're talking about the greatest automobile race ever put on anywhere on the face of the earth. Everything connected with it is going to be bigger and better than ever before.... This is going to be the greatest crowd attraction of all time."

Speaking with characteristic optimism was Carl Fisher, co-owner of Prest-O-Lite, an Indianapolis headlight manufacturer. He was also president of the Indianapolis Motor Speedway. In 1908 he had conceived the Speedway as a showcase where the manufacturers of automobiles and accessories could prove that their products were fast and durable. Fisher and his partners spent almost $200,000 to build the Speedway on some 300 acres of farmland located 15 minutes by car from downtown Indianapolis.

The Speedway opened in June, 1909. Two wooden grandstands, with seats for 15,000 spectators, faced a 2.5-mile loop of track. Since the track was not yet ready for car racing, the first event was a balloon race. Auto racing began at the Speedway in August, 1909. The opening event of the three-day program was a 5-mile dash that was won by a Stoddard-Dayton with an average speed of 57 miles an hour. The first day's main event was the 250-mile Prest-O-Lite Trophy

Racers at the Speedway have come a long way since 1910, when an Overland (opposite page, top) used a propeller in a 5-mile race against a plane flying above it. The car, averaging 60 miles an hour, lost by four seconds. Right: A modern Coyote-Foyt could traverse a football field in a second. Its engine, only slightly larger than a Volkswagen's, is turbocharged to exceed 200 miles an hour. Driving the car is Janet Guthrie, proving that more than cars have come a long way.

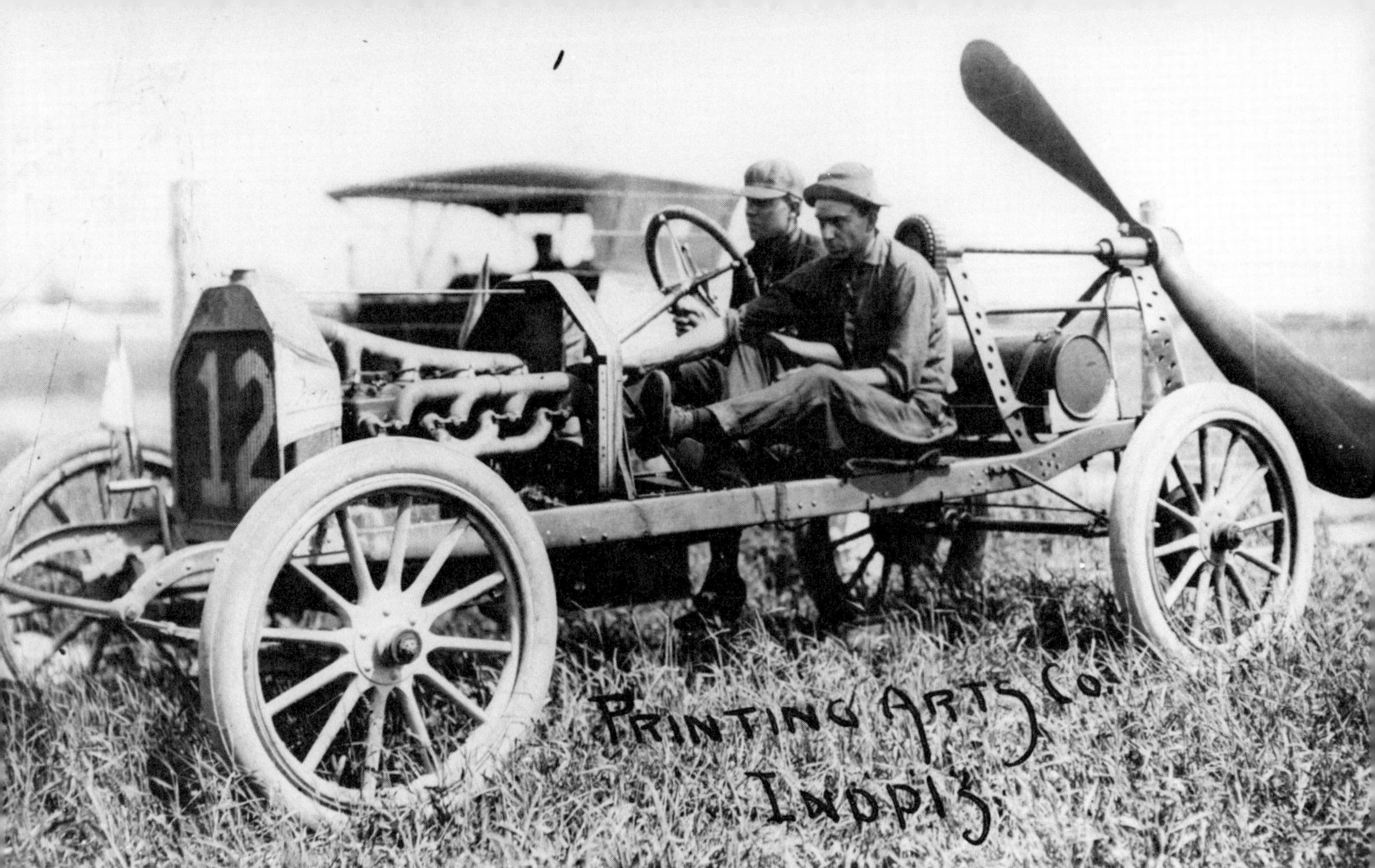
12
PRINTING ARTS CO.
INDPLS.

GILMORE
Racing Team
CHAMPION
GOODYEAR
1
1
PREMIER

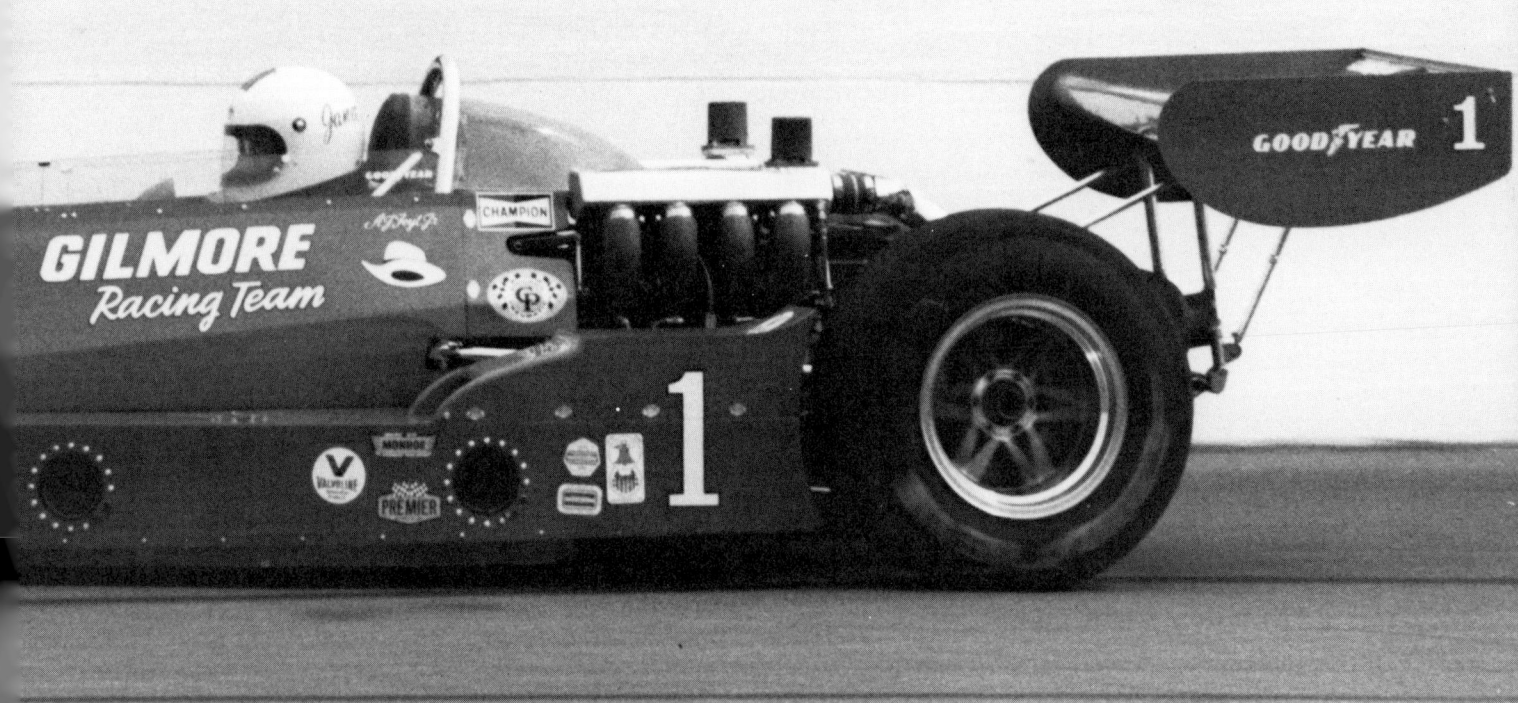

race. The tar-and-gravel track was soon pockmarked by the pounding of the cars' hard wheels. One driver was temporarily blinded when he was struck in the eye by a flying stone. Another driver and his riding mechanic were killed when their car hit a pothole and flipped. The race was won by Bob Burman, whose Buick averaged 53 miles an hour. Hasty track repairs permitted the second day's events—a series of shorter races—to proceed without serious accidents. Then came the climax of the three days of racing: the 300-mile Wheeler-Schebler Trophy race. Drivers ducked and dodged through dust and stones from the disintegrating track. One car plowed into a group of spectators, killing two of them and the car's mechanic. Another car hit a chuckhole and careened off the track. After 235 miles the race had to be halted. An embarrassed Fisher promised a new track.

Only 63 days later, more than 3 million bricks, each weighing ten pounds, had been laid over the old surface. In the setting sun's rays the bricks glowed red; they would give the Speedway a name it has kept—the Brickyard.

In 1910 the Speedway held a series of races on the Memorial Day, July 4, and Labor Day weekends. Crowds dwindled to as few as a thousand spectators. Fisher realized the Speedway had

Top left: The Speedway's first president, Carl Fisher. He and partners Jim Allison, Frank Wheeler, and Arthur Newby, Indianapolis businessmen, built the Speedway at a total cost of more than $500,000. Fisher later spent a fortune developing a Florida swamp called Miami Beach. He died in 1939. Opposite page, top: Speedway president Anton (Tony) Hulman delivers the traditional starting command: "Gentlemen, start your engines." Below and right: The main gate in 1909 and today. Now, as then, the Speedway won't disclose exactly how many fans go through its gates.

to provide "something different" from the usual programs offered by the speedways and dirt tracks that had popped up across the Midwest. He decided on one super race—a mammoth 500-mile grind over the bricks, the equivalent of a trip from Indianapolis to Washington, D.C. The race would be long enough to give those who paid the $1 general admission their money's worth, said Fisher, but would end before dusk. And the purse would be the biggest ever for an auto race: $25,000 would go to the top ten finishers, with $10,000—what most Americans earned in ten years—to be paid to the winner.

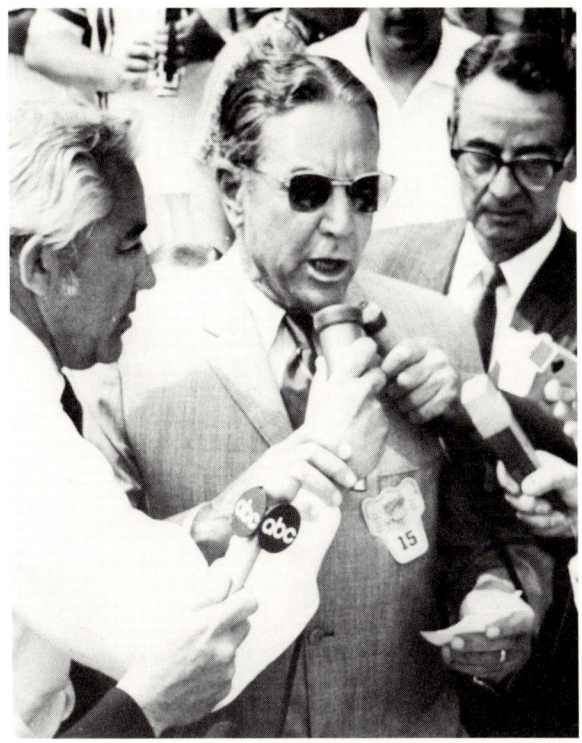

Today the race still claims to offer the biggest prize in sport—more than a million dollars. Most of the bricks have been glossed over with asphalt. Towering steel-and-concrete grandstands now look down on the starting line. Attendance at practice days, the two weekends of qualifying, and then the race—what has come to be called "Thirty Days of Indy"—totals close to a million. The Indianapolis 500 has outlived 500-mile races at other speedways and is still the most famous auto race in the United States. "There's only one Indianapolis," says A. J. Foyt, winner of three "500s." "It pays the biggest purse, it pulls the most drivers, and it's the biggest challenge of them all."

Driving a car at the Indy 500 has been described as a sensation akin to flying a jet past a row of trees, with three or four other jets at your nose and tail. The cars boom down the 3,300-foot straights at better than 200 miles an hour, streaking toward one of Indy's terrifying left-handed turns. As the cars swerve out of the banked turns, they swing frighteningly close to onrushing walls that can dismember a car with one metal-screeching kiss. In the 1960s drivers still eased off their throttles through most of the turns; but now drivers "stand on it" through two or even three turns. An extra mile an hour through the four turns—purchased with a nerve-testing brush of those deadly walls—can mean victory and a first prize of a quarter of a million dollars.

Today's fiberglass, winged creatures look no more like the steel boxes of the first "500" than a mosquito resembles a wheelbarrow. Most of

Below: An aerial view of the Speedway, looking north, taken in the 1960s. Each straightaway is five eighths of a mile long, each short "chute" an eighth of a mile, each turn a quarter of a mile. Counterclockwise from lower left, the turns are the southwest (No. 1) turn, southeast (No. 2), northeast (No. 3), and northwest (No. 4). Opposite page, top: The seven-foot-high Wheeler-Schebler Trophy; until 1932 it was awarded each year to the leader at the race's 400-mile point. Bottom: The four-foot-high Borg-Warner Trophy, valued at $75,000, bears the image of each winner since 1911 and has been the official "500" winning trophy since 1936.

the early engines were huge 600 cubic-inchers that produced about 200 horsepower, compared to the nearly 1,000 horsepower of today's turbocharged 160-inch engines. The driver of today reclines in a form-fitting cockpit; the early driver sat atop a hot, banging engine, his body bruised by the jarring ride on hard springs and wire-spoked wheels.

The track today is officially the same size as it was in 1909: 50 feet wide on the straightaways, 60 feet on the turns. But the turns are wider because there are no inside walls as there were in the early days. Today a driver can swerve out of trouble onto an apron or the infield grass. In 1911, with the turns like alleys, newspapers predicted blood and carnage for the first "500," as 40 cars banged around the oval. Perhaps knowing why some people come to an auto race—to see sudden death—Fisher predicted: "We're going to have the biggest damn crowd anyone in the country has ever seen." That prophecy was confirmed by the *New York Times,* which called the crowd at the 1912 race the "largest ever to attend a sporting event in America." Today's attendance—estimated at more than 300,000 on race day—is triple the crowd at a Super Bowl or Kentucky Derby and more than the total attendance at all the games of many World Series. It is still the largest attendance for any single day's sports event in the United States.

For the first "500"—on Memorial Day of 1911—some 80,000 people streamed to Indianapolis by train, car, and horse and buggy, jamming roads around the Speedway. They filled the wooden grandstands breasting the front straightaway and lined the infield fence. There were greying men who had fought at Gettysburg and younger men who had dashed up San Juan Hill with Teddy Roosevelt. Like millions of men and women in a mostly rural America, they were fascinated by those sputtering automobiles, the speedy new machines that could catapult them beyond the horizon that had penned them in for most of their lives.

They were equally fascinated by the daredevils who drove these machines—national idols like brash Barney Oldfield, the bronze-faced Ralph DePalma, and that unsmiling man in the pointy-tailed yellow Wasp, the one they called the Bedouin . . .

1911

A Wasp's Last Flight

The Bedouin snapped the goggles atop his leather helmet. He swept his eyes over the gleaming metal boxes lined up in front of him. The cars sat on the track in eight rows, five cars in a row. From the cockpit of his yellow Marmon, in the sixth row, the Bedouin could see David Bruce-Brown, a wealthy sportsman, in his maroon Fiat, and Spencer Wishart, another rich daredevil, in a grey Mercedes that had cost over $60,000.

The white Lozier beside him drew the Bedouin's longest looks. Behind the wheel was Ralph Mulford, considered to be the best road racer in America. But the best at spinning around tracks was the Bedouin. In his yellow Marmon he had won the previous year's Wheeler-Schebler 200-mile race and the 1910 American Automobile Association driving championship.

The Bedouin was Ray Harroun (the nickname came because of his Arabian ancestry), a 29-year-old engineer with a somber, no-nonsense manner. When he wasn't driving, he designed cars and engines for the Marmon company here in Indianapolis. He'd designed and built this yellow Marmon, called the Wasp by newspapers. Now—though he had retired from driving at the end of the 1910 season—Harroun had been persuaded by Howard Marmon to drive the Wasp in the new Indianapolis 500-mile race.

All the other cars in the race were two-seaters, hippy enough to carry a driver and a mechanic (who watched instruments and kept an eye on traffic coming from behind). Harroun's Wasp was sculpted long and narrow, the cockpit flared, its tail pointed, and it was a single-seater. Harroun figured the mechanic was only extra weight. Before the race other drivers had objected that Harroun's Wasp was a hazard because he couldn't see behind him. Threatened with disqualification, Harroun had bolted a mirror onto the front of the cockpit. He had given the Wasp—and automobiling—the first rearview mirror.

Cool gusts of wind scattered spectators' straw hats as the starting time neared. Nearly 80,000 fans had pushed and shoved through the Speedway gates since they had swung open at 6:30 A.M. About 50,000 people filled the four grandstands that breasted the straightaway, and the other 30,000 lined the railing on the infield. At exactly 10 o'clock an aerial bomb exploded. Mechanics whirled starting cranks, and black smoke ballooned as the thunder of 40 engines filled the air.

Led by Speedway owner Carl Fisher in a pace car, the cars swung toward the south turn, wrapped in a black cloud. They circled the track at 40 miles an hour in the tight eight-row formation. Dots loomed larger as the cars appeared out of the north turn at the top of the straightaway. Their distant buzz became a bellow as they sped by the stands in a flying start. The pace car swerved aside, the starter snapped the flag, and the first "500" had begun.

A big blue National, driven by Johnny Aitken, charged out of the front row and into the lead. Close behind was Ralph DePalma, one of the nation's most famous drivers, in a red Simplex. These two whirled around the oval at better than 80 miles an hour, only a couple of seconds apart.

The Bedouin hung back at a restrained 75

Cars in the front row puff smoke as the gentlemen start their engines for the first "500." Note right-hand steering wheels. At right is timers' stand. Electric devices registered the exact instant tires hit a wire laid across the track.

miles an hour. "I could open it up to 80," he had told Howard Marmon before the race, "but we're giving away more than a hundred inches to some of the others. We don't have their speed. But I think an average of 75 miles an hour will win this race. The bigger cars will probably try to run wide open all the way. If they do, they'll be spending a lot more time changing tires than I will." At 80 miles an hour, he had found, the hard-rubber tires were torn apart by the bricks after only a few laps. At 75 miles an hour, however, he could run for as long as two hours without a tire change.

On the 13th lap an Amplex swung out of the No. 2 turn and threw its rear wheels. The car flopped over on its back. The driver was pinned, his mechanic flung against a fence. The driver survived, but the mechanic, his body "horribly mangled," according to newspaper stories, was killed. The "500" had swallowed its first life.

In his maroon Fiat, David Bruce-Brown overtook Aitken and DePalma and stretched out his lead—at one point ahead by 7 miles. But Harroun held the Wasp's speed at 75. Like most of the other drivers, the Bedouin did not try to cover the full 500 miles of bricks himself. Some two hours into the race, he turned the Wasp over to relief driver Cy Patschke. Coming out of the pit in fifth place, Patschke steadily closed on the speedier cars, who were in the pits frequently for tire changes, and gave the Wasp back to Harroun at the 255-mile point in second place, only a mile behind Bruce-Brown's Fiat.

As the Wasp buzzed out to resume the chase, Harroun now at the wheel, the Fiat was swerving into the pit for a wheel repair. Harroun's Wasp popped into the lead, and by the time Bruce-Brown was back on the bricks, Harroun had put a lap between the Wasp and the Fiat. A few laps

Opposite page: The first pace car, a Stoddard-Dayton, whips around a banked turn before the race. Below: Frank Fox's Pope-Hartford goes by the $2.50 grandstand seats; it finished 22d. Bottom: The track maintenance "fleet." During the race crews sprinkled sand on the oily bricks to keep the track from getting too slick, but the sand whipped into drivers' eyes.

later the Fiat pitted again, for new plugs.

Now the Wasp had a new pursuer: the white Lozier, a stock car driven by Ralph Mulford. Running at 80 miles an hour, it was closing on the Wasp at a rate of three seconds a lap. When Harroun had to pit with a blown tire, the Lozier swept ahead. Then the Lozier pitted and the Wasp led. But with some 60 miles still to go, the Lozier whisked by the Wasp to retake the lead.

Harroun watched the Lozier pull away and become a distant, bobbing speck. But he coolly held the Wasp to its 75-mile-an-hour pace. At 80 miles an hour, he told himself, the Lozier would need new rubber before the finish. He was gambling the $10,000 first prize that he was right.

Only 23 laps to go...22.... Harroun saw the Lozier jounce toward the pit. It needed tires —its 14th change of the race, compared to only four for the Wasp.

Two minutes later—"Slow and clumsy work in the pit," wrote one reporter—the Lozier came out almost 2 laps behind the Wasp. Harroun sprinted for the checkered flag and Mulford couldn't close the gap. Harroun shot by the finish almost two minutes ahead to win the first "500."

The race had ended with one man dead and four injured. But as the *New York Sun* put it, "The predicted wholesale killings in the 500-mile auto race didn't come about."

The "500" would go on. And drivers like Ralph DePalma would discover just how bad racing luck can be.

Edward Towers:
Oil in the face

Looking back more than six decades, Edward Towers, who rode as a mechanic with W. H. (Wild Bill) Turner in the first Indy 500, recalled early auto-racing days. *The cars then looked inside much the same as now—a clutch, foot brake, foot throttle—although we also had a throttle on the wheel that you set when you got out to start the car. We had a speedometer and a temperature gauge we watched a lot for overheating. And we had to pump oil during the race. Piston rings weren't what they are now, and at high speeds the cars threw oil out their exhausts into the faces of the guys behind them. We had no windshields then and you sat up pretty high in those bucket seats, so the mechanic had to wipe the oil off the goggles of the driver. When cars got up to 90 miles an hour, oil flew into a lot of faces.*

1911's TOP TEN

Race open to cars with a piston displacement of 600 cubic inches or less.

NO.	DRIVER	CAR	ENGINE	CYL.	BORE	STROKE	PISTON DISPL.	TIME	MPH	WINNINGS*
32	Ray Harroun	Marmon	Marmon	6	4.500	5.000	447.1	6:42:08	74.59	$10,000
33	Ralph Mulford	Lozier	Lozier	4	5.375	6.000	544.6	6:43:51	74.29	5,000
28	David Bruce-Brown	Fiat	Fiat	4	5.000	7.500	589.0	6:52:29	72.73	3,000
11	Spencer Wishart	Mercedes	Mercedes	4	5.100	7.100	580.2	6:52:57	72.65	2,000
31	Joe Dawson	Marmon	Marmon	4	4.500	7.000	445.3	6:54:34	72.34	1,500
2	Ralph DePalma	Simplex	Simplex	4	5.750	5.750	597.2	7:02:02	71.13	1,000
20	Charlie Merz	National	National	4	5.000	5.687	436.8	7:06:20	70.37	800
12	W. H. Turner	Amplex	Amplex	4	5.312	5.000	443.3	7:15:56	68.82	700
15	Fred Belcher	Knox	Knox	6	5.000	4.750	559.1	7:17:09	68.63	600
25	Harry Cobe	Jackson	Jackson	4	5.000	5.500	431.9	7:21:50	67.90	500

* Speedway prizes for winning entries. Total awards in race, $27,550: Speedway prizes, $25,100; accessory prizes, $2,450.

Opposite page: A driver goggled and masked against the oil, sand, dust, and smoke. Left and below: Ray Harroun and the winning Wasp. "Gee, give me something to eat," he said as crowds clamored around him after the race. His winnings included $10,000 from the Speedway plus a few thousand from manufacturers. Harroun retired from driving, and the Wasp never again raced in a "500." Single-seaters were banned from the race, riding mechanics made mandatory. In the race's most harrowing incident, a mechanic fell from his car and into the path of onrushing vehicles. Trying to avoid hitting the man sprawled on the track, one driver lost control of his car. He and his mechanic were hurled through the air. The driver was hospitalized with "a possible skull fracture and nervous shock."

1912

DePalma Walks Home

Empty seats dotted the grandstands. Thousands of spectators streamed past the gates on their way out of the Speedway through the long shadows of the afternoon sun. Behind them they could hear the sonorous buzz of Ralph DePalma's ghostly grey Mercedes as it flew down the straightaway at close to 90 miles an hour. Hunched at the wooden wheel of the Mercedes, his mechanic beside him, DePalma ached from the strain of slamming over 475 miles of bricks without relief. But now he led by nearly 10 miles with 25 miles to go, and thousands had started home, sure he would win this "500" and the first prize of $20,000.

Carl Fisher, delighted by the huge crowd at the race in 1911, had doubled the Speedway prize money—from $25,100 to $50,000. To make the race safer, the field was limited to a maximum of 33 cars. But only 24 qualified in the trials, held on May 27, by running one lap at a minimum of 75 miles an hour. Among the fastest qualifiers was DePalma in his German Mercedes.

Starting positions were determined—as in 1911—by the cars' entry dates, and DePalma was given a front-row spot. Only 10 miles into the race, he caught Teddy Tetzlaff's Fiat and moved into the lead.

Lap by lap he pulled away from the field, its ranks thinned as engines quit and tires blew. Four cars crashed or spun, but no one was seriously hurt. The Mercedes sped through the first 100 miles in an hour and 13 minutes, a new record for an American speedway. Averaging 82 miles an hour, DePalma led 23-year-old Smiling Joe Dawson, an Indianapolis boy in an Indianapolis-made car, a blue National, by more than 10 miles with only 6 laps—15 miles—to go.

The 70,000 fans who had stayed to see the end of the race looked for DePalma's Mercedes to appear at the top of the straightaway of the 195th lap. Other colored dots appeared and sped closer —but no DePalma. "Where's DePalma?" Like a sigh the question swept the stands, and then there was an even stronger surge of excitement when the crowd saw the Mercedes. It was trailing a curling plume of white smoke.

The car had slowed to about 50 miles an hour, and the hammering engine told DePalma what had happened: A connecting rod had snapped and had torn a hole in the crankcase. As he approached the pit area, DePalma knew he could stop, patch the hole, and still finish in the top five or six. But he would lose the big prize.

He decided to go for first on that stammering engine. The car chugged by the pit. Moments later Joe Dawson shot by and stared at the puffing Mercedes. He was 4 laps behind. His crew was waving a blackboard sign at Dawson: "Go."

With the crowd roaring for Dawson on every lap, Smiling Joe went down hard on the throttle. He rushed by the Mercedes twice more to trail by 2 laps. DePalma was nursing the Mercedes gently around the track, but the car had slowed

DePalma (gripping the wheel) and his mechanic, Rupert Jeffkins, push the 2,500-pound Mercedes by the stands, trailed by officials. The *New York Times* called the crowd at this and the previous year's races "the largest number to witness any sports event in the U.S."

to 20 miles an hour. As DePalma approached the homestretch of the 199th lap, the engine, starved for oil, screeched, clanked, and died.

DePalma and his mechanic got out. With the desperation of men not knowing what else to do, they began to push the 2,500-pound machine around the banked turn and down the stretch. The blue National blurred by, completing its 197th lap. DePalma and his mechanic pushed the car into the pits, exhausted; they could go no more. From there they watched Dawson win the second "500," his average speed, 78 miles an hour, some 4 miles an hour faster than Ray Harroun's speed a year earlier.

Dawson won $20,000, DePalma about $380. The driver who pushed his car home would from this day on be the "500's" most famous loser.

DePalma and Dawson: "The game's all luck"

Hard-luck loser Ralph DePalma: *It was just tough luck and that's all. I made the race while I was in it, and I suppose if I had used just a little mule power on the last lap and pushed the car through the 200th lap, I could have gotten in the money for a thousand or so, but life is too short.*

Lucky winner Joe Dawson: *I've been up against the same thing as DePalma. The game's all luck. I just had a feeling I would win and I never had that feeling but once before. That was when I won the Cobe race trophy here in 1910. Today that feeling began to get pretty slim toward the end of this race, but you never can tell until the finish line is crossed.*

1912's TOP TEN

Race open to cars with a piston displacement of 600 cubic inches or less.

NO.	DRIVER	CAR	ENGINE	CYL.	BORE	STROKE	PISTON DISPL.	TIME	MPH	WINNINGS*
8	Joe Dawson	National	National	4	5.000	6.250	490.8	6:21:06	78.72†	$20,000
3	Teddy Tetzlaff	Fiat	Fiat	4	5.000	7.500	589.0	6:31:29	76.60	10,000
21	Hughie Hughes	Mercer	Mercer	4	4.375	5.000	300.7	6:33:09	76.31	5,000
20	Charlie Merz	Stutz	Stutz	4	4.750	5.500	389.9	6:34:40	76.01	3,500
18	Bill Endicott	Schacht	Schacht	4	4.750	5.500	389.9	6:46:28	73.81	3,000
2	Len Zengel	Stutz	Stutz	4	4.750	5.500	389.0	6:50:28	73.09	2,200
14	Johnny Jenkins	White	White	6	4.250	5.750	489.4	6:52:38	72.70	1,500
22	Joe Horan	Lozier	Lozier	4	5.375	6.000	544.6	6:59:38	71.49	1,400
9	Howdy Wilcox	National	National	4	5.000	7.500	589.0	7:11:30	69.52	1,300
19	Ralph Mulford	Knox	Knox	6	4.800	5.500	597.1	8:53:00	56.29	1,200

* Speedway prizes for winning entries. Total awards in race, $55,225; Speedway prizes, $50,000; accessory prizes, $5,225.   † New record.

Opposite page: Cars speed under bridges at the southeast (No. 2) turn. The bridges allowed pedestrians and cars to cross to the infield. Below: The start of the race. Carl Fisher pulls the Stutz pace car off the track (r.) as Gil Anderson, on the pole in No. 1, a Stutz, streaks through smoke and dust to take the lead. Bottom: The finish, as Smiling Joe (r.) takes the checker with a wave. After the race he rode a trolley to the YMCA, lolled in a steam bath to relieve the aches of his bruising ride over the bricks, then sauntered home in the fading light, puffing on a cigar. Dawson drove in only one more "500," in 1914, and finished 25th. He died in 1946.

Fuel is poured into a Mercedes-Knight. It finished fifth. Hotel rooms, "as usual," wrote one reporter, were impossible to find the night before the race. On race day farmers rented parking spaces in their fields.

1913

Castor Oil and Champagne

The blue Peugeot wobbled into the pit, its right rear tire shredded and smoking. The driver, the mustached, 25-year-old Jules Goux, pulled off his goggles. He glanced at Johnny Aitken, the American driver who had volunteered to advise the Frenchman in his first Indianapolis 500. Aitken spoke to an interpreter. "Tell him to keep it below 80 miles an hour this early in the race. Otherwise he's going to be coming back into the pit for new rubber."

The translator spoke. Goux nodded. A year earlier he had driven this car to victory at Le Mans and this year he had set a world record by going 106 miles an hour during a 100-mile run. But he would do as the American said. He snapped out some words in French.

"What did he say?" Aitken asked the interpreter as the Peugeot flew out of the pit. "He told me it's terribly hot on the track," said the interpreter, "and that we must have a bottle or two of chilled wine ready on his next pit stop."

"Forget the wine," growled Aitken. But the interpreter darted toward the stands. What Jules Goux, ace driver and son of the superintendent of the Peugeot factory, wanted, Jules got.

More than 90,000 spectators sweltered in the wooden grandstands or baked in the infield under a raw, white sun. Many had paid from $4 to $12 for tickets. A writer for *Motor Age* magazine estimated Speedway receipts at $250,000 and expenditures at $80,000. The next spring the Speedway would pay a cash dividend to its stockholders.

But there had been problems. Marmon and National, the manufacturers whose cars had won the previous "500s," had withdrawn from racing. Why should they risk their winning reputations in future races? To entice makers who were turning out smaller engines for passenger cars, the Speedway dropped maximum engine size from 600 to 450 cubic inches. And it dangled the handsome prize money before European car builders, who were tinkering with smaller engines. Seven of the 27 cars in this race had come here from Europe.

The two Peugeots from France had an engine, designed by Switzerland's Ernest Henry, that was considered revolutionary: Double overhead camshafts and four inclined valves per cylinder were among its features. American engines got 115 horsepower at 1,800 rpm, while the Peugeot got 160 horsepower at 2,200. It was the granddaddy of the racing engines of the 1970s. As a lubricant the French swore by castor oil—good, they said, for 250 more rpm than any other oil.

The 1913 race was ballyhooed as a confrontation between America's and Europe's racing cars. American drivers conceded that the Peugeots were faster but doubted that the engine could stand up under the wear and tear of 500 miles at sustained high speed. As if determined to prove them wrong, Jules Goux gunned the Peugeot into the lead in the 4th lap; but before long he had to pit after blowing a tire. Heeding Aitken, he slowed to 80 miles an hour and didn't have to pit again until the 150-mile mark. When he did, seven pints of champagne waited for him in an ice bucket. He sluiced two pints down his parched throat, then charged back onto the course.

This year the Speedway had brought back three trophies that were offered in 1909 and 1910 races. Goux led at 200 miles to win the Remy Trophy, at 300 miles to win the Prest-O-Lite, and at 400 miles to take the Wheeler-Schebler.

With 100 miles left in the race and the Frenchman 6 laps ahead (and refreshed by his fourth

23

Above: New stand for press, timers, and judges sits near the start. It replaced the two separate press and judges' stands. Its design gave it its name —the pagoda. Late in a race the bricks glowed blood-red in the sunlight. Right: Goux and the Peugeot, sans "the good wine."

pint of champagne), the crowd began to cheer for Charlie Merz, in an Indianapolis-built Stutz, to finish second. Merz roared into the 200th lap a straightaway ahead of Spencer Wishart's black Mercer. A tongue of orange flame licked out from the hood of the Stutz. Merz could have swerved into the pits, but he knew the stop would cost him second place. He stayed at the wheel of his flaming bomb for the last lap. Smoke and flame engulfed the car and Merz had to slow. Wishart sped by, but Merz clung to the wheel and finished third to tumultuous applause.

Goux's blue Peugeot won by better than 13 minutes. It had coasted the last 100 miles. Joe Dawson's 78-mile-an-hour record of a year earlier was safe, but American pride had been stung by this foreign victory at Indianapolis. A year later it would be stung again—and harder.

Jules Goux: "The good wine"

The first winner to go the 500 miles without a relief driver, Jules Goux told reporters: *We broke all records up to 250 miles. At every stop I say we can do much better time. But the manager refused to let me put the car to its highest speed. We proved the Peugeot could go the full 500 miles, eh? But as for me, without the good wine I would not have been able to win.*

1913's TOP TEN

Race open to cars with a piston displacement of 450 cubic inches or less.

NO.	DRIVER	CAR	ENGINE	CYL.	BORE	STROKE	PISTON DISPL.	TIME	MPH	WINNINGS*
16	Jules Goux	Peugeot	Peugeot	4	4.246	7.875	448.1	6:35:05	75.93	$20,000
22	Spencer Wishart	Mercer	Mercer	4	4.370	5.000	299.0	6:48:13	73.49	10,000
2	Charlie Merz	Stutz	Stutz	4	4.813	5.500	399.9	6:48:49	73.38	5,000
9	Albert Guyot	Sunbeam	Sunbeam	6	3.540	6.290	367.5	7:02:58	70.92	3,500
23	Theodore Pilette	Mercedes-Knight	Knight	4	3.937	5.118	251.3	7:20:13	68.15	3,000
12	Howdy Wilcox	Gray Fox	Pope-Hartford	4	4.750	5.500	389.9	7:23:26	67.65	2,200
29	Ralph Mulford	Mercedes	Mercedes	4	4.489	7.087	448.6	7:28:05	66.95	1,800
31	Louis Disbrow	Case	Case	4	5.100	5.500	449.0	7:29:09	66.80	1,600
35	Willie Haupt	Mason	Duesenberg	4	4.316	6.000	350.5	7:52:35	63.48	1,500
25	George Clark	Tulsa	Tulsa	4	4.752	5.500	340.1	7:56:14	62.99	1,400

* Speedway prizes for winning entries. Total awards in race, $55,875: Speedway prizes, $50,000; accessory prizes, $5,875.

Left: An ad by the McCue Company of Buffalo, New York, pointed out that Goux, Wishart, and 12 other drivers rode wire-wheeled racers. The ad claimed wire wheels were "faster and more resilient" and would "increase the life of your tire wear from 25 to 50 percent." This was one of the first efforts by makers of tires and other automotive products to tie "500" success to safer, better, or more economical motoring for the highway driver. Bottom: Jules Goux (r.) and his mechanic (l.) pose with two visitors from France.

Four ladies watch the race with varying displays of interest. Motorists drove from as far as New York for the race and complained of speed traps. With Indianapolis hotels filled, visitors slept in parks.

1914

"A Bad Day for America"

"Two men in an iron bathtub" was how one writer of the time described racing cars. Of the 30 that lined up for the start of the 1914 race, 12 were challengers from Europe. At the wheel of his blue Peugeot sat Jules Goux, confident that he would win his second "500" in a row. In the one-lap trials—only the 30 fastest cars would start—he had whipped around the oval at 98.13 miles an hour, 10 miles an hour faster than any previous car had ever qualified for the "500." But that record was shattered by another French driver, Georges Boillot, who averaged 99.86 in a Peugeot. Arthur Duray, driving what was dubbed a "baby" Peugeot—the engine had a piston displacement of only 183 cubic inches—buzzed around the course at 90 miles an hour.

America's hopes on this cool, cloudy Memorial Day rode with Barney Oldfield in a Stutz, Joe Dawson in a Marmon, and Eddie Rickenbacker in a Duesenberg (Fred and August Duesenberg had begun building their own cars in a Minnesota shop). With the order of the start determined by a drawing on the eve of the race, not one of the fast French cars was in the first two rows—setting off some Gallic mutterings.

Barney Oldfield ended up in the last row. Seldom seen without a cigar in his mouth, Barney was one of America's most famous drivers. The American Automobile Association, racing's ruling body, often had to suspend the rotund, loud Barney for driving on outlaw tracks against airplanes, horses, and anything else that moved. This was Barney's first "500."

Two of the French drivers, Rene Thomas in a Delage and Duray in the baby Peugeot, shot out of the pack at the start to go by the slower American cars and run one-two, only 22 seconds apart, at the 100-mile mark.

In a clump of cars behind Thomas and Duray lurked Smiling Joe Dawson, the 1912 winner, in his Marmon. An Isotta just in front of Dawson blew a tire and cartwheeled onto its back. As Dawson roared down on the wreck, he saw the Isotta's mechanic crawling across the track. Dawson jerked the Marmon toward the infield. He struck a pile of dirt and his car tumbled end over end. Dawson and his mechanic were pulled from the wreck badly cut but alive, as were the Isotta's driver and mechanic.

From then on Thomas and Duray pulled away. Their closest pursuers were two other Frenchmen—Albert Guyot in another Delage, Goux in the bigger Peugeot. Pulling down trophies at 100, 200, 300, and 400 miles, Thomas moved away from Duray's baby Peugeot to win by 10 miles in the fastest "500" to date—just a shade over six hours at a record average speed of 82.47 miles an hour. The first American to finish was Oldfield, 30 miles behind Thomas.

"Today has been a bad day for America," intoned *The Automobile*'s correspondent at the race. Of the 13 cars that finished, six were foreign, and the magazine estimated the foreigners' winnings at $61,125, Thomas alone taking $37,050, including special prizes for the leader at each 100 miles of the race.

But it was a pivotal day for racing, as *The Automobile* also noted. "The baby Peugeot," it reported, "ran a race that put to shame the big specially constructed racing machines that were

Barney Oldfield, a cigar—his trademark—poking from his mouth, poses at the wheel of a Peugeot before the 1913 race. Known as "the man who never looked back" during his 17 years of racing, he finished fifth in 1914 and 1916, his only "500s." He retired from racing after World War I and died in 1946.

designed to come just under the displacement requirement of 450 cubic inches."

The baby Peugeot had shown that the smaller, high-rpm engine—already under the hoods of European cars—would be tomorrow's engine.

Loren Hodge:
No escape

A mechanic, Loren Hodge rode home 12th in 1911 and third in 1912 and 1913. In the 1914 race he rode with Eddie Rickenbacker, who finished tenth. *Before World War I there were three '500s'—the one in Indianapolis on the bricks and ones in Sheepshead Bay and Chicago on board tracks. The board tracks were banked high and much smoother than Indianapolis. At Indianapolis you got up to 118, 120 on the straightaway, but then you had to shut down—get off the accelerator—to slow down on the turns. On the boards you didn't have to shut down on the curves, and so you could get up to 160 miles an hour. But at those speeds the boards splintered. After a race we pulled splinters out of our clothes. They were like little darts flying through the air. Today's track at Indianapolis is the same track we rode on, 50 feet wide on the turns, 60 on the straights, the only difference being the surface is smoother with the bricks now covered. And they took away the inside walls on the four turns. In the old days if a car broke up, you were caught between the inside wall and the outside wall. Now, with no inside wall, you can escape down low to the grass.*

1914's TOP TEN
Race open to cars with a piston displacement of 450 cubic inches or less.

NO.	DRIVER	CAR	ENGINE	CYL.	BORE	STROKE	PISTON DISPL.	TIME	MPH	WINNINGS*
16	Rene Thomas	Delage	Delage	4	4.130	7.080	380.2	6:03:45	82.47†	$20,000
14	Arthur Duray	Peugeot	Peugeot	4	3.070	6.180	183.0	6:10:24	80.99	10,000
10	Albert Guyot	Delage	Delage	4	4.130	7.080	380.2	6:14:01	80.21	5,000
6	Jules Goux	Peugeot	Peugeot	4	3.940	7.080	345.0	6:17:24	79.49	3,500
3	Barney Oldfield	Stutz	Stutz	4	4.800	6.000	434.3	6:23:51	78.15	3,000
9	Josef Christiaens	Excelsior	Excelsior	6	3.800	6.200	446.6	6:27:24	77.44	2,200
27	Harry Grant	Sunbeam	Sunbeam	6	3.140	5.900	273.0	6:36:22	75.69	1,800
5	Charles Keene	Beaver Bullet	Case	4	5.100	5.500	449.4	6:40:57	74.82	1,600
25	Billy Carlson	Maxwell	Maxwell	4	4.200	8.000	445.3	7:02:42	70.97	1,500
42	Eddie Rickenbacker	Duesenberg	Duesenberg	4	4.400	6.000	360.5	7:03:34	70.83	1,400

* Speedway prizes for winning entries. Total awards in race, $51,675: Speedway prizes, $50,000; accessory prizes, $1,675. † New record.

Opposite page: Two Peugeots, Goux in No. 6, Boillot in No. 7, battle wheel to wheel. Above and right: Rene Thomas and his Delage. He drove in three more "500s" but never won again. He died in 1975.

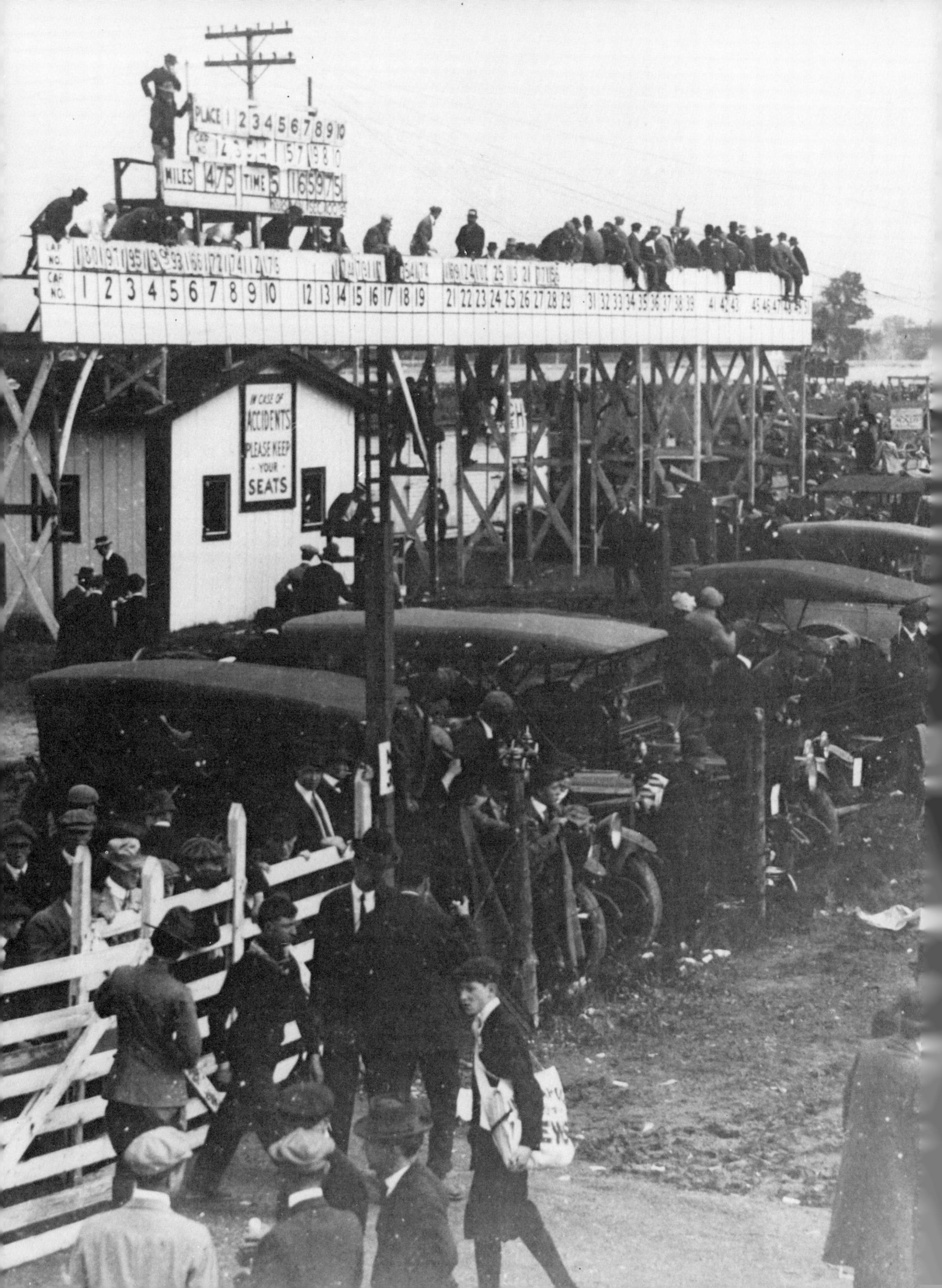

1915

Twice-Told Tale—with a New Ending

The bronzed, oil-spattered face of Ralph DePalma hung over the steering wheel as the white Mercedes bellowed down the backstretch of the 197th lap. With only 8 miles to go, DePalma sped closer to the first prize that he'd lost in 1912 when a connecting rod had snapped only 5 laps from the finish line.

DePalma swung the Mercedes into the No. 3 turn. The car bucked. Rapping sounds erupted from under the hood. Incredibly, as in the 1912 nightmare, a connecting rod had snapped under DePalma as he closed on the checkered flag. Within minutes the engine would be bled dry, its chambers a mass of hissing, hot metal. DePalma hit the throttle. He would try to boot his banging engine around the course three more times.

The day was a cool May 31, the sun obscured by clamlike clouds. The race had been scheduled for May 29 because May 30, Memorial Day, was a Sunday. But five days of steady rain had pushed the race back to Monday. Indianapolis hotels spilled over with people, and restaurants ran out of food. Visitors went door to door, begging bed and board.

The Speedway opened a seventh grandstand—G—for this year's race. It was the fourth to be erected or enlarged since 1911. Three tunnels now ducked under the brick track to carry people and cars to the infield. Carl Fisher and his partners were determined to keep the Indianapolis Motor Speedway as attractive as speedways that had opened in Brooklyn and in Chicago, where a 500-mile race was to be run in July on a new 2-mile board track.

Piston displacement had again been reduced—to 300 cubic inches—to attract smaller European designs. Although European armies were locked in trench warfare, the Peugeot factory sent over three cars. One, driven by young Dario Resta, had won the Vanderbilt Cup and Grand Prix races on the West Coast prior to coming to Indianapolis, where Resta qualified the car at 98.47 miles an hour. This year, for the first time at the "500," cars were lined up in order of qualifying speed, the fastest in the first row. Resta was in the front row but lost the No. 1 spot, the pole position, to Howdy Wilcox, who rammed his Stutz around the one lap at 98.90 miles an hour. Also in the front row was Ralph DePalma, driving a heavy Mercedes.

The race was expected to be a duel between DePalma's Mercedes and Resta's Peugeot, and that was what happened. Some 80 miles into the race, Resta popped to the front with DePalma hanging to his tailpipe. They whirled around the oval never more than a hundred yards apart. With 175 miles to go DePalma veered in for his second pit stop, changed tires, and came out 90 seconds later trailing by a lap. He could not close on Resta, but he knew that Resta would have to make a second stop to change tires.

Resta waited too long. The Peugeot blew the right rear tire, spun, skidded to a stop, and had to waddle to the pit. It came out 70 seconds later,

The scoreboard shows No. 2, DePalma, leading after 475 miles with No. 3, Resta, in second. More than 10,000 autos were parked at the Speedway, probably the heaviest concentration of cars anywhere in the world that day.

A smiling Eddie Rickenbacker (in cap and white overalls) poses with members of the Prest-O-Lite team before a "500." Later to be famous as "Mr. 500," Rickenbacker drove in only three of the grinds, from 1914 to 1916, his best finish a tenth in 1914.

a lap behind the Mercedes. But the spin had damaged Resta's steering gear and he had to brake gingerly on the turns. DePalma began pulling away.

With 8 miles to go, ahead by 3 laps, DePalma banged down the backstretch of the 197th lap, then heard the hammering of his bleeding engine. He had to think bad luck would cost him a second "500." Again, as in 1912, he tried to hurry the car around the oval before the engine's hot innards seized. This time he was lucky. He rolled by the checkered flag, and the Mercedes lumbered to the garage, where DePalma flung open the hood and watched its death throes. He had traveled the 500 miles a half hour faster than Rene Thomas's record of a year earlier. For the third straight year a foreign car had won in the heartland of America. The foreign cars' days of dominance here were numbered—but Ralph DePalma's days of bad "500" luck were not.

Peter DePaolo: The best tip

Of his uncle Ralph DePalma, Peter DePaolo—the 1925 winner of the "500"—recently recalled: *I don't think there's any question: He was the greatest driver America and the world ever produced. He entered more than 2,000 races and won more than 2,000. He won only one '500,' but he still is the all-time leader in laps led at Indianapolis—more than 600. He stood out physically among the other drivers—a man who didn't drink or smoke, when some of the boys hit the bottle pretty hard. And he dressed like a million dollars. He was a bear on physical fitness. 'Take care of your body,' he'd say, 'you can't be a good driver if you're not fit.' He taught me a lot about driving—not getting excited, waiting for your opportunity—but that's what I remember him telling me most: 'Peter, take care of your body.'*

1915's TOP TEN

Race open to cars with a piston displacement of 300 cubic inches or less.

NO.	DRIVER	CAR	ENGINE	CYL.	BORE	STROKE	PISTON DISPL.	TIME	MPH	WINNINGS*
2	Ralph DePalma	Mercedes	Mercedes	4	3.620	6.500	274.0	5:33:55	89.84†	$20,000
3	Dario Resta	Peugeot	Peugeot	4	3.620	6.670	276.0	5:37:24	88.91	10,000
5	Gil Anderson	Stutz	Stutz	4	3.800	6.480	295.3	5:42:27	87.60	5,000
4	Earl Cooper	Stutz	Stutz	4	3.800	6.480	295.3	5:46:19	86.62	3,500
15	Eddie O'Donnell	Duesenberg	Duesenberg	4	3.980	6.000	299.0	6:08:13	81.47	3,000
8	Bob Burman	Peugeot	Peugeot	4	3.650	7.100	296.0	6:13:19	80.36	2,200
1	Howdy Wilcox	Stutz	Stutz	4	3.816	6.484	298.5	6:14:19	80.14	1,800
10	Tom Alley	Duesenberg	Duesenberg	4	3.980	6.000	299.0	6:15:08	79.97	1,600
19	Billy Carlson	Maxwell	Maxwell	4	3.750	6.750	298.0	6:19:55	78.96	1,500
7	Noel Van Raalte	Sunbeam	Sunbeam	4	3.700	6.300	274.0	6:35:23	75.87	1,400

* Speedway prizes for winning entries. Total awards in race, $51,200: Speedway prizes, $50,000; accessory prizes, $1,200.   † New record.

Left: DePalma waves as he goes under the finish bridge. Bottom: He sits at the right-hand wheel with mechanic Louis Fontaine. DePalma (below) drove in ten "500s" during his racing career.

Top: Cars buzz through the No. 1 turn. Above: Eddie Rickenbacker at the wheel of an earlier racer. In this race he and another Prest-O-Lite team member, Pete Henderson, were the first drivers to wear crash helmets.

1916

The "500" Goes 300

"Who the hell does he think he is?" Carl Fisher snapped at T. E. (Pop) Myers, the Speedway's new general manager. Myers had just told Fisher that Ralph DePalma, the premier attraction in racing, had demanded "appearance money"—at least $5,000—to enter the 1916 race.

Fisher's partners wanted to give DePalma the money. Some of the shine of the race had faded as other speedways staged 500-mile races. This year Fisher had decided to shorten the race to 300 miles. He had made the decision for a number of reasons. Some fans had argued that a "300" would be more exciting. Moreover, with the guns of World War I still barking across Europe, no new machines would come across the Atlantic; and in America only Arthur and Louis Chevrolet and the Duesenberg brothers, Fred and August, were rolling new racers out of their shops. Most of the 1916 entries, as a result, would be older cars, and Fisher thought that few would survive a 500-mile grind over the bricks.

His partners argued that since a 300-mile race might not draw the throngs that had jammed downtown Indianapolis and its hotels for the previous races, the presence of DePalma would help to swell the attendance. But Fisher was adamant: He would not pay DePalma or anyone else.

A few days later Barney Oldfield—he and DePalma were jealous rivals—asked Fisher for the same fee that DePalma was getting. Fisher assured Barney that DePalma was not receiving a fee. "We don't need DePalma or anyone else that much," Fisher said. Barney entered. DePalma tried to sign up after the entry deadline had passed, but Fisher curtly turned him away. The race had asserted itself as bigger than its parts.

Only 21 cars lined up for the start of the "300." The crowd was noticeably sparser than in previous years—70,000 was one optimistic estimate. Favored to win was the hawk-faced Eddie Rickenbacker, like DePalma and Oldfield a pioneer racer on dirt tracks and at county fairs. His white Maxwell, designed by Ray Harroun, was partly owned by Fisher. Rickenbacker had won two big races, in Brooklyn and Tacoma, to bring home more than $50,000 in the past 12 months for himself and Fisher's Prest-O-Lite racing team.

Rickenbacker had won a front-row spot by qualifying at better than 96 miles an hour. On the pole was Johnny Aitken in an old Peugeot and right behind him was stumpy Dario Resta, "a driving master," one critic had called him, in another Peugeot.

At the start Rickenbacker arrowed his white Maxwell into the lead and began to edge away from the two pursuing Peugeots. But near the 25-mile point Rickenbacker veered off the track with a broken steering knuckle, his car through for the day (Rickenbacker finished sixth in the other Maxwell as a relief driver). Aitken's Peugeot slipped into the lead. But when Aitken stopped for 20 seconds to change a tire, he came out in second, Resta's Peugeot a gleaming blue and white speck in front of him.

Streaking through the sunshine, Resta's Peugeot roared over the first 100 miles in an hour and seven minutes. Behind him clung Aitken's Peugeot. After 172 miles Aitken peeled off into

Right: Resta takes the checker. Below: He poses with goggles and behind the wheel of the winning Peugeot. Resta did not race in another "500" until 1923. He died in 1924 on a speedway in England.

DARIO RESTA — 1916

Spectators get a view of the race perched atop the family car. Automobile prices were on their way down, newspapers said, but a Reo cost $1,500, a sum many Americans didn't earn in a year. There were two smashups in the race. One driver fractured his thigh, another his skull.

the pit with a broken valve, his car one of ten that would not finish the race. Eight miles ahead of the second-place car, a Duesenberg, Resta raised high a hand, a signal to his pit that he would come in on the next lap. He pointed at the right rear tire; he wanted it changed. The treads looked sound, but a blown right rear tire had cost him the race a year earlier. In the pit he also took on fuel, losing a minute, but he screeched back onto the track still far ahead. Over the next 125 miles he held the Peugeot at 80 miles an hour and finished with an average speed of 84 miles an hour, well below the record of 89. For the fourth straight year a foreign car had won.

It had been a dull race. Fisher decided to switch back to a 500-mile contest—but he would have to wait three years to see it.

Edward Towers:
Slipshod scoring

Ralph Mulford, who finished third in 1916, had come in second in 1911. Edward Towers, a riding mechanic, later said: *Mulford always insisted he won that first '500' in 1911. In those days the scoring was slipshod. They'd have a scorer assigned to watch one or two cars to check on their speed and how many laps they'd covered. But the scorers weren't experienced men. And Ray Harroun and Joe Dawson were from Indianapolis driving Indianapolis cars. I know the car I was in, with Wild Bill Turner, we were placed eighth in that 1911 race, but we were pretty sure we finished sixth. Oh, yes, sir, there was some hometown scoring.*

1916's TOP TEN

Race open to cars with a piston displacement of 300 cubic inches or less.

NO.	DRIVER	CAR	ENGINE	CYL.	BORE	STROKE	PISTON DISPL.	TIME*	MPH	WINNINGS†
17	Dario Resta	Peugeot	Peugeot	4	3.620	6.650	274	3:34:17	84.00	$12,000
1	Wilbur D'Alene	Duesenberg	Duesenberg	4	3.750	6.750	299	3:36:15	83.24	6,000
10	Ralph Mulford	Peugeot	Peugeot	4	3.600	6.700	274	3:37:56	82.59	3,000
14	Josef Christiaens	Sunbeam	Sunbeam	6	3.180	5.900	299	3:46:36	79.44	2,000
15	Barney Oldfield	Delage	Delage	4	3.720	6.300	275	3:47:19	79.18	1,700
4	Pete Henderson	Maxwell	Maxwell	4	3.750	6.750	298	3:49:56	78.28	1,400
29	Howdy Wilcox	Premier	Premier	4	3.600	6.700	274	3:54:31	76.75	1,200
26	Art Johnson	Crawford	Duesenberg	4	3.750	6.750	298	4:01:54	74.41	1,000
24	William Chandler	Crawford	Duesenberg	4	3.750	6.750	298	4:02:43	74.16	900
9	Ora Haibe	Osteweg	Wisconsin	4	4.340	5.000	296	4:03:10	74.02	800

* For 300 miles.   † Speedway prizes for winning entries. Total awards in race, $31,350: Speedway prizes, $30,000; accessory prizes, $1,350.

1919

Another Tortoise and a Hare

In November, 1918, only a few days after World War I ended, Carl Fisher left by train from Miami Beach, where he was carving a resort out of a swamp, for Indianapolis to plan the 1919 race. During the war the Speedway's gates had been shut to the public; its garages sheltered Army planes, its brick track was a landing strip. When Fisher announced that the race would be resumed on Memorial Day, 1919, some editorialists called the Speedway's "race to death" an insult to the dead of World War I. Fisher ducked some of the darts by holding the race on Saturday, May 31, the day after Memorial Day.

Again the race would stretch 500 miles for a purse of $50,000 plus accessory prizes. French factories shipped over four new Ballots, valued at $120,000. Driving one was the 1914 winner, Rene Thomas. The Chevrolet brothers entered four of their new Frontenacs, and the Hudson factory sent five new six-cylinder stock cars. The Duesenbergs, who had moved their shop to New Jersey, entered four cars. Ralph DePalma came in a ponderous 12-cylinder Packard, its displacement of 299.2 cubic inches just under the limit of 300.

Rene Thomas piloted his Ballot through a qualifying lap at 104.7 miles an hour—a Speedway record—as the 100-mile-an-hour barrier was penetrated by seven cars. Thomas won the pole position. (This year the qualifiers on the first day were placed ahead of later qualifiers who might have faster times, a rule that still stands.)

Estimates of the race day crowd, on a sunny morning, ranged between 75,000 and 125,000. The packed stands contradicted predictions that postwar America had become too sophisticated for auto racing. After band music, aerial bombs, the playing of "Back Home in Indiana," and the national anthem, the crowd saw the popular favorite—DePalma—blast his big Packard to the front. He whizzed around the first 100 miles at 92 miles an hour, a record for the Speedway. Hanging close behind was Louis Chevrolet, in one of his Frontenacs. Far back, in a patched old blue and white Peugeot, the happy-go-lucky Howdy Wilcox restrained his enthusiasm and his heavy foot as he noodled along at a steady 85 miles an hour.

On the 44th lap Arthur Thurman's car overturned and he was killed. An hour later a Roamer exploded, cremating the driver and mechanic on the track. These were the first deaths at the Speedway since 1911.

At the 150-mile mark DePalma veered in for a pit stop and Chevrolet zoomed into the lead. Behind him the expensive French Ballots shook apart as they pounded over the bricks. Cars streamed into the pits and many did not come out (only 14 of the 33 cars finished the race). Near the halfway point both Chevrolet and DePalma had to make lengthy pit stops, and they watched Wilcox roll by in the Peugeot to take the lead. Cars rushed at Wilcox, then had to swing in for repairs and came out too far behind. Wilcox held

CARS ARE TESTED IN OTHER RESPECTS THAN AS TO SPEED

A cartoonist sketched scenes at a "500" before and during the race, sometimes with an acid comment (above) on the size of the spectators. Front pages on this Memorial Day bannered headlines reporting on the flight of a U.S. seaplane from New York to Lisbon with stops along the way. Flying time was 57 hours. Watching the race was Mrs. Arthur Thurman, who fainted when her husband crashed. She came to and learned he was dead.

Dust, smoke, and noise in their wake, cars curve around the banked southwest (No. 1) turn. The turn worried drivers because it had a nasty bump. Some drivers rode high on the bank to avoid it. No. 3 is Howdy Wilcox's Peugeot. No. 31 is Rene Thomas's Ballot. One car's broken wheel snapped a timing wire stretched across the track. The cut wire flew up, slashing a driver across the neck. Doctors saved him from bleeding to death.

the lead for the last 200 miles to win with an average speed of 88 miles an hour. DePalma's 1915 record was still intact.

He "made no exceptionally fast laps," *Motor Age* magazine said of Wilcox, who came in for only three pit stops while other drivers made as many as 12. "He won because others, who drove faster while on the track, could not keep going."

Only hours after the race, Carl Fisher announced that future "500s" would be limited to cars with 183-cubic-inch displacement or less. That was equivalent to the three-liter limit newly set for the French Grand Prix and so would attract Grand Prix cars to Indianapolis. "Racing," Fisher said, "is primarily for the purpose of developing and improving the cars in everyday use. There are many more cars in use having small-displacement engines than those with 300-cubic-inch displacements." And he added: "Today's race proved that 300-cubic-inch cars are too fast for the track and the track too rough for the big cars."

Wilcox's victory extended the dominance of foreign cars, winners now of five Indy races in a row. But Americans like the Duesenbergs, Tommy Milton, Jimmy Murphy, and an eccentric genius named Harry Miller were about to cast their shadows over the "500."

Howdy Wilcox: Planned just so

Minutes after the race Howdy Wilcox told reporters: *I planned this race just right, and each of my pit stops came when I'd planned. I had very good, fast work from my pit men—19 seconds the first time, to change a tire. My two biggest problems were a left front frame horn that cracked late in the race and we had to tape it together and hope she'd hold. Thank the Lord it did. The other thing was that No. 1 turn at the bottom of the stretch. There's a bump in it and you got to go high on the bank. Hit it and you could land in downtown Indianapolis.*

1919's TOP TEN

Race open to cars with a piston displacement of 300 cubic inches or less.

NO.	DRIVER	CAR	ENGINE	CYL.	BORE	STROKE	PISTON DISPL.	TIME	MPH	WINNINGS*
3	Howdy Wilcox	Peugeot	Peugeot	4	3.600	6.700	274.6	5:40:42.87	88.05	$20,000
14	Eddie Hearne	Durant	Stutz	4	3.810	6.500	298.6	5:44:29.04	87.09	10,000
6	Jules Goux	Peugeot	Premier	4	3.600	6.700	274.6	5:49:06.18	85.93	5,000
32	Albert Guyot	Ballot	Ballot	8	2.920	5.520	296.0	5:55:16.27	84.44	3,500
26	Tom Alley	Bender	Bender	4	3.625	7.000	289.0	6:05:03.92	82.18	3,000
4	Ralph DePalma	Packard	Packard	12	2.657	4.500	299.2	6:10:10.64	81.04	2,200
7	Louis Chevrolet	Frontenac	Frontenac	4	3.875	6.375	299.5	6:10:10.92	81.04	1,800
27	Ira Vail	Hudson	Hudson	6	3.500	5.000	288.6	6:12:42.00	80.49	1,600
21	Denny Hickey	Stickel	Hudson	6	3.500	5.000	288.6	6:13:57.24	80.22	1,500
41	Gaston Chevrolet	Frontenac	Frontenac	4	3.875	6.375	299.5	6:17:21.79	79.50	1,400

* Speedway prizes for winning entries. Total awards in race, $55,275: Speedway prizes, $50,000; accessory prizes, $5,275.

Left: Howdy Wilcox at the wheel of his winning Peugeot. The car's carburetor was built in the Los Angeles shop of Harry Miller, presaging Miller's dominance of future "500s." Wilcox (above) also drove in stock-car and hill-climbing races. He was killed on a track at Altoona, Pennsylvania, in 1923.

1920

Good for America, Bad for DePalma

Ralph DePalma twisted the creamy Ballot through the turn at better than 80 miles an hour. As the Ballot arrowed down the stretch, DePalma grinned at his mechanic and nephew, Peter DePaolo. They had just won $100, and on each whirl around the 2.5-mile track they could win another $100. The Golden Age of Sport was dawning, and the gold had already begun to rain on Indianapolis's pride, its Speedway. This year Indianapolis merchants offered $100 to the leader of each and every one of the 200 laps. So far DePalma had won almost $8,000 in lap prizes. As he clicked through the south turns, the nose of his Ballot was only 50 miles away from the $20,000 first prize. And Ralph DePalma was only a half hour away from becoming the first driver to win two "500s."

The huge crowd, estimated at around 120,000 (another new grandstand—H—had been added) watched as DePalma disappeared into the turns. The crowd cheered as several American cars swarmed by, Gaston Chevrolet in his new Monroe the closest to DePalma. In the last five races, the winners had been foreign cars, and Americans wanted a winner made in the country that had saved the world for democracy.

But all the cars, foreign and American, had delighted spectators who welcomed the drop in piston displacement from 300 to 183 cubic inches. "The lightweight, small-engined racing car made good here today," wrote Lambert G. Sullivan of *Motor Age* magazine after the race. "It went through a racking, grinding 500 miles of extreme speed in a way... which demonstrated clearly that the designers of today are able to get quite as much speed [and] endurance out of the lightweight, small-engined cars as their predecessors were out of much larger machines." The race, he added, "proved that light cars can be built which are in every way the equal of their heavier brothers of the present."

This year, however, no passenger car manufacturer, like Packard or Hudson, entered a stock car against the custom-built racers assembled by the Chevrolets, the Duesenbergs, and the French Ballot factory. But manufacturers of batteries, tires, and other accessories had come to the Speedway waving cash prizes at drivers who would use their products. Before the war most cars had used Goodrich Silvertown cord tires, and Goodrich had let that be known ("Goodrich Wins," proclaimed newspaper ads across the country the day after a "500.") Now Firestone was here with its Oldfield tires. The Delco company had offered $50,000 to be split among drivers in the top ten who used its new battery ignition system. Carl Fisher objected —he didn't want the lavish prizes of big companies to drive smaller companies from the Speedway—and Delco reduced the prize.

All told, the drivers set their sights on nearly $100,000 in prize money—almost double the money of a year ago. As Ralph DePalma swooped the Ballot into the 186th lap, he had only 35 miles to go to collect more money than any previous driver had ever won in a single race.

Then that demon bad luck once more alighted, grinning, on the DePalma hood. Coming out of the backstretch the Ballot sputtered and stopped. Thinking the car was out of gas, mechanic DePaolo sprinted across the infield to lug back a can of fuel. DePalma, meanwhile, removed the cap from the gas tank and saw the tank was still a quarter full. As cars sped by, DePalma lifted the hood and found a failed magneto. He jerked the spark plugs from the four rear cylinders and re-

The working press sit on the hard-wheeled truck that took them around the track for interviews. At a victory dinner the night after the race—still a "500" tradition—$93,550 in prizes was handed out, the fattest purse offered up to then in automobile racing.

An aerial view of the Speedway after World War I, the southwest (No. 1) turn in the top left corner, the No. 2 turn at bottom left, the No. 3 turn at bottom right, the No. 4 turn at top right. Present-day West 16th Street flanks the track on the left, West 30th on the right.

started the car; it rattled through the No. 4 turn and onto the straightaway.

In his green and white Monroe, Gaston Chevrolet scooted by the struggling Ballot (which had picked up the panting DePaolo near the pits) to take the lead. Other cars passed DePalma—he would finish fifth—but none could catch Chevrolet. He took the checker with an average speed of 88.62 miles an hour, under DePalma's 1915 record but slightly faster than the bigger-displacement Peugeot of a year ago. Chevrolet had won $36,000, including a prize from Firestone for wearing its Oldfields. They were the first tires to go the full 500 miles on a winner without a change —and for the next 46 years, every winning car would ride on Firestones.

An American car had won at the Speedway for the first time since 1912. Gaston Chevrolet would relish the honor only briefly: Six months later he was dead, killed on a Beverly Hills speedway. But because of this tragedy another driver would begin a run toward two "500" triumphs. His name was Tommy Milton.

Peter DePaolo:
"I was damn tired"

When Ralph DePalma's Ballot faltered near the end of the 1920 race, riding mechanic DePaolo made a frantic dash to the pits for gas. A half-century later, DePaolo recalled his famous sprint: *We'd stopped between the third and fourth turns. I ran about a mile and a quarter to the pits. I was damn tired when I got there and I drank a lot of water, which I shouldn't have. Then I started back, hauling one of those five-gallon milk cans filled with gasoline. I'd have to stop every 20 yards and sit down, and I was sick now from the water I drank. Then I see Uncle Ralph coming down the straightaway. I threw the can away, seeing he's not out of gas, and ran to the car. When I got there he yells, 'Go back and get that can or we'll be disqualified.' I went back, of course, but you can imagine what I felt like. I got into the car and we finished fifth, chugging along.*

Below: Winner Gaston Chevrolet, who would soon die in a racing accident in California. Opposite page: He sits in the winning Monroe, designed by brother Louis. Note the bullet nose, the pinched tail for streamlining. The car ran out of gas 3 laps from the finish, luckily could coast to the pit, was hastily refueled, then beat it to the checker.

1920's TOP TEN

Race open to cars with a piston displacement of 183 cubic inches or less.

NO.	DRIVER	CAR	ENGINE	CYL.	BORE	STROKE	PISTON DISPL.	TIME	MPH	WINNINGS*
4	Gaston Chevrolet	Monroe	Frontenac	4	3.125	5.937	182.5	5:38:32.00	88.62	$20,000
25	Rene Thomas	Ballot	Ballot	8	2.560	4.410	181.0	5:44:51.60	86.99	10,000
10	Tommy Milton	Duesenberg	Duesenberg	8	2.500	4.625	181.5	5:45:02.48	86.95	5,000
12	Jimmy Murphy	Duesenberg	Duesenberg	8	2.500	4.625	181.5	5:52:31.35	85.10	3,500
2	Ralph DePalma	Ballot	Ballot	8	2.560	4.410	181.0	6:05:19.15	82.12	3,000
31	Eddie Hearne	Duesenberg	Duesenberg	8	2.500	4.625	181.5	6:10:21.55	81.00	2,200
26	Jean Chassagne	Ballot	Ballot	8	2.560	4.410	181.0	6:15:16.65	79.94	1,800
28	Joe Thomas	Monroe	Frontenac	4	3.125	5.937	182.5	6:21:41.55	78.60	1,600
33	Ralph Mulford	Mulford	Mulford	8	2.500	4.625	181.5	7:17:14.25	68.61	1,500
15	Pete Henderson	Revere	Duesenberg	4	2.500	4.625	181.5	7:23:53.95	67.58	1,400

* Speedway prizes for winning entries. Total awards in race, $93,550: Speedway prizes, $50,000; accessory prizes, $23,550; lap prizes, $20,000.

Gaston Chevrolet, Winner 1920

1921

Too Hot To Last

A skyrocketing aerial bomb exploded. Band music floated on a light breeze. Along the nearly mile-long row of wooden grandstands facing the track, people glanced at their watches. Almost time. On the track, high in his white Ballot, sat Ralph DePalma, his car on the pole in the front row. Far behind him, in the next to last row, crouched Tommy Milton, in the cockpit of a plum Frontenac.

A year earlier the fiery-tempered Tommy, who had poor vision in one eye, had shot a snubnosed Duesenberg over the sands of Daytona Beach at 156 miles an hour to break DePalma's world record of 149. Tommy had come here determined to break another DePalma record—his 1915 average of 89.94 miles an hour for the "500."

Tommy had thought he had the car to break the record—he'd been, in his positive way, sure of it. The car had a straight-eight engine built for Milton by Harry Miller, a Los Angeles carburetor designer, and Miller's shop superintendent, Fred Offenhauser. Milton, Miller, and Offenhauser had combined the prewar Peugeot's multiple inclined valves and hemisphere-like cylinder with the postwar Duesenberg engine. For better breathing, Miller modified the Duesenberg design: Instead of a single camshaft and three valves per cylinder, Miller built two camshafts and four valves per cylinder.

Milton had placed the new Miller engine (he paid for it with $5,000 borrowed from Barney Oldfield) into a chassis borrowed from wealthy sportsman Cliff Durant and called the car the Durant Special. But the new car wasn't ready in time for the 1921 Indianapolis qualifying trials.

Instead Milton accepted a ride in one of the straight-eights of Louis Chevrolet, filling the opening left in the Frontenac team by the death of Gaston Chevrolet, who had won the 1920 race. In the 4-lap time trials Milton could get only 93 miles an hour out of the Frontenac while DePalma's French-built Ballot won the pole at a little better than 100.

Another aerial bomb exploded. Ten o'clock. The 23 cars ran toward the first turn behind the pacer. Minutes later DePalma blew by the grandstands to win the first lap prize. His Ballot whizzed through the first 200 miles at an average of 93 miles an hour, breaking nearly all the track records and winning for DePalma almost $8,000 in prize money. In fourth place, some 8 miles behind, Milton pushed the Frontenac along at 90.

At a little past 12:30 P.M., DePalma zoomed toward the 100th lap, the race's halfway mark. The Ballot grunted and slowed. DePalma's mechanic circled his head with his arms—the signal they would pit on the next lap.

For four minutes mechanics' hands clawed at the Ballot's engine. Cars whirled by, cutting DePalma's lead to 2 laps, then one. Roscoe Sarles's grey Duesenberg popped by the pits to take the lead. DePalma rushed onto the track and caught the Duesy. But again the Ballot faltered, slowed, and rolled off. DePalma stepped grimly out of the cockpit. The scorching pace had burned out the Ballot's bearings. Once more DePalma's "500" luck had been bad.

His finely tuned Frontenac sliding smoothly around the track, Tommy Milton closed relent-

Top: Roscoe Sarles at the left-hand wheel of the Duesy that diced with Milton to bring the crowd to its feet in the latter part of the race. Bottom: A car that leaped but didn't clear the wall on the No. 4 turn. Neither driver Louis Fontaine nor his mechanic was badly hurt.

lessly on Sarles's Duesy and took the lead on the 111th lap. Behind them other cars smoked into the pits, burned out by the day's heat and De-Palma's pace. Only eight cars would last the 500 miles.

Clicking off laps at a steady 90 miles an hour, Milton pulled away to sprint home first with an average speed of 89.62, only a smidgen off De-Palma's record. It was the second straight victory for a Chevrolet-built car. Milton and Louis Chevrolet shared almost $36,000 in prize money. Around them on the vast infield, the cars of spectators spit and coughed as they started up amid clouds of dust to head homeward in the afternoon sunlight. A grinning Milton walked through the dust. Next year he would ride his own car, the Durant Special with its Miller engine, and next year, he told friends, that DePalma record and a second straight "500" victory would be his.

Ira Vail: "An awful beating"

Ira Vail, who finished seventh, spoke a half-century later about the physical rigors of driving a "500." *I'd go into a '500' weighing 135 pounds and come out eight to ten pounds lighter. Steering those heavy cars was hard work and took a lot out of you. And the shock absorbers we had in those days—they were Hartfords and worked like scissors—didn't give you the soft ride they get today on shocks. I'd come out of a race bruised, yes, and the heavier men took an awful beating. Some, like Chevrolet, had to wear corsets and bind themselves with tape.*

Left: Winner Tommy Milton. Below: Milton at the wheel of the winning Frontenac. Barney Oldfield, with cigar, stands next to Milton. Louis Chevrolet is on Barney's left. Chevrolet's Frontenacs finished first, third, and ninth. Opposite page: A contemporary poet's ode to war ace Eddie Rickenbacker and other "500" heroes.

What The Little Birds Saw.
BY WILLIAM HERSCHELL.

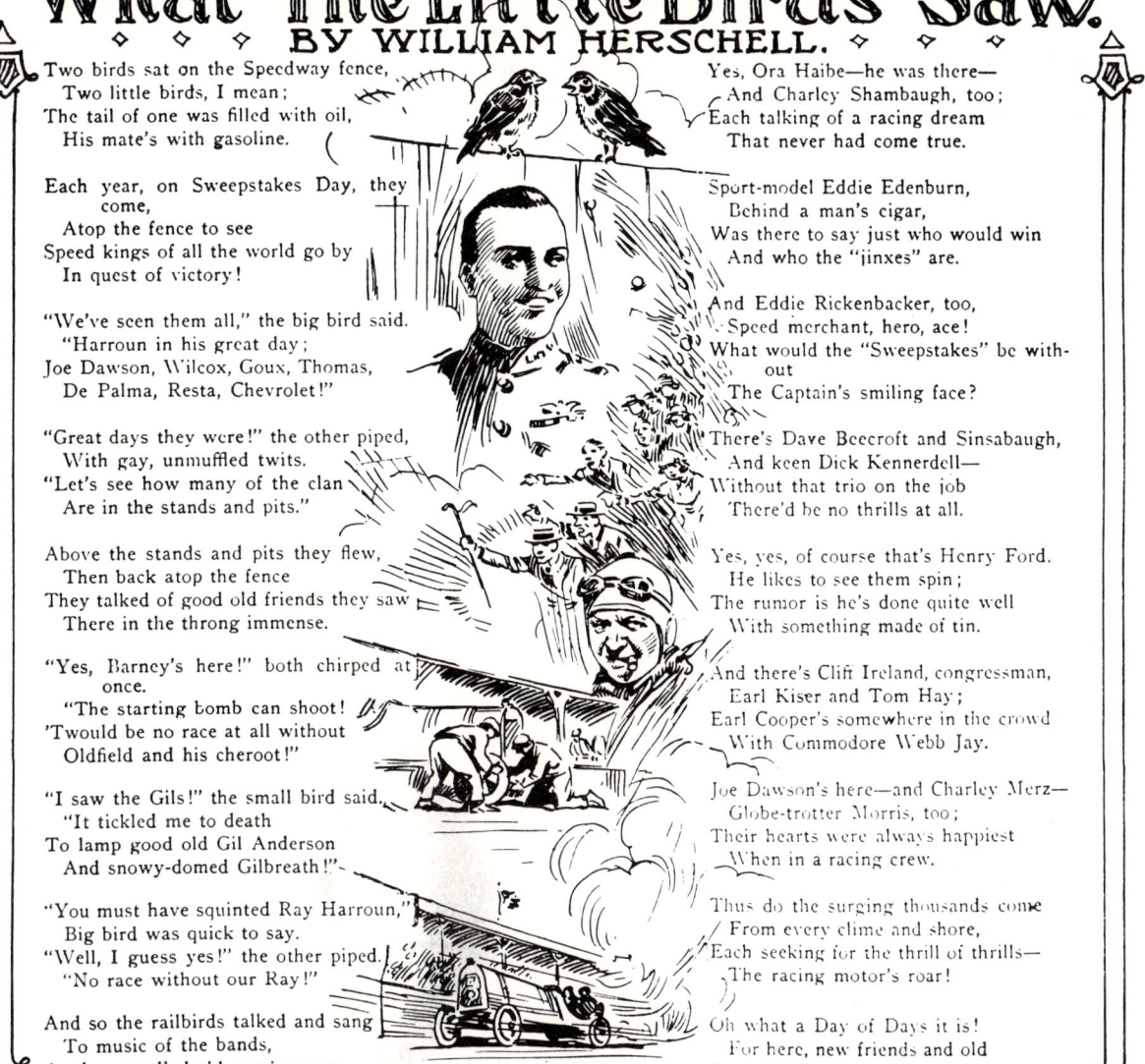

Two birds sat on the Speedway fence,
   Two little birds, I mean;
The tail of one was filled with oil,
   His mate's with gasoline.

Each year, on Sweepstakes Day, they come,
   Atop the fence to see
Speed kings of all the world go by
   In quest of victory!

"We've seen them all," the big bird said.
   "Harroun in his great day;
Joe Dawson, Wilcox, Goux, Thomas,
   De Palma, Resta, Chevrolet!"

"Great days they were!" the other piped,
   With gay, unmuffled twits.
"Let's see how many of the clan
   Are in the stands and pits."

Above the stands and pits they flew,
   Then back atop the fence
They talked of good old friends they saw
   There in the throng immense.

"Yes, Barney's here!" both chirped at once.
   "The starting bomb can shoot!
'Twould be no race at all without
   Oldfield and his cheroot!"

"I saw the Gils!" the small bird said.
   "It tickled me to death
To lamp good old Gil Anderson
   And snowy-domed Gilbreath!"

"You must have squinted Ray Harroun,"
   Big bird was quick to say.
"Well, I guess yes!" the other piped.
   "No race without our Ray!"

And so the railbirds talked and sang
   To music of the bands,
As they recalled old cronies seen
   Around the pits and stands.

Yes, Ora Haibe—he was there—
   And Charley Shambaugh, too;
Each talking of a racing dream
   That never had come true.

Sport-model Eddie Edenburn,
   Behind a man's cigar,
Was there to say just who would win
   And who the "jinxes" are.

And Eddie Rickenbacker, too,
   Speed merchant, hero, ace!
What would the "Sweepstakes" be without
   The Captain's smiling face?

There's Dave Beecroft and Sinsabaugh,
   And keen Dick Kennerdell—
Without that trio on the job
   There'd be no thrills at all.

Yes, yes, of course that's Henry Ford.
   He likes to see them spin;
The rumor is he's done quite well
   With something made of tin.

And there's Clift Ireland, congressman,
   Earl Kiser and Tom Hay;
Earl Cooper's somewhere in the crowd
   With Commodore Webb Jay.

Joe Dawson's here—and Charley Merz—
   Globe-trotter Morris, too;
Their hearts were always happiest
   When in a racing crew.

Thus do the surging thousands come
   From every clime and shore,
Each seeking for the thrill of thrills—
   The racing motor's roar!

Oh what a Day of Days it is!
   For here, new friends and old
Pay tribute to a steed of steel
   Manned by a heart of gold!

1921

1921's TOP NINE*

Race open to cars with a piston displacement of 183 cubic inches or less.

NO.	DRIVER	CAR	ENGINE	CYL.	BORE	STROKE	PISTON DISPL.	TIME	MPH	WINNINGS†
2	Tommy Milton	Frontenac	Frontenac	8	2.625	4.093	182.5	5:34:44.65	89.62	$20,000
6	Roscoe Sarles	Duesenberg	Duesenberg	8	2.500	4.625	183.8	5:38:34.03	88.61	10,000
23	Percy Ford	Frontenac	Frontenac	4	3.125	5.937	182.1	5:52:50.30	85.02	5,000
5	Eddie Miller	Duesenberg	Duesenberg	8	2.500	4.625	183.8	5:54:24.98	84.65	3,500
16	Ora Haibe	Sunbeam	Sunbeam	8	2.560	4.415	181.3	5:55:58.20	84.28	3,000
9	Albert Guyot	Duesenberg	Duesenberg	8	2.500	4.625	182.6	6:01:17.70	83.03	2,000
3	Ira Vail	Leach Special	Miller	8	2.687	4.000	181.4	6:14:17.47	80.15	1,800
21	Bennett Hill	Duesenberg	Duesenberg	8	2.500	4.625	183.3	6:19:06.74	79.13	1,600
8	Ralph Mulford	Frontenac	Frontenac	8	2.625	4.093	182.5	Flagged	177 laps	1,500

* Tenth place not awarded. † Speedway prizes for winning entries. Total awards in race, $86,650; Speedway prizes, $50,000; accessory prizes, $19,300; lap prizes, $17,350.

1922

Two Blows

Tommy Milton rolled his Leach Special into its starting position in the next to last row of cars. Up ahead of him—on the pole—sat the sad-eyed, dwarfish Jimmy Murphy in his green and white Murphy Special. Seeing young Murphy so far ahead of him, a mass of metal between them, had to be two sledgehammer blows to the heart of Tommy Milton.

Jimmy Murphy had once been Tommy Milton's mechanic. Milton had talked Fred Duesenberg into putting Murphy behind a wheel. A year later Murphy had streaked in a Duesenberg to an unofficial world speed record, infuriating Milton, who had expected to have first chance at steering the car to the record. Now Murphy and Milton did not speak to each other.

By the end of 1921, they were rated America's greatest drivers. Murphy had barreled in a Duesenberg to victory in the 1921 Le Mans road race, becoming the first American to win a European Grand Prix event. And Milton—the world's speed king after setting the official record of 156.046 miles an hour in the Duesenberg—had won the 1921 "500" and enough other races to gain the national driving title a second straight year.

The car that had carried Milton to the 1921 driving championship was his own Durant Special, which had been completed too late to compete in the 1921 Indy race. Looking toward Indianapolis in 1922, Milton had felt sure the Durant Special, powered by the straight-eight engine conceived and built by himself, Harry Miller, and Fred Offenhauser, could win for him a second straight "500" crown. But a few months before the "500," the American Automobile Association's Contest Board had decreed that Milton could not drive the Durant Special because a Durant dealer had advertised that Tommy had won races in a Durant factory car. A frustrated Milton sold the car to Cliff Durant, who was also a driver. Milton then bought another Miller eight to put in a new car, the Leach Special. But, lacking time to tune the engine properly before the "500," he'd averaged only 94 miles an hour in the time trials.

Fastest qualifier, at better than 100 miles an hour, was Jimmy Murphy in his Murphy Special —which had in its Duesenberg chassis one of the new Miller engines that Tommy Milton had helped to design. He'd been beaten to the pole, Milton could tell himself, by his own engine in a car driven by an ungrateful protégé.

At the flying start the one-time protégé blasted his Murphy Special into the lead. Murphy fled through the first 100 miles of this tenth running of the "500" at an average speed of 94.07 miles an hour to break Ralph DePalma's record of a year earlier. Harry Hartz, a rookie, snuggled his Duesenberg in behind Murphy, and behind him clung another rookie, Peter DePaolo, Ralph DePalma's nephew. Far behind bumped Tommy Milton in his Leach Special, its clogged fuel line hiccuping gas to the engine. After 100 miles Milton angrily jerked the car out of the race and sat in the pits to watch Murphy battle for the lead.

Near the 200-mile mark, the sun beating down on a track that shimmered heat waves, Murphy had to pit twice within ten minutes. Hartz pushed his white Duesenberg into the lead. At 300 miles

50

The pace car (upper l. corner), a National 8 driven by Barney Oldfield, nears the line for the flying start. Portions of the race, including the start, were broadcast over the radio —a first—to listeners in the Midwest.

1922's TOP TEN

Race open to cars with a piston displacement of 183 cubic inches or less.

NO.	DRIVER	CAR	ENGINE	CYL.	BORE	STROKE	PISTON DISPL.	TIME	MPH	WINNINGS*
35	Jimmy Murphy	Murphy Special	Miller	8	2.685	4.000	181.4	5:17:30.79	94.48†	$20,000
12	Harry Hartz	Duesenberg	Duesenberg	8	2.508	4.500	181.9	5:20:44.39	93.53	10,000
15	Eddie Hearne	Ballot	Ballot	8	2.560	4.218	180.1	5:22:26.06	93.04	5,000
17	Ralph DePalma	Duesenberg	Duesenberg	8	2.531	4.500	181.1	5:31:04.65	90.61	3,500
31	Ora Haibe	Duesenberg	Duesenberg	8	2.490	4.578	177.1	5:31:13.45	90.57	3,000
24	Jerry Wonderlich	Duesenberg	Duesenberg	8	2.503	4.500	181.5	5:37:52.84	88.79	2,200
21	I. P. Fetterman	Duesenberg	Duesenberg	8	2.490	4.625	180.2	5:40:55.54	88.00	1,800
1	Ira Vail	Disteel-Duesenberg	Duesenberg	8	2.501	4.656	183.3	5:48:19.16	86.13	1,600
26	Tom Alley	Monroe	Frontenac	4	3.125	5.937	181.5	5:55:53.46	84.30	1,500
10	Joe Thomas	Duesenberg	Duesenberg	8	2.507	4.500	181.2	6:03:24.23	82.55	1,400

* Speedway prizes for winning entries. Total awards in race, $70,575: Speedway prizes, $50,000; accessory prizes, $12,550; lap prizes, $8,025. † New record.

Left: Jimmy Murphy. Opposite page: Murphy in the winning car with his mechanic, Ernie Olson. Above: One of the two Fronty-Fords that entered the race. The cars had Model T Ford planetary transmissions and Ford rear axles and semi-elliptic front springs, but the engine blocks had 16-valve Frontenac heads from Louis Chevrolet. Against much more powerful racing cars, the Fronty-Fords ran steadily to finish 14th and 18th.

Murphy rammed over the brick straightaways at close to 100 miles an hour to scoot ahead when Hartz had to pit. From there on Murphy opened up bricks to pluck off lap prizes and finish 5 miles ahead of Hartz. He had averaged better than 94 miles an hour—almost 5 miles an hour faster than DePalma's old record, set back in 1915. And although lap and accessory prizes were half what they had been in 1920, he'd won almost $28,000. Murphy's record-busting run in the Miller put a stack of new orders for his engine onto the desk of Harry Miller, a dour, double-chinned man who claimed he sometimes heard "voices" telling him what to do. This victory would begin a decade-long battle between Miller and the Duesenbergs for supremacy at Indianapolis. For a glum Tommy Milton, there could be only the hope of revenge next year.

Ernie Olson: "No head"

Ernie Olson was Jimmy Murphy's riding mechanic. In California 54 years later he talked about their winning ride. *We had the pole and I think we led for every lap except one. The officials said that Harry Hartz was leading for part of the race, but we always thought that was crap. Jimmy Murphy, along with Tommy Milton, they were probably the two best drivers in the world at that time. ... At Indianapolis there were only four or five drivers who knew how to fix a car to get the most out of it. DePalma was a good driver, but he had no head when it came to knowing how to fix a car to get more miles per hour out of it. Milton did. Murphy did. And later on Frank Lockhart did —he was the best of them all.*

1923

No More "500s"?

Tommy Milton stood on the throttle of the H.C.S. Special as it hurtled a little high off the No. 4 turn and onto the straightaway in front of the grandstands. A yellow and black Durant Special jumped by him on the inside and the two cars screamed by the packed stands nose to nose. Here they were, Jimmy Murphy and Tommy Milton—America's best drivers and bitter rivals—locked in a duel to decide who would be the first to win two "500s."

This year's cars were lighter and sleeker because of two new rule changes. Single-seat bodies were allowed for the first time since 1911, so each of the 24 drivers left the weight of his mechanic in the pits. And engines were smaller, piston displacement shaved to 122 cubic inches, or two liters, as the Speedway kept pace with smaller, higher-rpm Continental designs. During the 4-lap trials, the light cars bounced and leaped over the bricks; bone-sore drivers pleaded for more effective shock absorbers. But five cars qualified at over 100 miles an hour, and Tommy Milton's H.C.S. Special whirled to a new record of better than 108 miles an hour.

Most every driver had wanted a Miller straight-eight engine under his hood after Jimmy Murphy's record-breaking ride atop a Miller a year earlier. Cliff Durant entered a team of eight Miller cars, Harry Miller now building chassis as well as engines. The Duesenberg brothers entered three cars, but only one qualified. The Germans were back for the first time since the war with three Mercedes. Former "500" winners Ralph DePalma and Dario Resta were driving Packards. But the favorites were those two rivals—Jimmy Murphy, in one of the Durant cars, and Tommy Milton, steering a Miller that, after two years of frustration, he'd finally made ready to run in a "500."

Some 50,000 fans filled the grandstands and an estimated 100,000 stood on the vast infield as the 24 cars started on a cool, breezy Memorial Day. For the first 50 miles Milton passed Murphy and then Murphy passed Milton in a furious lead-swapping battle that swallowed up the track at an average of better than 96 miles an hour. Murphy tried to blast off the turns with the quickness of Milton but, lacking the master's touch, he shredded his tires and had to pit early. Glancing over his shoulder and seeing Murphy go off, Milton slowed to save his rubber and Howdy Wilcox squeezed into the lead.

Bodies and nerves were rubbed raw by the pounding in the light cars (only four of the 11 drivers who finished went the 500 miles without relief). By the race's halfway mark, Milton held a slight lead, but his hands were painfully blistered. He came to the pit and Howdy Wilcox, whose own car had dropped out, took the wheel in relief. Harry Hartz slipped ahead while the change of drivers was being made, but when Milton returned from having his hands bandaged at the field hospital, Wilcox had moved by Hartz to retake first. Wilcox got an "IN" sign, bringing him to the pit, and Milton took the wheel. He came out still ahead of Hartz, but Murphy was third and closing. Milton guessed that Murphy would have to pit before the end of the race because he'd made that early stop for rubber. Milton held the H.C.S. Special at about 90 miles an hour and, sure enough, Murphy had to cut in for a tire change.

The Duesenberg 8 pace car waits as the field lines up. There was an early rush for the lap prizes. "The inner field," wrote a witness, "is a sea of automobile tops, the license plates . . . the colors of the nation." Note overhead suspension bridge.

For the last 50 miles Milton spun off the laps to finish comfortably ahead of Hartz and almost 8 miles ahead of Murphy, his average for the race a lackadaisical 90 miles an hour.

Tommy Milton's faith in the Miller engine was confirmed: Of the first seven finishers, six carried Millers. And 30-year-old Tommy Milton had become the first driver to win two "500s."

During the race a car had barreled through a fence, killing a 16-year-old boy who'd been watching through a knothole. Newspapers demanded an end to this "Memorial Day madness." The American Legion instituted legal action to stop the race. Suddenly, the day after the race, Carl Fisher seemed to bow to the critics. The Speedway, he announced, was for sale, and he questioned whether there should be another "500."

Tommy Milton: A driver's last thoughts

What goes through a driver's mind when he is about to crash? This was Tommy Milton's reply a few years after his last "500": *In a race in California, my front axle broke as I led at a high speed. The car spun, hit the top rail, spun around again, and hit the lower wall. I had no control whatsoever. This thought ran through my mind: 'Well, old fellow, you've carried the pitcher to the well once too often. This is the time it gets broke. I'm not afraid to meet the Maker, but life is fun.' However, I was driving the next race.*

1923's TOP TEN

Race open to cars with a piston displacement of 122 cubic inches or less.

NO.	DRIVER	CAR	ENGINE	CYL.	BORE	STROKE	PISTON DISPL.	TIME	MPH	WINNINGS*
1	Tommy Milton	H.C.S. Special	Miller	8	2.344	3.500	120.7	5:29:50.17	90.95	$20,000
7	Harry Hartz	Durant Special	Miller	8	2.344	3.500	120.7	5:33:05.90	90.06	10,000
5	Jimmy Murphy	Durant Special	Miller	8	2.344	3.500	120.7	5:40:36.54	88.08	5,000
6	Eddie Hearne	Durant Special	Miller	8	2.344	3.500	120.7	5:46:14.23	86.65	3,500
23	L. L. Corum	Barber-Warnock Special	Fronty-Ford	4	3.115	4.000	122.0	6:03:16.81	82.58	3,000
31	Frank Elliott	Durant Special	Miller	8	2.531	3.000	120.8	6:04:52.87	82.22	2,200
8	Cliff Durant	Durant Special	Miller	8	2.344	3.500	120.7	6:05:06.30	82.17	1,800
15	Max Sailer	Mercedes Special	Mercedes	4	2.765	5.020	119.4	6:11:49.60	80.68	1,600
19	Prince de Cystria	Bugatti Special	Bugatti	8	2.362	3.468	121.7	6:26:24.78	77.64	1,500
34	Phil Shafer	Duesenberg Special	Duesenberg	8	2.374	3.422	121.4	6:40:04.98	74.98	1,400

* Speedway prizes for winning entries. Total awards in race, $83,425: Speedway prizes, $50,000; accessory prizes, $21,325; lap prizes, $12,100.

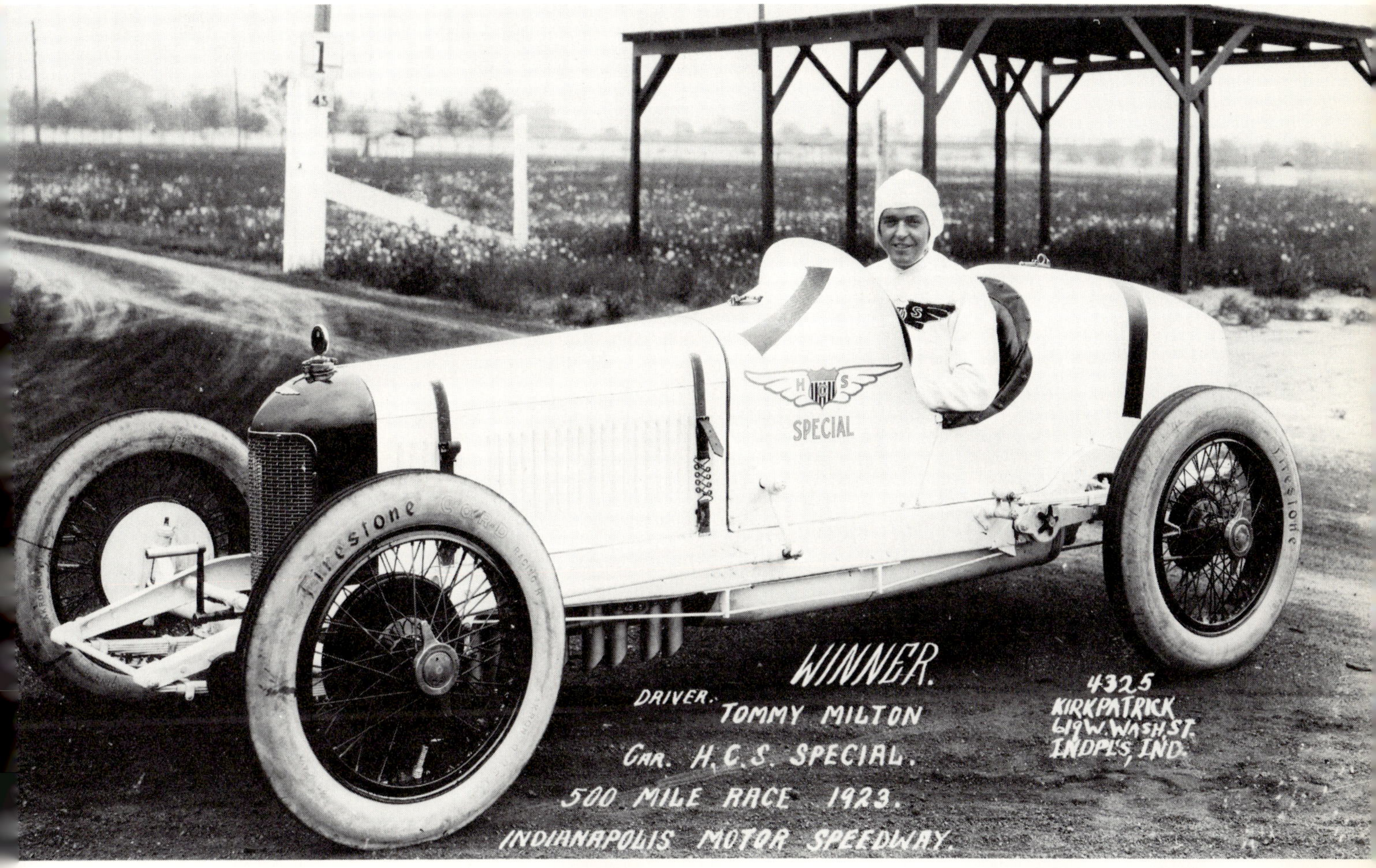

WINNER.
DRIVER. TOMMY MILTON
CAR. H.C.S. SPECIAL.
500 MILE RACE 1923.
INDIANAPOLIS MOTOR SPEEDWAY.

4325
KIRKPATRICK
419 W. WASH. ST.
INDPLS, IND.

Tommy Milton (above) in the winning H.C.S. Special (it was named for manufacturer Harry C. Stutz) and (r.) rival Jimmy Murphy in his Durant Special. By now it had become in at always trendy Indy to dub cars Specials. Opposite page, top: An artist's view of Milton taking the checker. Bottom: The helmeted Milton. Many spectators came to picnic and only glanced occasionally at the race. They roared as cars buzzed by each other, not knowing or caring that one car might be a dozen laps behind the other. "Thousands will tell you they never miss a race," declared a writer, "and yet they have little concept of what is going on."

1924

Here Come the Howlers

His topcoat flapping in the cool breeze as he stood in the pit, Fred Duesenberg frowned as he watched the four leading cars buzz by the 250-mile point of this "500." The four leaders were powered by Miller engines. In fifth place hung a Duesenberg. Angrily, Fred Duesenberg waved in the car. He turned to Joe Boyer, famous for his heavy foot, and told him to replace the driver, L. L. Corum. "Catch them," he snapped at Boyer, pointing to the distant Millers, "or burn this ship."

The Duesenberg brothers had come to the race determined to blunt the rush to Harry Miller's new engines—nearly half the entries carried them— and make a Duesenberg a winner after eight years of trying. They showed Gasoline Alley something new: Three of their four entries were equipped with superchargers, or, as they were soon called on the Alley, "blowers." At high-rpm levels, cylinder gases packed a weaker punch. Blasts of air from a blower strengthened that punch, European racers had found, but the Alley's mechanics wondered if the new contraptions would hold up over 500 miles.

The three supercharged Duesenbergs impressed few in the trials, 104 miles an hour their best showing. Little Jimmy Murphy won the pole in a Miller with a 108-mile-an-hour run, and his rival and former mentor, Tommy Milton, took the No. 3 spot (with a 105) in another Miller.

The trials took place only because Henry Ford and other car makers had talked Carl Fisher into continuing the "500." As his involvement in developing resorts in Miami Beach and Long Island increased, Fisher had lost interest in the race. The Speedway's grandstands needed renovating, but Fisher was reluctant to siphon $200,000 from investments sunk into real estate to pay for the work. And he expressed doubts about the value of the race if it were to be primarily a sporting event rather than a test of automotive performance. But, swayed by Ford, he continued the race while he and his partners looked for someone to buy the Speedway.

Gunning for a second "500" victory, which would put him even with Tommy Milton, Jimmy Murphy had shot into the lead in the 2d lap. At the end of 250 miles, Murphy's closest pursuer was Earl Cooper. (Tommy Milton had dropped out early with a broken gas-tank strap.) But then Joe Boyer, responding to Fred Duesenberg's exhortations, came out of the pit at the wheel of the supercharged Duesenberg to chase after Murphy, Cooper, and two other Miller-powered cars. Boyer whipped by one Miller, then a second. At the 400-mile point he howled by the grandstands a mile behind Cooper's green Studebaker Special and Murphy's blue Miller, closing relentlessly with 104-mile-an-hour bursts on the straightaways.

Murphy heard Boyer's footfalls and saw he couldn't match the supercharged Duesy's straight-

An artist on the scene tells the story of this "500," despite erratic spelling. "Henry" (top r.) is Henry Ford, the honorary referee.

AT 7 P.M. THURSDAY, CARS WERE LINED UP TWO MILES TO GET THE BEST PLACES WHEN THE GATES WERE OPEN FRIDAY A.M.

9:20 BAND COMES DOWN THE TRACK LED BY STARS AND STRIPES

HENRY, AS REFEREE INSPECTS THE TRACK IN THE COLE PACEMAKER

9:43 CARS START LINING UP

9:45 FIRST BOMB

9:57 BATTLE-IN-THE-CLOUDS BOMB

10:00 THEY'RE OFF IN A CLOUD OF DUST BEHIND THE PACEMAKER

MANY OLD TIMERS MISSED THE SAGGY OLD SUSPENSION BRIDGE

JOE BOYER A FREQUENT STOPPER LOOSES 2 GASTANK CAPS

COOPER GAINES ON MURPHY WHO HAS HELD LEAD FOR 41 LAPS AND PASSES MURPHY IN LAP 42 AT BETTER THAN 100 M.P.H.

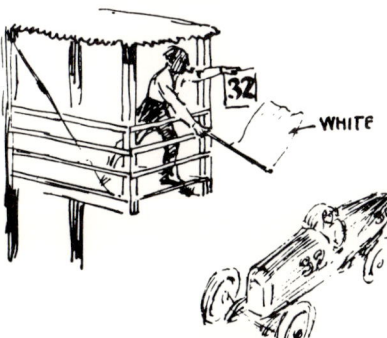
CAR 32 FLAGGED FOR DRIVING TOO HIGH ON THE TURNS

MURPHY STOPS AT PITS 15 SECONDS FOR TIRE CHANGE GIVING BENNIE HILL SECOND PLACE

The sketches picture the ending of the race, won by Corum (below, l. inset) and Boyer (r. inset). The Contest Board of the American Automobile Association ruled that Boyer would get credit for being a co-winner after driving nearly half the race, but Corum would get all of the driver's share of the first-prize money. With lap prizes reduced—$50 for each of the first 125 laps, nothing for the remaining laps—Boyer netted only $50. Three months later he was killed at Altoona, Pennsylvania. The Corum-Boyer victory brought congratulations pouring down on owner Fred Duesenberg, the first American builder to equip his cars with superchargers.

away speeds. He began to bite deeply into the turns, but ripped a tire and had to pit. Cooper blasted the Studebaker into the lead. But he, too, couldn't match the speed of that screaming Duesy on the straights. He dug lower into the turns, tore a tire, and wobbled to the pit. The Duesy stormed triumphantly into the lead.

But Cooper zoomed out of the pits, flashed through the turns, and crept to within a few feet of the maroon Duesenberg. With the grandstand crowd standing for one of the most sensational finishes ever seen at the Speedway, both cars blurred into the No. 1 turn—inches apart, only 30 miles to go. Cooper swung for an opening and skidded. He fought the nose and straightened, but he'd ripped a tire; he veered to the pit. Easing on the throttle to save his own rubber, Boyer cruised the rest of the way to win with an average speed of 98.23, a new "500" record, almost 4 miles an hour faster than the 1922 record.

The Duesenbergs had triumphed, and their blowers had proven their power and durability. But eccentric genius Harry Miller would be back in 1925 with his engines—and a new idea.

A view of a fan who put his money on the wrong driver.

Joe Boyer: "Let 'er all out"

The first co-winner of a "500," Joe Boyer told after the race how he got from the pit to the checker: *I started the race in the No. 9 Duesenberg and won the first lap. But then I came in for a tire change and Fred Duesenberg called me out and sent Ernie Ansterberg into my car.... I was in the pits about 4 laps when Corum came in in car No. 15 for the usual halfway stop. Duesenberg called Corum out and there I was back in the race. I was so glad to have a ride I thought, 'Let 'er all out.'*

1924's TOP TEN

Race open to cars with a piston displacement of 122 cubic inches or less.

NO.	DRIVER	CAR	ENGINE	CYL.	BORE	STROKE	PISTON DISPL.	TIME	MPH	WINNINGS*
15	L. L. Corum and Joe Boyer	Duesenberg Special	Duesenberg†	8	2.380	3.422	121.9	5:05:23.51	98.23‡	$20,000
8	Earl Cooper	Studebaker Special	Miller	8	2.343	3.500	120.7	5:06:47.18	97.79	10,000
2	Jimmy Murphy	Miller Special	Miller	8	2.343	3.500	120.7	5:08:25.39	97.27	5,000
4	Harry Hartz	Durant Special	Miller	8	2.343	3.500	120.7	5:10:44.39	96.54	3,500
3	Bennett Hill	Miller Special	Miller	8	2.343	3.500	120.7	5:11:00.07	96.46	3,000
12	Peter DePaolo	Duesenberg Special	Duesenberg	8	2.380	3.422	121.9	5:18:08.55	94.30	2,200
14	Fred Comer	Durant Special	Miller	8	2.343	3.500	120.7	5:21:06.91	93.42	1,800
6	Ira Vail	Ira Vail Special	Miller	8	2.343	3.500	120.7	5:24:30.07	92.45	1,600
32	Antoine Mourre	Mourre Special	Miller	8	2.343	3.500	120.7	5:26:55.62	91.76	1,500
19	Bob McDonogh	Miller Special	Miller	8	2.343	3.500	120.7	5:31:26.73	90.51	1,400

* Speedway prizes for winning entries. Total awards in race, $86,850: Speedway prizes, $60,000; accessory prizes, $20,600; lap prizes, $6,250. † Supercharged.
‡ New record.

1925

Needed Were Some More Bricks

"If we could go through each turn in two and a half seconds less—without ruining our tires—the average for the '500' would go up at least 10 miles an hour."

Speaking was little Jimmy Murphy. He was explaining to a friend why he wanted Harry Miller to build a racer with the power transmitted to the front wheels rather than the rear wheels as in conventional cars. A front-drive car, Murphy reasoned, would be pulled around the four Speedway turns faster than a rear-drive car could be pushed—and with fewer skids and less tire wear. In the summer of 1924 Miller began building a front-drive for Murphy. But Jimmy never saw it. In September he died on a Syracuse dirt track. Their feud ended, Tommy Milton accompanied Murphy's crushed body to California for burial.

At the Speedway the next May, Miller's front-drive car—the Junior 8 Special—attracted gaping crowds. Ever since single-seaters had returned to the "500," cars had been sculpted lower and more streamlined. With no drive shaft running under the cockpit to the rear wheels, the Junior 8's driver's seat was set so low that people joked that the driver's elbows would scrape the track. Only 36 inches high, the Junior 8 weighed less than 1,500 pounds dry. Mechanics and drivers worried that the small, front-heavy car would spin its tail on turns.

After the previous year's victory by a supercharged Duesenberg, most of the 1925 cars ran with blowers. "You're going in naked without one," said a driver. And nearly all the cars rode over the bricks faster and smoother on new low-pressure balloon tires introduced by Firestone.

Of the 22 qualifiers that lined up on a simmering morning before an estimated 145,000 spectators, one car would be pulled and 15 pushed by Miller engines. A Miller had won the pole with a record-breaking 113.196 miles an hour, but No. 2 in the front was Peter DePaolo in a Duesenberg. In the second row, having qualified at 109 miles an hour, sat Dave Lewis, Harry Miller's brother-in-law, in the supercharged front-drive Junior 8.

Early in the race DePaolo jumped away from the pack, and for the first 100 miles he and Earl Cooper, in a Miller, battled for first. Then Phil Shafer, in another Duesenberg, shot ahead. But DePaolo forged back into the lead and still led at the 250-mile mark, his average a record 103 miles an hour. Whizzing through the turns, only a lap behind, was Dave Lewis in the front-drive.

DePaolo, his hands bloody and blistered, came out for a relief driver at 250 miles. Only 50 miles later Dave Lewis steered the Miller front-drive past the Duesenberg. The two cars hurtled by the stands at better than 130 miles an hour, the howl of the superchargers singing through the noise of the throng. The Miller gained on the turns and began to pull away. Fred Duesenberg called in the relief driver and out whirled Peter DePaolo, hands bandaged, at the wheel of the Duesenberg. "Driving like a wild man," as one observer later put it, DePaolo set his sights on Lewis's blue Miller.

Lewis clung to the wheel, exhausted after his bone-bruising 400-mile ride over the bricks. His speed began to waver. His crew signaled him to the pit. Head wobbling, he overshot the pit and had to scoot around one more lap. As he braked, he was lifted out of the cockpit. Into the seat jumped Bennett Hill, a recent college graduate, whose Miller had limped out of the race.

As Hill roared onto the track, he saw the Duesenberg far ahead and leading now by a lap

Flames and smoke engulf the pagoda, race headquarters for press, timers, and judges since its erection in 1913. The fire erupted on the morning of June 1, two days after the race. Plans began immediately for a new pagoda.

63

MEMORIAL
DAY
MAY 30, 1925
THIRTEENTH
INTERNATIONAL
SWEEPSTAKES
RACE

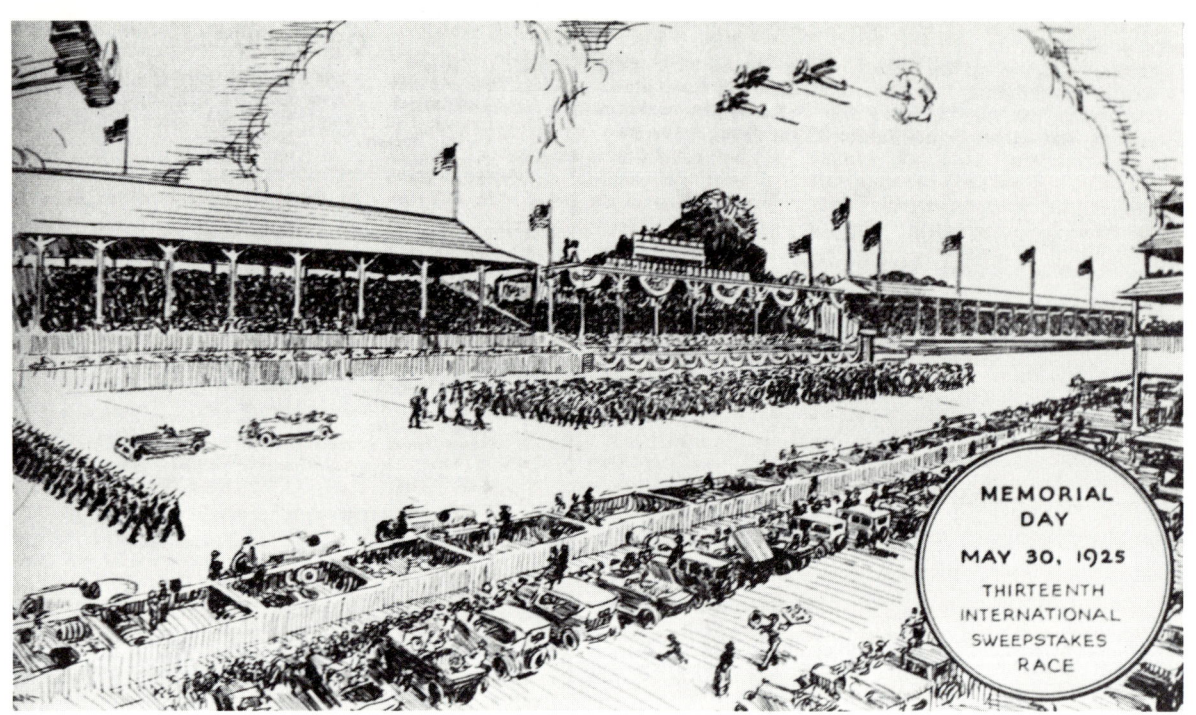

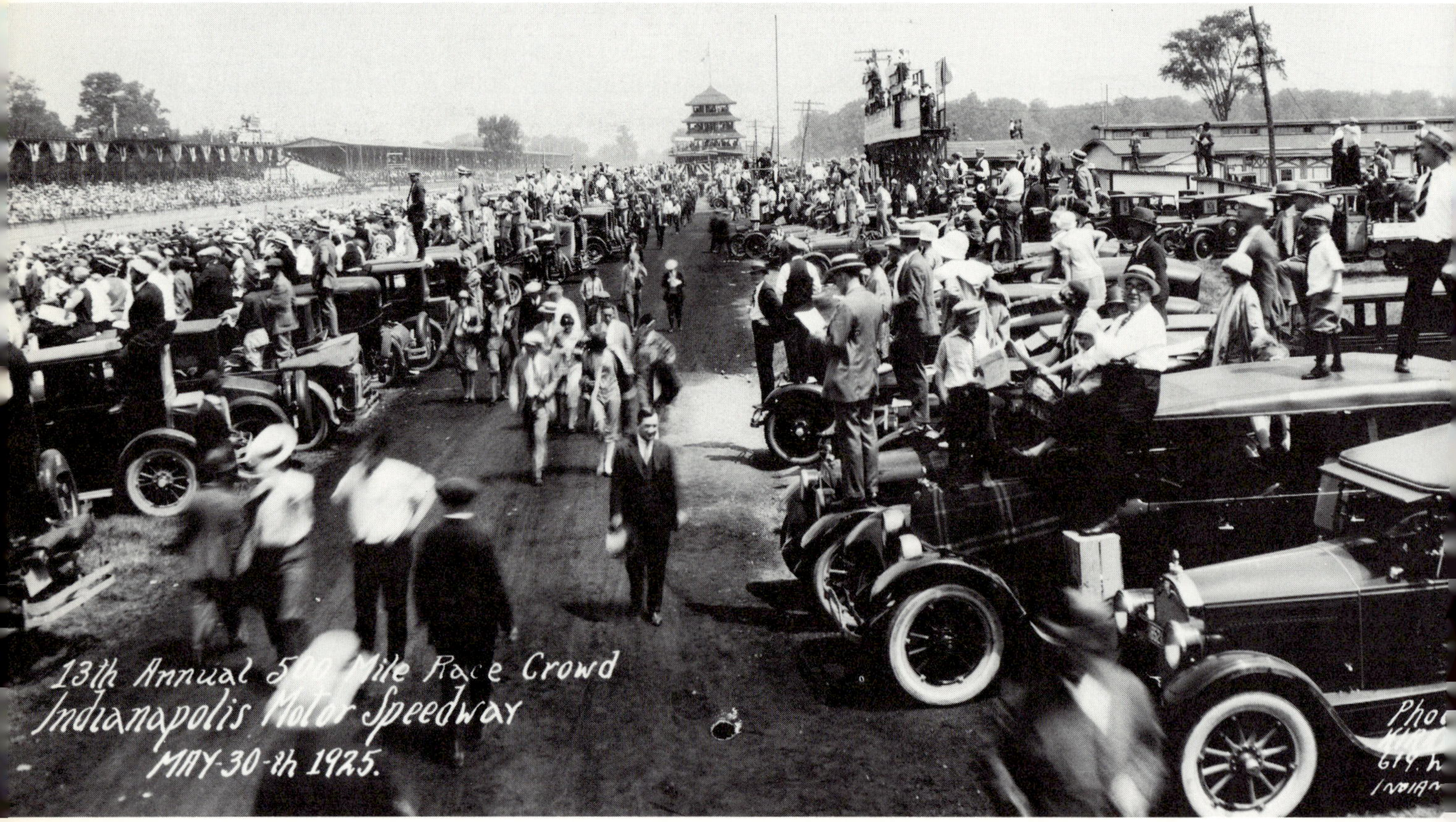
13th Annual 500 Mile Race Crowd
Indianapolis Motor Speedway
MAY-30-th 1925.

and a half with some 50 miles left in the race. Twisting the front-drive through the turns, Hill swept by the Duesenberg to trail by a lap. On each go-round he was blasting seconds off the Duesenberg's lead—but then he ran out of bricks. DePaolo booted the Duesenberg by the checker, the first driver to cover the 500 miles in under five hours, more than an hour and a half faster than Ray Harroun's time of 14 years earlier. And DePaolo was the first to finish with an average of better than 100 miles an hour. The first four finishers, in fact, broke the previous year's record.

For a second straight year, Duesenberg had triumphed over Miller. But the Miller front-drive had proven its skill through the turns and one day would be a king of the "500." Even sooner would Harry Miller lord it over the Duesenbergs.

Peter DePaolo: "OK, Daddy"

Looking back on his victory, Peter DePaolo remembered two conversations with Fred Duesenberg: *Mr. Duesenberg was a wonderful man. We called him Daddy. In 1924 I finished sixth behind Joe Boyer, who was the first to win with a supercharger. After the race I said, 'Daddy, could I have a supercharger?' He was so happy about Boyer winning and me coming in sixth he said, 'Kiddo, you can have the factory.' So in 1925 I got the supercharger. While my hands were bandaged, Norm Batten had dropped my car back to fifth. Fred said to me in the pit, 'Kiddo, you're going to have to go.' 'OK, Daddy,' I said, 'we'll make it.' And we did.*

Opposite page: An artist and a photographer view the Speedway minutes before the race. Above: A low-to-the-track Dave Lewis peers around the front-end assembly of the Miller front-drive Junior 8. Its wheelbase was 100 inches, its weight a frisky 1,500 pounds. With the car Miller brought back an idea as old as the 1893 de Dion-Bouton cars: independent suspension. Right, top: One view of a DePaolo fan. Bottom: Side view of a Miller front-drive, Bennett Hill at the wheel. The rotund Harry Miller, hands in pockets, savors its low-slung lines.

13th Annual 500-Mile Race
Indianapolis Motor Speedway

PETE'S UNUSUAL FEAT

$7,800 LAP MONEY

$20,000 PRIZE MONEY

1925's TOP TEN

Race open to cars with a piston displacement of 122 cubic inches or less.

NO.	DRIVER	CAR	ENGINE*	CYL.	BORE	STROKE	PISTON DISPL.	TIME	MPH	WINNINGS†
12	Peter DePaolo	Duesenberg Special	Duesenberg	8	2.380	3.421	121.7	4:56:39.46	101.13‡	$20,000
1	Dave Lewis	Junior 8 Special	Miller§	8	2.343	3.500	120.7	4:57:33.15	100.82	10,000
9	Phil Shafer	Duesenberg Special	Duesenberg	8	2.373	3.406	120.5	4:59:26.79	100.18	5,000
6	Harry Hartz	Miller Special	Miller	8	2.343	3.500	120.7	5:03:21.59	98.89	3,600
4	Tommy Milton	Miller Special	Miller	8	2.342	3.500	120.7	5:08:25.72	97.27	3,000
28	Leon Duray	Miller Special	Miller	8	2.343	3.500	120.7	5:09:34.01	96.91	2,200
8	Ralph DePalma	Miller Special	Miller	8	2.343	3.500	120.7	5:09:46.06	96.85	1,800
38	Peter Kreis	Duesenberg Special	Duesenberg	8	2.373	3.406	120.5	5:11:26.86	96.32	1,600
15	W. E. Shattuc	Miller Special	Miller	8	2.343	3.500	120.7	5:13:20.48	95.74	1,500
22	Pietro Bordino	Fiat Special	Fiat	8	2.375	3.437	121.0	5:16:37.97	94.75	1,400

* All supercharged. † Speedway prizes for winning entries. Total awards in race, $87,750: Speedway prizes, $60,000; accessory prizes, $12,750; lap prizes, $15,000. ‡ New record. § Front-drive.

Opposite page, top: Cars line up behind the pace car, a Rickenbacker 8, for the start of the race. Bottom: A cartoonist portrays the heavy swag taken away by DePaolo for himself and the Duesenberg team. Above: That team surrounds DePaolo (also at l.) and the winning Duesenberg. Its balloon tires needed only one change. "The day of the balloon tires has come," commented *Motor Age* magazine. "Perhaps the supercharger and the front-wheel drive are not far distant as regular features of passenger vehicles. New things are often tried out in this great outdoor automotive laboratory."

1926

Run in the Rain

The raindrops on the hood of the blue Miller twinkled in the sunlight. From the cockpit Dave Lewis glanced over his shoulder at clouds massed like hovering elephants. Rain had spattered the bricks an hour earlier, but the sun had flashed between the cloud banks and now was drying the track. Dave Lewis, Harry Miller's brother-in-law and a missionary for this car, wasn't all that worried about slick bricks. His front-drive Miller, he told people, would claw its way around the turns faster than "any of the pigs in this race."

This year's racers carried the smallest engines ever for a "500"—91.5 cubic inches (1.5 liters)—as the Speedway tried to keep the ever faster cars from soaring out of the brickyard. Harry Miller shrank displacements and produced cars that cost $15,000 for front-drive and $10,000 for rear-drive. The Duesenberg brothers, busy cranking out expensive passenger sedans for the *nouveau riche* of the gaudy twenties, had time to modify only two cars for the race, but in one of the Duesies sat Peter DePaolo, the 1925 winner. All 28 cars in the starting field boasted improved superchargers, and nearly all rode on recently developed 5.25 x 30 Firestone balloon tires. Some cars weighed a bantam 1,200 pounds. As a result, even with the smaller engines, qualifying times were wickedly fast. Veteran Earl Cooper won the pole; his Miller Special averaged better than 111 miles an hour, a shade below the record. In his low-slung front-drive Miller, Dave Lewis sat right behind Cooper, in the second row. Far back in the seventh row, wrapped in a conventional rear-drive Miller, was blond, 23-year-old Frank Lockhart, a Los Angeles mechanic and dirt track driver who had come to Indianapolis begging for a ride and had been given the Miller when its driver, Pete Kreis, was flu-stricken. During time trials, Lockhart had failed twice before narrowly qualifying for his first "500."

Puddles splotched the mucky infield, and the crowd—estimated at 125,000—seemed thinner than last year's. With a "fearful roar and popping," in the words of one reporter, and amid clouds of smoke, the cars started, rolled one lap behind the pacer, then burped and blasted by starter Seth Klein's flag. At the 50-mile mark Dave Lewis whirled the Miller front-drive out of the No. 4 turn and into the lead; but swaying along in his wake was the Miller piloted by young Lockhart. At 150 miles Lewis zipped in for a tire change and watched Lockhart's white Miller howl by in first place. Minutes later sheets of rain slanted from the clouds and the starter waved a white flag from the platform overhanging the course, sending the cars to the pits. It was the first interruption of a "500."

The cars stood, hooded, for an hour and 15 minutes. Mechanics were forbidden to put even a finger on the cars. When the rain stopped, the racers filed out in the order they'd held at the flag and shot off again. With 300 miles to go, Lockhart led by a lap with Harry Hartz and Dave Lewis struggling to catch up. Lewis's front wheel suddenly bucked and slowed, a valve splintered, and his front-drive Miller was out of the race.

In his grey Miller, veteran Harry Hartz closed on this kid Lockhart racing in his first "500." Only 20 yards apart, the two Millers whizzed by the grandstands, a pair of grey and white bullets. Hartz inched ahead of Lockhart on the backstretch to lead by 25 yards . . . then by 35 yards

Top: A cartoon of the times makes the claim that the gods might not always care for that racket down below and could call on their pluvial nature to drown out the race. This was the first time it had rained in Indianapolis during a "500," and although this would not be the last race shortened by rain, people in Indianapolis believed then—and still do—that the "500" is lucky with the weather. Above (l. to r.): Official timers Odis Portor, S. J. Williams, and Chester Ricker hover over their instruments in the new pagoda, erected where the old one had stood.

... "and in the stands," said one observer, "people stamped their feet and went loco." But with 240 miles to go, Hartz had to coast to the pits, and young Lockhart flashed ahead. Hartz scooted out of the pit and tried to close. But Lockhart moved neatly through the turns and blasted down the straights to keep him at bay. "He can drive, that fellow," admired *Motor Age* magazine's reporter. Rain again sprinkled the track, and a frustrated Hartz saw Lockhart get the checker, the race ended at 400 miles. Lockhart's average speed was well off the record, but he had become only the fourth driver—Rene Thomas, Jules Goux, and Ray Harroun were the others—to win the "500" as a rookie.

Another winner was Firestone. Only 18 tires were changed during the race, compared to 36 a year earlier and 88 in 1913. Also a winner was Harry Miller, nine of his cars among the first ten finishers. A loser was Fred Duesenberg, but one more "500" victory was down the road, his last.

Ira Vail:
Win or lose

Vail drove in five "500s" before retiring in 1925, his best finish a seventh place in 1921. During part of his racing career, Vail maximized his earnings by owning the car he drove. *The car I drove, I bought it from Harry Miller for about $10,000. That was what they all cost, a Miller or a Duesenberg, from $8,000 to $10,000, which was a lot of money at a time when a very good passenger car cost only a little more than $1,000. But you could win $30,000 or more at Indianapolis and as much as $5,000 at a cement track in Minneapolis-St. Paul or tracks in Hartford, Boston ... everywhere. You'd be guaranteed $2,000 or $3,000 even if you didn't win, depending on the deal you made with the track's promoter. The deal depended on how many people you could draw. I got guarantees at most tracks and I'd drive at 15 or 20 tracks during the year.*

1926's TOP TEN

Race open to cars with a piston displacement of 91.5 cubic inches or less.

NO.	DRIVER	CAR	ENGINE*	CYL.	BORE	STROKE	PISTON DISPL.	TIME†	MPH	WINNINGS‡
15	Frank Lockhart	Miller Special	Miller	8	2.187	3.000	90.2	4:10:14.95 (160)	95.904	$20,000
3	Harry Hartz	Miller Special	Miller	8	2.187	3.000	90.2	4:10:50.49 (158)	94.482	10,000
36	Cliff Woodbury	Boyle Special	Miller	8	2.344	2.625	90.2	4:11:46.55 (158)	94.131	5,000
8	Fred Comer	Miller Special	Miller	8	2.187	3.000	90.2	4:11:49.99 (155)	92.323	3,500
12	Peter DePaolo	Duesenberg Special	Duesenberg	8	2.286	2.750	90.3	4:10:41.90 (153)	91.544	3,000
6	Frank Elliott	Miller Special	Miller	8	2.344	2.625	90.6	4:10:46.64 (152)	90.917	2,200
14	Norman Batten	Miller Special	Miller	8	2.344	2.625	90.6	4:10:53.91 (151)	90.276	1,800
19	Ralph Hepburn	Miller Special	Miller	8	2.344	2.625	90.6	4:11:59.68 (151)	89.883	1,600
18	John Duff	Elcar Special	Miller	8	2.344	2.625	90.6	4:11:51.19 (147)	87.551	1,500
4	Phil Shafer	Miller Special	Miller	8	2.187	3.000	90.2	4:11:26.66 (146)	87.097	1,400

*All supercharged. † Race stopped at 400 miles due to rain; figures in parentheses show number of laps run. ‡ Speedway prizes for winning entries. Total awards in race, $88,100: Speedway prizes, $60,000; accessory prizes, $12,100; lap prizes, $16,000.

Opposite page: Spectators perch on cars, stepladders, and a pole. Top: Frank Lockhart and the winning car and crew. They won $39,000. The driver usually got 30 to 40 percent, the crew less than ten percent, the owner the rest. Lockhart finished 18th the next year, was dead before the 1928 race. Right: An artist shows the race's end.

1927

A Last Hurrah

The boyish-faced Frank Lockhart nodded at the mechanic, who twirled the starting crank. Lockhart's Perfect Circle Miller Special belched noise and smoke. Behind him ten rows of cars, three abreast, exploded into life with a staccato popping. The sun blazed from a cloudless sky. Perched in the press pagoda, timing judges and reporters squinted out at the 33 starters, the biggest field since 1919. In the grandstands and the infield, sweltering spectators—straw-hatted, colorfully attired—waited for a LaSalle to take the field around the pace lap.

A year earlier the blond Lockhart had sat in a back row, an unknown dirt track racer from California who'd squeezed into the race on his last qualifying try. He'd won that rain-shortened "500" as well as later races on board tracks and speedways across the nation. Today he was as famous as Peter DePaolo, Harry Hartz, or Tommy Milton. And for this race he sat on the pole, the fastest qualifier.

The speed of the qualifiers had amazed Speedway railbirds (thousands paid 25¢ and 50¢ to watch the trials, held a few days before the race). Harry Miller, the Duesenberg brothers, and other car designers had injected more speed into the little 91.5-cubic-inch engines introduced a year earlier. Better superchargers and intercoolers had whipped engine speeds from 7,000 rpm to better than 8,000 rpm and lifted straightaway speeds to as high as 150 miles an hour. All 33 qualifiers, for the first time, had exceeded 100 miles an hour, compared to only one as recently as 1922 and 16 in 1926. And Frank Lockhart had sped his Miller to a new record for the 4 laps: 120.1 miles an hour.

Young drivers from midget-car racing, dirt tracks, and board tracks had swarmed to Indy hungry for the fame and money attained a year before by Lockhart. Among them was George Souders, a 24-year-old former Purdue student with no long-distance experience. He was riding a Duesenberg, one of five in the race (compared to 28 Millers). In a nearby car was another rookie, Wilbur Shaw.

Lockhart was the popular favorite, thousands rooting for the "youthful daredevil," as the papers called him, to win a second straight "500." The grandstand crowds applauded as he streaked into the lead at the start and clicked off lap after lap to snare one prize after another. (This year, for the first time since 1920, lap prizes were up to $20,000—$100 to the leader on each lap.) By the halfway point he'd won almost $10,000. But with 80 laps to go, his Miller threw a connecting rod and Lockhart smoked into the pits. He stepped out, shrugged, smiled, and asked for a hot dog.

On the track a pack of cars snapped hungrily for the lead. Peter DePaolo (driving in relief for Bob McDonogh after his own car dropped out) snatched it for a while, but a supercharger failed and his Miller spent three precious minutes in the pits. The grind over the bricks and the intense heat pulverized the small engines (only 12 of the 33 starters were running at the end). With 60 laps left in the race, the crowd let out an excited yell as an unknown rookie, for the second straight year, rammed his way through the pack to lead. It was George Souders in a grey and black Duesenberg. He pulled away from Egbert (Babe) Stapp, in another Duesy, and led by 2 laps as he coasted by the checker with the slowest average speed for the full 500 miles since 1923—97.545 miles an hour. Behind him, Babe Stapp was only a lap and

Norman Batten's Car on Fire

The tail of his car a torch, Norman Batten steers his Miller Special away from the pits after its gas tank burst afire on the straightaway in front of the stands. He stayed at the wheel until the car had slowed down and was clear of the pits and stands. Then—badly burned —he leaped to safety. After the race, drivers and mechanics contributed almost $5,000 as a gift to Batten. There were four crashes or fires during the race—but no deaths. A week before, newspapers had told how Paris crowds swarmed to the airport to greet Charles Lindbergh's Spirit of St. Louis when it landed after a solo hop across the Atlantic. "And no bad news," wrote a commentator, "could slow the market's sweep upward."

The Start

Top: At the start Jim Hill's Nickel Plate Special (No. 42) is off from the last row to taste the smoke and dust of the leaders. Above and right: George Souders and his Duesenberg and crew. Souders's winnings totaled about $30,000.

1927's TOP TEN

Race open to cars with a piston displacement of 91.5 cubic inches or less.

NO.	DRIVER	CAR	ENGINE*	CYL.	BORE	STROKE	PISTON DISPL.	TIME	MPH	WINNINGS†
32	George Souders	Duesenberg	Duesenberg	8	2.250	2.343	90.0	5:07:33.08	97.545	$20,000
10	Earl Devore	Miller	Miller	8	2.187	3.000	90.2	5:19:35.95	93.868	10,000
27	Tony Gulotta	Miller	Miller	8	2.187	3.000	90.2	5:22:05.88	93.139	5,000
29	Wilbur Shaw	Jynx Special	Miller	8	2.343	2.625	90.6	5:22:12.05	93.110	3,500
21	Dave Evans	Duesenberg	Duesenberg	8	2.281	2.750	90.5	5:30:27.71	90.782	3,000
14	Bob McDonogh	Cooper Special	Miller‡	8	2.187	3.000	90.2	5:31:49.34	90.410	2,200
16	Eddie Hearne	Miller Special	Miller	8	2.187	3.000	90.2	5:33:05.74	90.064	1,800
6	Tommy Milton	Detroit Special	Miller‡	8	2.187	3.000	90.2	5:52:36.21	85.081	1,600
25	Cliff Bergere	Miller Special	Miller	8	2.343	2.625	90.6	6:15:20.07	79.929	1,500
5	Frank Elliott	Junior 8 Special	Miller‡	8	2.343	2.625	90.6	6:23:25.69	78.244	1,400

* All supercharged. † Speedway prizes for winning entries. Total awards in race, $89,850: Speedway prizes, $60,000; accessory prizes, $9,850; lap prizes, $20,000. ‡ Front-drive.

a half away from second place, $10,000, and a one-two finish for the Duesenberg team when he broke a rear axle. But for the third time in the past four years, a Duesenberg, outnumbered by Millers, had triumphed. This victory, however, would be the Duesenbergs' last hurrah at the "500." As for Harry Miller, his already impressive record at the "500" would get even shinier.

George Souders: "An awful spill"

Nearly 50 years after his surprising win at the "500," George Souders reminisced about his racing career: *I quit Purdue when my father died. I worked in a garage and rode on dirt tracks. All my life I've been a mechanical nut. That car I rode in 1927, it was smooth handling. And the engine was the smallest ever to win at Indianapolis. The piston displacement was just under 90. The car was the most expensive the Duesenbergs ever built for racing. It cost around $50,000, I was told. A year later I finished third at Indianapolis. In the summer of '28 I raced in Detroit— a $1,000 race, nothing much, and was guaranteed $750 just for showing up, but you have . . . you want to win. Anyway, I had an awful spill. I was unconscious six months and I never raced after that.*

The scoreboard shows No. 2, Frank Lockhart, leading after 250 miles. The people atop the scoreboard, which was behind the pits, could see the race, but those perched on the cars saw little more than each other. The traffic jam as cars squeezed into the Speedway that morning was described in newspapers as "immense."

1928

One for a Plugger

Slanted on a stretcher in the pits, Peter DePaolo could see the cars lined up for the start. During the trials he had bounced out of a spinning car and fractured his skull. Now he waved at the crowd as it signaled with applause its delight at seeing him intact. "The little Italian," wrote one reporter, "is lucky to be alive."

Not as lucky was another Speedway winner. Frank Lockhart, racing's golden boy after his victory as a rookie in 1926, had gone to Daytona Beach chasing a world record and died in blood and sand. Of the 15 winners and co-winners of this race, six had died young and with their goggles on—Dario Resta, Howdy Wilcox, Gaston Chevrolet, Jimmy Murphy, Joe Boyer, and now Lockhart.

Gone also from "500" racing was Carl Fisher. He had found a buyer for the Speedway. In the fall of 1927, former driver and World War I ace Eddie Rickenbacker had joined a combine of Detroit businessmen to pay $700,000 in bonds and an unrevealed sum of cash for the 18-year-old plant. Rickenbacker was appointed Speedway president and T. E. (Pop) Myers stayed on as general manager.

On the pole for this race, on a cloudy and cool Memorial Day, hunched Leon Duray in a front-drive Miller Special. He had zipped through the trials at better than 122 miles an hour, a new record. Well back in the pack of 29 supercharged cars sat 23-year-old Louis Meyer, a California mechanic who had come here looking for a ride as a relief driver (a year earlier he'd driven in relief of Wilbur Shaw). For $5,000, a wealthy Boston friend had bought a used Miller that had finished third in 1927's race and put Meyer at the wheel.

From the start, as the railbirds had figured, Duray shot his front-drive Miller into the lead and whisked through the first 100 miles in a record-breaking 56 and a half minutes. Then his engine overheated and he fell back into the pack. At 200 miles Jimmy Gleason's Duesenberg snatched first place and set a frantic pace; at the 300-mile point, Gleason's average of 103 miles an hour was another new record. By now Louis Meyer had crept from ninth place to third as cars fell into the pits. Only 19 were still running.

Gleason decided to pit for fuel and rubber and as he went in, Tony Gulotta's Stutz flashed by to take the lead. One of Gleason's mechanics accidentally spilled water on a magneto, but it was wiped off and Gleason whizzed out to try to catch the Stutz. The two whirled around the track at better than 100 miles an hour, two colored blobs never more than a few hundred yards apart. Back in third hung Meyer, watching the specks battle in the distance. He'd pitted once and he figured his tires and fuel would carry him the rest of the way at a steady 100 miles an hour.

The Stutz and Duesenberg blew by the 400-mile point clinging to one another. At 425 miles, a soft drizzle brought out the yellow flag, locking the cars into their respective positions and slowing the pace to 80 miles an hour. But the rain soon stopped and, with 50 miles to go, Gulotta still led, with Gleason right behind him. Far back, in third, buzzed Meyer.

Gulotta's Stutz roared toward the No. 3 turn. Suddenly it shuddered and coughed to a stop, a fuel line clogged. Gleason's Duesenberg whined

What it was like to be young and at the "500" in the twenties is shown here by the photographer's camera and the artist's pen. Dashing men were "cake eaters," sexy women were "flappers." But this was also the time of Prohibition, and what the vendor is clutching isn't a bottle of beer.

1928's TOP TEN

Race open to cars with a piston displacement of 91.5 cubic inches or less.

NO.	DRIVER	CAR	ENGINE*	CYL.	BORE	STROKE	PISTON DISPL.	TIME	MPH	WINNINGS†
14	Louis Meyer	Miller Special	Miller	8	2.187	3.000	90.2	5:01:33.75	99.482	$20,000
28	Lou Moore	Miller Special	Miller	8	2.187	3.000	90.2	5:02:17.64	99.241	10,000
3	George Souders	S.A.I. Special	Miller	8	2.187	3.000	90.2	5:06:01.04	98.034	5,000
15	Ray Keech	Simplex Piston Ring Special	Miller	8	2.187	3.000	90.2	5:21:28.45	93.320	3,500
22	Norman Batten	Miller Special	Miller	8	2.187	3.000	90.2	5:21:47.51	93.228	3,000
7	Babe Stapp	Miller Special	Miller‡	8	2.187	3.000	90.2	5:23:50.40	92.638	2,200
43	Billy Arnold	Boyle Valve Special	Miller	8	2.187	3.000	90.2	5:29:16.09	91.111	1,800
27	Fred Frame	S.A.I. Special	Duesenberg	8	2.281	2.750	90.5	5:33:02.38	90.079	1,600
25	Fred Comer	Boyle Valve Special	Miller‡	8	2.187	3.000	90.2	5:37:29.89	88.889	1,500
8	Tony Gulotta	Stutz Special	Miller	8	2.187	3.000	90.2	5:37:30.11	88.888	1,400

* All supercharged.   † Speedway prizes for winning entries. Total awards in race, $90,750: Speedway prizes, $60,000; accessory prizes, $15,750; lap prizes, $15,000.   ‡ Front-drive.

by in the lead. Minutes later Gleason roared into his 195th lap—13 miles to go for all the glory and the first-place prize money.

And then it was Gleason who felt the life ebb out of his car. The water on the magneto had seeped through to kill the engine. Gleason coasted into the pit. Mechanics frantically tried to restart the car but couldn't, and Louis Meyer rolled by in his used Miller to take the checker. His average was an unspectacular 99.482 miles an hour. Meyer won, said one observer, by "steady plugging."

No longer was Louis Meyer a penniless relief driver. "Another young dirt track pilot," wrote a romantic reporter, "has taken the ride to fame and fortune."

For Meyer, one of the lucky "500" drivers, the ride had only begun.

Cliff Bergere: A little more patience

Hollywood stunt man Cliff Bergere drove in 16 "500s," a record (shared with Chet Miller) until A. J. Foyt entered his 17th in 1974. Until 1975, when again Foyt topped him, Bergere had driven more Speedway miles than anyone else—6,142.5. But he never won a "500." In 1976 he talked about why. *I never had the sense of pace that a driver like Louis Meyer had. He had an uncanny sense of how fast to go. He never took the early lead. He drove consistently and steadily to pick off worn-out cars and push into the lead. Even in my last '500,' in 1947, I made the mistake of starting out in front, and my car broke down. Louis Meyer had patience, and if I had had some of his patience, maybe I would have won like he won.*

Right: The view from the pits during the race, the Duesenberg team in the foreground. At far right is the new pagoda, built in 1926 after the original, built in 1913, burned down.

Louis Meyer and the used Miller that won about $30,000. Meyer won no lap money since no prizes were awarded after the 144th lap.

Exhaust smoke billows into the warm air as the engines cough to life and crews wait to shove off the cars. In the first row, behind the Studebaker pacer, are Cliff Woodbury on the pole, Leon Duray in the middle, and Ralph Hepburn on the outside.

1929

—And Sudden Death

What Steve Hannagan, the Speedway's press agent, hailed as the "largest band ever assembled"—there were 1,500 pieces from marching bands all over the Midwest—serenaded the arriving crowd on a warm Memorial Day. This was a time of superlatives; everything was the best and getting better as Americans took a joyride atop a booming economy. The winner of this race, reporters said, could earn more money for a five-hour trip than any driver ever before—$20,000 in first-prize money, $20,000 in lap prizes, more than $15,000 in accessory prizes.

At the start Leon Duray, eager for the lap money, scorched around the first 4 laps at 110 miles an hour. At 20 miles Deacon Litz charged at Duray. The two cars whirled into the No. 4 turn. Litz reached for the lever of his hand brake. He grasped air: The lever had fallen off. Litz saw Duray's tail rush toward him. Litz swung his Rusco-Durac Brake Special down the banked turn. The car skidded sideways, then straightened, and Litz fishtailed out of the spin in first place.

A lap later Bill Spence's Duesenberg skidded and did not straighten. The car careened into the wall. It bounced backward, a whirling red ball, and overturned. The 24-year-old Spence was hurled onto the track. He died on the way to the hospital—the first driver to die in the race since 1919 (a driver was killed in the trials in 1926).

Deacon Litz whirled through the first 100 miles to win almost $5,000 in lap prizes. Then his Miller burned a rod and it chugged, smoking, out of the race.

Minutes later the leader was Louis Meyer, gunning his black and white Miller Special toward a second straight "500" win. Near the 375-mile point he swung into the pit for his second stop. He took on new tires and fuel—enough, by his precise, slide-rule calculations, to take him the rest of the way. But the engine stalled in the pit. Seven minutes later his sweating mechanics restarted the car and the Miller zoomed back onto the track in pursuit of the new leader, pudgy-faced, 28-year-old Ray Keech.

Two years ago Keech had been scrapping for a living on eastern dirt and board tracks. Then, in 1928, he had flashed across the sands at Daytona at 207 miles an hour to be acclaimed the world speed king. Today he steered a Miller car—the Simplex Piston Ring Special—that had once been the pride of Frank Lockhart, the 1926 winner, who had died at Daytona in 1928. Lockhart, a marvelous mechanic as well as a driver, had pepped up the Miller to better than 170 horsepower. Now, with Meyer buzzing after him, Keech tramped down hard on the throttle and pulled away from Meyer and everyone else to win by 9 miles, collecting over $40,000. Two weeks later he joined his benefactor, Frank Lockhart, in death, killed on a midwestern dirt track.

For Harry Miller this race was another triumph. Seven of the first ten finishers were Miller-built racers. In ten years Miller had won five "500s," the Duesenbergs three. Their $25,000-and-up thoroughbreds had been groomed for the Speedway, and other auto makers hesitated to challenge their speed, quickness, and durability. Of the 33 cars in this race, for example, 26 were either Millers or Duesenbergs.

But Eddie Rickenbacker thought the race—if it was to continue to draw people—needed a greater variety of cars. And it also needed what many fans wanted to see: faster and faster speeds. The 91.5-inch engines, as intended, had kept speeds

1929's TOP TEN

Race open to cars with a piston displacement of 91.5 cubic inches or less.

NO.	DRIVER	CAR	ENGINE*	CYL.	BORE	STROKE	PISTON DISPL.	TIME	MPH	WINNINGS†
2	Ray Keech	Simplex Piston Ring Special	Miller	8	2.187	3.000	90.2	5:07:25.42	97.585	$20,000
1	Louis Meyer	Miller Special	Miller	8	2.187	3.000	90.2	5:13:49.21	95.596	10,000
53	Jimmy Gleason	Duesenberg Special	Duesenberg	8	2.286	2.750	90.1	5:20:10.46	93.699	5,000
43	Carl Marchese	Marchese Special	Miller	8	2.344	2.500	91.5	5:20:42.95	93.541	3,500
42	Fred Winnai	Duesenberg Special	Duesenberg	8	2.195	3.000	91.0	5:37:52.05	88.792	3,000
48	W. H. Gardner	Chromolite Special	Miller	8	2.187	3.000	90.2	5:39:24.27	88.390	2,200
6	Louis Chiron	Delage Special	Delage	8	2.196	2.992	89.9	5:41:57.85	87.728	1,800
9	Billy Arnold	Boyle Valve Special	Miller	8	2.187	3.000	90.2	5:57:31.77	83.909	1,600
25	Cliff Bergere	Armacost-Miller Special	Miller‡	8	2.187	3.000	90.2	6:11:44.00	80.703	1,500
34	Fred Frame	Cooper Special	Miller‡	8	2.187	3.000	90.2	Flagged	193 laps	1,400

* All supercharged.   † Speedway prizes for winning entries. Total awards in race, $95,150: Speedway prizes, $60,000; accessory prizes, $15,150; lap prizes, $20,000.   ‡ Front-drive.

Opposite page: "The largest band ever assembled." Below and left: Ray Keech and the winning Miller. Keech won $40,100. His face appeared in hundreds of newspaper ads the next morning smoking a cigarette under the headline "Gimme a Tareyton." Drivers agreed in advance to these ads for products. Bottom: The view from the last row before the start. No. 27 dropped out after 50 laps.

lower—Peter DePaolo's 1925 record, set with a 122-inch engine, still stood—but Rickenbacker knew people came to see records broken. For the 1930 race he announced that cars with a piston displacement of up to 366 cubic inches would be eligible and that the old two-seat bodies were back. Rickenbacker wanted passenger-car makers —General Motors, Chrysler, Ford, Hupmobile, Hudson, and the rest—to challenge the Millers and the Duesenbergs.

They would. And Rickenbacker's decision, made before the 1929 stock market crash, turned out to be one of his luckiest and wisest.

Louis Meyer: Good and lean years

The winner of three "500s" (1928, 1933, and 1936), Louis Meyer finished second in 1929. *In all my races I figured my job was to finish and not break the car, and what place I was in after 500 miles, that was it. But sometimes it's relatively easy to lead without going so fast that you break the car, and that's what happened in '29, when I led most of the way. But then I had to go to the pits and I couldn't catch Keech. But I won a lot of lap money in '29, when the country was going good. I think I won more money in '29 than in '33, when I won the race but got only a little prize money because the country was going bad.*

1930

Even a Model T Can Win

The engines emitted a full-throated roar as they warmed up for the start of the race on a grey, frosty Memorial Day morning. Missing from the din were the howls and shrieks of superchargers. And back again, for the first time since 1922, were hippy two-seaters that carried a driver and a mechanic.

Eddie Rickenbacker's new rules had thrown open the race to engines as big as 366 cubic inches. Superchargers were banned from the conventional four-cycle engines, and cars had to weigh at least 1,750 pounds. As Rickenbacker had hoped, the new rules had brought the big-car makers—Buick, Chrysler, Studebaker, and Ford among them—back to the race to challenge the custom racers of the Duesenbergs and Harry Miller.

The rule changes had been a lucky move by Rickenbacker. In 1930, with the nation caught in the panic of the Depression, even wealthy sportsmen were wary of gambling $25,000 on a race car. But owners were willing to invest in the cheaper modified stock cars (sometimes called "junk cars") since they seemed likely to outrun the racers, which the new rules had shorn of their superchargers. A total of 38 cars, the biggest field since 1911, waited, engines vibrating, behind the pacer. In a middle row was a $2,500 Model T Ford, slicked up for racing with a Fronty engine. There was a $2,000 Stutz, stripped of its fenders and running boards but carrying its cigarette lighter. And two of Fred Duesenberg's entries were built mostly with stock parts from the old Duesenberg Model A.

Many observers, before the race, had thought that the semistocks, as the juiced-up factory cars were called, would run away from Harry Miller's smaller-displacement racers, which had won the last two "500s." But one veteran driver, Harry Hartz, staked most of his life's savings on a Miller. With $6,000 of "shouldn't-touch" money he built a front-drive car, the kind that Jimmy Murphy, back in 1924, had predicted would cut the corners at the Speedway. Hartz put a five-year-old Miller engine under the hood, its 122 cubic inches stretched to 151.5 but still only half the size of some of the semistocks. Hartz, his driving nerves not yet steady after a bad accident, hunted for a driver, but most veterans were leery of the nose-heavy front-drive. Finally Hartz found stumpy, tough, 23-year-old Billy Arnold, who eagerly blasted the front-drive through the trials at 113 miles an hour, a new record for a nonsupercharged car, to win the pole.

Led by Arnold, the pack snarled toward the first turn at the start of the race. A Duesenberg skidded toward the inside. Had it skidded to the outside, at least half the 38 cars in the field would have piled up on top of it.

In his off-white Miller-Hartz Special, Billy Arnold began to lap laggards. Near the 60th mile he weaved his way through a tangle of spinning and crashed cars—seven piled into each other, but the worst injury was Deacon Litz's broken wrist—and, averaging better than 106 miles an hour, began to pull away from his closest pursuers, Louis Meyer and William (Shorty) Cantlon.

Minutes later Cy Marshall whipped a Duesenberg through the No. 3 turn. The Duesy skidded, slammed into the wall, and shot over it. The car hit the ground nose first and overturned. Cy survived but his mechanic—his brother—died.

With his front-drive Miller-Hartz pulling tightly through the turns, Billy Arnold droned away from

Bleachers built atop a sedan seat eight spectators. Even though stock market and car prices had dropped ($590 for a Plymouth), "500" tickets sold fast and attendance was estimated at 170,000—a record.

Shorty Cantlon. Billy stopped once, near the halfway point, for gasoline, oil, water, and front tires, and still pounded back onto the track some 9 miles ahead. At the 400-mile mark Billy eased back on the throttle to conserve his car and buzzed home first by seven minutes. In the most one-sided "500" ever, he had led for 198 of the 200 laps. His average speed, 100.448 miles an hour, was only a hair below Peter DePaolo's 1925 record of 101.13.

This victory by a front-drive car had finally made Jimmy Murphy's 1924 prediction come true. And a Miller engine had won again, this time over the bigger semistocks. As for Harry Hartz, he and Arnold collected over $50,000—$20,000 for first, almost $17,000 in lap prizes, and another $15,000 from manufacturers. The money was probably divided 60 percent for Hartz, 40 percent for Arnold, the usual owner-driver split. Hartz now had the money for a second car, and in 1931 he would need a second car to get in the money.

Frank DelRoy:
Thanks enough

A riding mechanic in the 1930 race, Frank DelRoy, later a United States Auto Club official, recalled one of the "500's" most unusual incidents: *Chet Miller was driving one of the Fronty-Fords and broke a front spring. He didn't have a spare. Miller and a mechanic ran to the infield and found a Model T Ford parked there by a spectator. They jacked up the Ford, took out the spring, and left a message on the windshield for the owner to see them after the race. The Fronty-Ford ran the rest of the way on the borrowed spring and finished 13th. After the race Miller put the spring back into the Model T and offered to pay the owner. 'No, thanks,' said the owner. 'It's enough for me to say that part of my car ran in the "500."'*

Above: Shorty Cantlon holds the 183-cubic-inch four-cylinder Miller that powered him to second place. Below: Billy Arnold and his wife. Bottom: Billy and mechanic at the wheel of the winner. Of the semistocks, top finishers were a Stutz (10th) and Chet Miller's Fronty-Ford (13th). Opposite page: A view of the infield facing the homestretch, taken at the 1929 race, showing how cars littered some of the Speedway's 433 acres.

1930's TOP TEN

Race open to cars with a piston displacement of 366 cubic inches or less.

NO.	DRIVER	CAR	ENGINE	CYL.	BORE	STROKE	PISTON DISPL.	TIME	MPH	WINNINGS*
4	Billy Arnold	Miller-Hartz Special	Miller†	8	2.625	3.500	151.5	4:58:39.72	100.448	$20,000
16	Shorty Cantlon	Miller-Schofield Special	Miller	4	3.750	4.125	183.0	5:05:57.18	98.054	10,000
23	Louis Schneider	Bowes Seal Fast Special	Miller	8	2.344	3.500	121.0	5:10:04.21	96.752	5,000
1	Louis Meyer	Sampson Special	Miller	16	2.312	5.000	201.0	5:14:57.07	95.253	3,500
6	Bill Cummings	Duesenberg Special	Duesenberg	8	2.875	4.625	243.5	5:20:35.11	93.579	3,000
24	Dave Evans	Jones & Maley Special	Miller†	8	2.500	3.750	138.0	5:24:04.50	92.571	2,200
15	Phil Shafer	Coleman Special	Miller†	4	3.750	4.125	183.0	5:29:57.37	90.921	1,800
22	Russ Snowberger	Russell 8 Special	Studebaker	8	3.500	4.375	336.0	5:36:26.96	89.166	1,600
25	Leslie Allen	Allen-Miller Special	Miller	4	3.750	4.125	183.0	5:49:51.51	85.749	1,500
27	L. L. Corum	Stutz Special	Stutz	8	3.375	4.500	322.0	5:51:32.09	85.340	1,400

* Speedway prizes for winning entries. Total awards in race, $96,250; Speedway prizes, $60,000; accessory prizes, $19,250; lap prizes, $17,000.   † Front-drive.

1931

To the Wall

Eddie Rickenbacker was amazed. Seventy cars had entered the 1931 race—almost double the number of a year earlier. As Rickenbacker had hoped, the factory cars had come back to the race, Buick, Studebaker, Hudson, Ford, and Reo among the entries. These semistocks were built mostly with factory parts, but the bodies were streamlined and the engines beefed up for racing. Russ Snowberger's Special, with a Studebaker engine, cost only $1,500. While only 13 semistocks had qualified the year before, almost half of this year's field were what some drivers called "stockers" (others called them "junk-formula" cars).

The fastest 40 qualified. Cars had to average at least 90 miles an hour for 4 laps, and with so many entries the qualifying runs occupied a week before Memorial Day—and snuffed out the lives of a driver and a mechanic.

Thin-faced, greying Harry Hartz saw his 1930 winner, the front-drive Miller-Hartz Special, speed through the qualifying run in the fastest time—116 miles an hour—the impetuous Billy Arnold again applying a heavy foot. Hartz also entered a Duesenberg—a race car, not a semistock. It was driven by Fred Frame.

A steady drizzle kept the cars in the garages until noon, the first time the race had not started at 10:00 A.M. When the cars finally grumbled off toward the southwest turn, Billy Arnold broke away to skim over the first 75 miles at a record 109 miles an hour. Then the rain spilled down again, the yellow flag was waved, and the drivers were locked into their positions at 80 miles an hour. As Billy led the parade toward the 175-mile point, the skies cleared, the track dried, and the field saw the green flag.

Arnold stretched out his lead. With only 100 miles to go and far ahead, he streaked toward a second straight "500" victory, never yet achieved by any driver. From the pit Harry Hartz flashed "E-Z" on the blackboard. But Billy bulleted into the northwest turn at better than 100 miles an hour. The rear axle snapped. The Miller-Hartz skidded on its belly, screeched into the wall, was rammed by another car, and exploded in midair. The car, a ball of orange flame and black smoke, cometed over the wall and thudded to the ground. A wheel soared over an outer fence and steamrollered over an 11-year-old boy playing on his lawn, killing him. Amazingly, Billy, his mechanic, and the crew of the ramming car survived. But Billy's broken hip kept his restless body in a hospital bed for six months.

When the track was cleared of debris, Tony Gulotta snapped up the lead but held it only briefly. He, too, cracked into that unlucky northwest wall. He walked away from the wreck and watched Louis Schneider, a 23-year-old former motorcycle cop in Indianapolis, swoop by in a blue and red Bowes Seal Fast Special. Schneider sped through the final 75 miles at a steady 100 to win with the slowest clocking, 96.629 miles an hour, since 1926. With lap and accessory prizes shrunk by the Depression, he won only $29,250.

Harry Hartz had seen his Miller front-drive go out in flames, but his other entry, the Duesenberg driven by 36-year-old Fred Frame, whipped in second, 44 seconds behind Schneider. For the fourth straight year, a Miller had won the "500." The first four finishers were racers, but Russ Snowberger's $1,500 semistock finished fifth and of the 15 cars that finished, eight were semistocks.

In the sporty getups of the time, an American Automobile Association official (l.) and the "500's" chief steward, W. D. (Eddie) Edenburn, wait for the start of the race. Waving the starting flag was racing's one-time bad boy, cigar-chomping Barney Oldfield.

1931's TOP TEN

Race open to cars with a piston displacement of 366 cubic inches or less.

NO.	DRIVER	CAR	ENGINE	CYL.	BORE	STROKE	PISTON DISPL.	TIME	MPH	WINNINGS*
23	Louis Schneider	Bowes Seal Fast Special	Miller	8	2.625	3.500	151.0	5:10:27.93	96.629	$20,000
34	Fred Frame	Hartz-Duesenberg Special	Duesenberg	8	2.718	3.156	150.3	5:11:11.12	96.406	10,000
19	Ralph Hepburn	Harry Miller Special	Miller	8	3.125	3.750	230.0	5:18:23.35	94.224	5,000
21	Myron Stevens	Jadson's Special	Miller	8	3.125	3.750	230.0	5:18:40.09	94.142	3,500
4	Russ Snowberger	Russell 8 Special	Studebaker	8	3.500	4.375	336.0	5:18:50.70	94.090	3,000
33	Jimmy Gleason	Duesenberg Special	Duesenberg	8	2.895	4.625	243.0	5:20:29.76	93.605	2,200
25	Ernie Triplett	Buckeye Special	Duesenberg	8	2.750	3.156	151.0	5:22:26.24	93.041	1,800
36	H. W. Stubblefield	Jones-Miller Special	Miller	4	3.750	4.125	183.0	5:24:35.37	92.424	1,600
28	Cliff Bergere	Elco Royale Special	Reo	8	3.375	5.000	358.0	5:26:39.62	91.839	1,500
27	Chet Miller	Marr Special	Hudson	8	2.875	4.500	233.6	5:34:53.75	89.580	1,400

* Speedway prizes for winning entries. Total awards in race, $81,800; Speedway prizes, $60,000; accessory prizes, $10,650; lap prizes, $11,150.

Right: A mechanic ponders what to do with a car Milton Jones smeared against a wall during practice. A year later Jones went over a wall in another car and was killed. Below: No. 32, Wilbur Shaw at the wheel, skies over the northwest wall. Drivers thought Shaw was dead, but he landed safely and walked to the pits. Minutes later he popped back into the race in another grey Duesenberg. "Drivers saw me and their jaws dropped," Shaw said. "They thought they saw a ghost."

After the race Harry Hartz's blackened Miller was towed into Gasoline Alley. Someone offered Hartz $5,000 for the wreck. He refused—a decision that would once more send Billy Arnold flying over that northwest wall.

Earl Unversaw:
"I want to do this again"

One of the last of the riding mechanics—he rode in seven "500s" during the thirties—Earl Unversaw, 45 years later, recalled his first "500" ride: *I was with Wild Bill Cummings. We broke an oil line about halfway through the race. Then we replaced Deacon Litz and his mechanic in their Maley. The mechanic carried a piece of leather which he touched to the tires to feel any bumps coming on. You pumped fuel to the carburetor—there was no fuel pump—and you watched the general condition of the car. We moved up into second place behind Schneider with about 50 miles to go. Then we broke a tie rod and slammed into both walls, top and bottom, on a turn at better than 110 miles an hour. The car was wrecked but we walked away. I thought, 'Hey, I want to do this again.' And I did until 1937, when they said mechanics couldn't ride any more. So I quit racing.*

Above: Louis Schneider and mechanic Jigger Johnson in the winner. Right: The Cummins Diesel, which set a record in this race—equaled since only once—by going the 500 miles without a stop. Driver was Dave Evans. It averaged 86 miles an hour to finish 13th and used only 31 gallons of fuel—better than 16 miles per gallon. The Cummins company wanted to prove diesel durability. Two decades later its diesel entry would be a favorite to win the "500."

1932

Bold Billy Flies Again

The Memorial Day morning was cool and clear. "A perfect day for the race," Eddie Rickenbacker told friends as he sat in the Lincoln pace car with honorary referee Edsel Ford. But Rickenbacker had to frown when he looked up at the wooden grandstands and saw patches of empty seats. In these hard times, there were no mob scenes around the gates as there had been in the twenties, when speculators had sold tickets for $20 and $30. Despite the Depression, Rickenbacker had raised Speedway prizes to $70,000, the money to be split among the 40 starters. Rickenbacker confided to friends that the Speedway would lose money on this 20th renewal of what the papers now called "the 500 classic."

Lap prizes had dropped from $100 to $50 a lap, and would have been lower except for the $5,000 personal check at the last minute from Henry Ford, here to watch Edsel drive the pace car.

Sixteen of the 40 starters were semistocks, including five entered by the Studebaker company. But in the garages that lined Gasoline Alley, most bets were on one of the 19 Miller-powered cars in the race. Veteran Lou Moore sat on the pole in the Boyle Valve Special, which carried an eight-cylinder Miller. Next to him was Billy Arnold, the 1930 winner, at the wheel of the front-drive Miller-Hartz Special that had soared over the northwest wall, aflame, the previous year. It had been, in the lexicon of Gasoline Alley, "unbent." Well back in the pack was another Harry Hartz entry, driven by 37-year-old Fred Frame, who had qualified with a mediocre 113 miles an hour, 4 miles slower than the fastest time. He, too, was piloting a Miller front-drive.

At the start Frame tried to keep up with the scorching pace set by Arnold, his teammate. Arnold wheeled the front-drive over the first 150 miles at an average of 111 miles an hour. As Arnold twisted into the northwest turn, where he'd left the track a year earlier, he boldly tried to elbow his way between a lapped Studebaker and the wall. The Studebaker swung right, the door shut, and the Miller-Hartz shot into the wall, snaked over it, and crashed upside down. A year before, Billy had been carted away with a broken hip, and his mechanic, Spider Matlock, with a broken shoulder; this time Billy had the broken shoulder, Matlock the broken hip. It was Billy's last race; he went west and became a rich contractor.

From the pit Harry Hartz could see Fred Frame, piloting the surviving car of his team, way back in tenth place. But the ski-nosed Frame wiggled the Miller through the pack, the front-drive cutting the corners. At 250 miles he was seventh and at 300 miles second, behind Wilbur Shaw. Then Shaw broke an axle and Frame sprang to the front. Young Howdy Wilcox II, the son of the 1919 Indianapolis winner, pressed in on Frame, but Frame held him off to win by 44 seconds. Frame's average of 104.144 miles an hour broke Peter DePaolo's seven-year-old record by slightly more than 3 miles an hour.

By leading this race at the 400-mile mark, Frame won for owner Harry Hartz the Wheeler-Schebler Trophy, which had first been awarded in 1909. Because his cars were the first to win the trophy three times, Hartz was given permanent possession of the seven-foot-high silver cup, valued at $10,000. In these Depression times, no one rushed forward offering another.

Over the past decade, Harry Miller had come

The old bricks are a course for a different kind of race. It was called the pushmobile—kids in tiny cars propelled by muscle power. Held on a day during race week, pushmobile races had a short history.

Giants of the U.S. auto industry meet at the "500." Below: Henry Ford (l.) and Harvey Firestone, Sr. Right: Assembled at the Lincoln pace car are (l. to r.) Eddie Rickenbacker, Henry Ford, Edsel Ford (at the wheel), Harvey Firestone, Jr., Henry Ford II, Benson Ford, and Harvey Firestone, Sr. They saw a race that was free of deaths, but a driver and a mechanic were killed during practice runs in the days before the race.

to loom almost godlike in the eyes of race car owners. It was to Harry's shop that they went if they would be Speedway winners. But the eccentric Miller, burdened by debts and hearing "voices" that told him to move on, sold his factory to his superintendent, Fred Offenhauser. In the thirties, Miller would design racers for Henry Ford that were revolutionary—and failures. (He died a sickly recluse in a Detroit rooming house in 1942.) The name Offenhauser would eventually become even more famous than the name Miller on Gasoline Alley—just as, within the next few years, the names of Louis Meyer and Wilbur Shaw would become the most famous on this old red saucer of bricks.

Clay Ballinger: Last shake of a dice

Mechanic Clay Ballinger rode with Louis Schneider in 1931, when he won, and in 1932, when he finished 23d. In 1976 he talked about drivers he had known. *Schneider was ... well, adventuresome. And he could get emotional during a race. Wilbur Shaw was also that way. Like if someone passed Shaw, Shaw went out and caught him and passed him; then if that driver came back to pass Shaw, oh boy, Shaw would get mad. I remember with Schneider in 1932, we had a dice with Shaw—we went ahead, Shaw passed us, then we went by Shaw on a straight ... back and forth it went. Once as we go by Shaw, I look over and there's Shaw—oh, was he mad—shaking his fist at us.*

Right: Fred Duesenberg, who died in a highway accident a few months after the race, when his car skidded and overturned. He was famous as a builder of both racers and passenger cars, the Duesenberg name synonymous with expensive elegance and precise engineering. His brother, August, withdrew the Duesenbergs from racing after Fred's death.

1932's TOP TEN

Race open to cars with a piston displacement of 366 cubic inches or less.

NO.	DRIVER	CAR	ENGINE	CYL.	BORE	STROKE	PISTON DISPL.	TIME	MPH	WINNINGS*
34	Fred Frame	Miller-Hartz Special	Miller†	8	2.875	3.500	182.0	4:48:03.79	104.144‡	$20,000
6	Howdy Wilcox II	Lion Head Special	Miller	4	4.062	4.250	220.0	4:48:47.45	103.881	10,000
22	Cliff Bergere	Studebaker Special	Studebaker	8	3.500	4.375	336.7	4:52:13.24	102.662	5,000
61	Bob Carey	Meyer Special	Miller	8	3.250	3.750	249.0	4:55:57.90	101.363	3,500
4	Russ Snowberger	Hupp Comet Special	Hupmobile	8	3.500	4.687	361.0	4:57:38.72	100.791	3,000
37	Zeke Meyer	Studebaker Special	Studebaker	8	3.500	4.375	336.7	5:04:38.52	98.476	2,200
35	Ira Hall	Duesenberg Special	Duesenberg	8	2.895	4.625	243.0	5:05:28.72	98.207	1,800
65	Fred Winnai	Foreman Axle Shaft Special	Duesenberg	8	2.750	3.187	151.0	5:07:53.49	97.437	1,600
2	Billy Winn	Duesenberg Special	Duesenberg	8	2.750	3.156	151.0	5:07:56.43	97.421	1,500
55	Joe Huff	Highway Parts Special	Cooper†	16	2.187	3.000	183.0	5:42:31.25	87.586	1,400

* Speedway prizes for winning entries. Total awards in race, $93,900: Speedway prizes, $70,000; accessory prizes, $13,200; lap prizes, $10,700. † Front-drive. ‡ New record.

Right: Fred Frame. Below: Frame seated behind the wheel of the winning Miller-Hartz. With him is his mechanic, Jerry Houck. The front-drive car had been built in 1928 by Tommy Milton—at a cost of more than $100,000—for wealthy driver Cliff Durant, who drove it to a 16th-place finish in 1928. Harry Hartz bought it in 1931 and put in a new engine and frame. In later "500s" it finished second, third, fourth, and eighth.

Spectators watch a long line of scorekeepers, who juggle numbers to show who stands where. The top row of numbers places car No. 5, driven by Billy Arnold, in first, with Howdy Wilcox II in second, Fred Frame in third, Lou Moore fourth, and Louis Meyer fifth. The race is at the 100-mile point, according to the next row of figures, with the time figures apparently being changed. The bottom rows show what lap each car is on.

1933

Unsafe at Any Speed?

The red and white Kemp-Mannix Special nosed out of control and skidded toward the concrete wall on the No. 1 turn. Metal screamed against concrete and sparks flew as the car climbed the wall, teetered a moment, then flipped toward the track and hung there, upside down. The driver, 30-year-old Mark Billman, and his mechanic were flung from the car. Billman was pinned against the wall by the car's left front wheel. Rescuers worked for 20 minutes to pry him free. His legs were broken, his left arm torn off. Within an hour, Billman was dead.

Later in the race, with the green flag flying again, a pack of cars swerved into that same southwest turn. A driver let off his throttle and slowed too suddenly. At the wheel of his Universal Service Garage Special, Malcolm Fox saw the rear of the slowed-up car swell toward him. He swerved upward on the banked track—directly into the path of Les Spangler, in a Miller Special. Spangler rammed Fox. Spangler's Miller rocketed over Fox's car and thudded into the wall at a cockeyed angle. "Spangler and his mechanic were so badly crushed," reported one newsman, "that their friends had some difficulty in telling which was which."

These men were the third, fourth, and fifth to die this year at the Speedway; two others had been killed trying to qualify. Ironically, there were new rules to make the race safer. Each car could carry only six gallons of oil and could not replenish its supply during the race. The purpose was to send to the pits the "leakers" that slicked the bricks with oil. Another rule shrank gas tanks to a 15-gallon capacity, compared to the 40-gallon tanks carried by most cars the year before. This meant the cars would have to stop more often to top off their tanks, and crews could inspect for tire wear.

Most Speedway railbirds thought that the semistocks in this year's race would outlast the race cars because the racers dripped oil faster than the semistocks. "Hardly anybody," commented *Motor* magazine, "believed that a racing car could run the distance on only six gallons of oil." By contrast, Cliff Bergere had run the 1932 race in a Studebaker and used only two quarts.

A recurring sign of the times—banks closed by the Depression—had put some worry lines into Eddie Rickenbacker's face. Contributions from merchants to the lap fund had dropped to $3,150 (it would be an all-time low), and accessory prizes were $11,100, the smallest since 1927. Rickenbacker, with ticket sales slow, cut the Speedway's prizes to $40,200—the thinnest purse since 1911.

Drivers grumbled, but 63 cars entered. And 42—the biggest "500" field ever—qualified by averaging better than 100 miles an hour through 10 laps (the qualifying distance was increased this year from 4 laps to draw more spectators to the trials at 25¢ and 50¢ a ticket). The fastest qualifier, at over 118 miles an hour, was Wild Bill Cummings, in a Miller-powered Boyle Products Special.

At the start Wild Bill streaked away from the pack. His 113-mile-an-hour pace soon tore apart Cummings's car. It faded into the pack and then dropped out. The 1928 winner, Louis Meyer, steered his red Tydol Special—another Miller car—from seventh place into the lead at 325 miles. "I figured if I held it at 110, it would be enough to win," he said later. But as he roared by the 400-mile point his pit crew signaled "E-Z" on a blackboard, and Meyer drew back on the throttle.

Two drivers, Ernie Triplett (l.) and Deacon Litz, paddle on the track a few days before the race. A creek that runs under the track near the No. 1 turn had overflowed, but the flood receded by race day.

Even so, he finished with a new record average —104.162 miles an hour, a fraction faster than Fred Frame's speed of a year earlier. Meyer became the second driver (Tommy Milton was the first) to score two "500" victories.

For the first time ever, the first six finishers had all looped around the track at speeds exceeding 100 miles an hour. But five men were dead in their wake. The streamlined dreadnoughts with their mastiff engines had become too fast for

Top: Louis Meyer. Right: Meyer at the wheel of the winning Tydol Special with mechanic Lawson Harris. Bottom: Standing (l. to r.) are track publicity director Steve Hannagan, Eddie Rickenbacker, designer Gar Wood, and W. D. (Eddie) Edenburn, the "500's" chief steward since 1919.

human drivers, declared Harold F. Blanchard in *Motor*. "The cars," he wrote, "are too fast for reasonable safety, but what can be done to slow them down is a problem."

Malcolm Fox:
A wrong guess

Malcolm Fox, the driver who cut into the path of Les Spangler, described after the race the narrow line between life and death on the Speedway: *My car was careening toward the fence as I tried to pull it away from that car that slowed down. The way I was swinging, if Spangler had tried to pass inside me instead of up above me, he would have made it. And he'd still be alive. But he had only two guesses to make, and he guessed wrong.*

1933's TOP TEN

Race open to cars with a piston displacement of 366 cubic inches or less.

NO.	DRIVER	CAR	ENGINE	CYL.	BORE	STROKE	PISTON DISPL.	TIME	MPH	WINNINGS*
36	Louis Meyer	Tydol Special	Miller	8	2.312	3.750	258	4:48:00.75	104.162†	$12,000
17	Wilbur Shaw	Mallory Special	Miller	4	4.062	4.250	220	4:54:42.64	101.795	6,000
37	Lou Moore	Foreman Axle Shaft Special	Miller	4	4.125	4.500	255	4:55:16.79	101.599	3,000
21	Chet Gardner	Sampson Radio Special	Miller	16	2.312	3.000	201	4:56:29.71	101.182	2,100
8	H. W. Stubblefield	Shafer 8 Special	Buick	8	3.125	4.625	284	4:57:43.82	100.762	1,800
38	Dave Evans	Art Rose Special	Studebaker	8	3.187	4.250	260	4:58:43.82	100.425	1,800
34	Tony Gulotta	Studebaker Special	Studebaker	8	3.500	4.375	336	5:02:48.75	99.071	1,450
4	Russ Snowberger	Russell 8 Special	Studebaker	8	3.500	4.375	336	5:02:59.84	99.011	1,300
9	Zeke Meyer	Studebaker Special	Studebaker	8	3.500	4.375	336	5:05:44.49	98.122	1,200
46	Luther Johnson	Studebaker Special	Studebaker	8	3.500	4.375	336	5:08:22.22	97.286	1,150

* Speedway prizes for winning entries. Total awards in race, $54,450: Speedway prizes, $40,200; accessory prizes, $11,100; lap prizes, $3,150.   † New record.

Right: Zeke Meyer (l.) crouches in Studebaker that finished ninth, its tear-shaped tail typical of new streamlining. Below: A tire is changed on L. L. Corum's Studebaker. Before the race, Speedway doctors disqualified the popular Howdy Wilcox II. Drivers threatened not to race, but minutes before the start Rickenbacker faced them down. A rookie replaced Howdy and came in 35th. His name: Mauri Rose.

1934

Wanted: More Miles Per Gallon

Impossible, snarled some of the drivers. Can't be done, mechanics growled the length of Gasoline Alley. They were enraged by a rule passed by the American Automobile Association (AAA) and the Speedway to make the "500" safer. The 1934 cars were limited to 45 gallons of fuel (most cars ran on secret, garage-made blends of gasoline). The cars in last year's race needed at least 50 gallons to go the 500 miles, drivers claimed. But the AAA and the Speedway were adamant. Drivers and mechanics pulled out extra carburetors, tinkered with compression ratios, and mixed new blends in locked garages. Could they get the 11-plus miles per gallon needed to go 500 miles and still run at 100-plus miles an hour? "They'll have to slow down," was the general prediction, "and death will take a holiday at this '500.'"

Death, instead, came early. During the 10-lap trials, Pete Kreis's Miller-Hartz Special skidded off the southwest turn, climbed the wall, and slammed into a tree. The car snapped in two, mangling Kreis and his mechanic.

With prosperity rumored, incorrectly as it turned out, to be lurking around the corner, an optimistic Eddie Rickenbacker had restored the Speedway prizes to $60,000—$50,000 to be spread among the first ten finishers, $10,000 among the rest of the field. But lap prizes, donated by merchants and various companies, were down to a paltry $25 or $50, and for many laps there were no prizes at all.

As another safety measure, the field was thinned to a maximum of 33 starters, the number it has remained ever since. Young Kelly Petillo won the pole with a clocking of 119 miles an hour. Perched in his streamlined Red Lion Special, he led for the first 10 miles of the race. But Petillo—and every other driver—was concerned about his fuel supply. As a result, the pace for the first 50 miles was only 106 miles an hour, compared to the previous year's 114. By the race's halfway point, the diminutive, mustached Mauri Rose had pushed his black and white Duray Special to the front. But pecking at his tailpipe was a front-drive Miller named the Boyle Products Special. At the wheel, thin mustache over white teeth, hunched Wild Bill Cummings. In the daytime Wild Bill loved to roar down roads on his motorcycle and at night he relished the raucous sounds of his Indianapolis nightclub.

At 325 miles Cummings grabbed the lead as Rose refueled. Then Cummings had to refuel and change tires, and from the pit he watched Rose jump into the lead. Wild Bill swerved back onto the course, closed steadily, and popped by Rose with 70 miles to go. By now both drivers, confident they had the fuel to finish, had upped their straightaway speeds to better than 140 miles an hour. Wild Bill was averaging 104 miles an hour as he knocked off lap records set a year earlier by Louis Meyer. Still he could not shake the bulldog clutch of little Mauri, though Mauri could not lunge past Wild Bill. The cars hummed by the grandstands never more than 30 seconds apart. With a record average speed of 104.863 miles an hour, Cummings slid past the checker only 27 seconds ahead of Rose—the closest one-two finish in the 22 runnings of the "500."

As Wild Bill came to a stop—after two precautionary laps to make sure he'd gone the 500 miles—he was kissed by his mother. Wild Bill asked for a bottle of beer and a cigarette. As he gulped the beer, someone shouted, "Here's your wife, kiss her!" Wild Bill did—as Louis Meyer

Like partridges in a pear tree, spectators cling to a tree on the infield to watch the race. They saw the Cummins Diesel again try to go the distance without a stop, as it did in 1931, but this time it broke down after 81 laps.

Before the race a military band prances down the straightaway in front of the stands. By now it had become traditional for bands to serenade the arriving fans with "On the Banks of the Wabash" and "Back Home in Indiana." Right: Veteran racing official Fred Wagner (l.) chats with a retired driver—Ralph DePalma. Wagner started the first "500" 23 years earlier. DePalma's last "500" was in 1925, but well into the 1970s he still held the record for total laps led at the "500"—613. He died in 1956.

had kissed his wife a year earlier. A tradition had been established that would later go Hollywood.

Few things, seemingly, had changed. For the third time in five years, a Miller front-drive car had won the "500." For the seventh straight year a Miller car—the Millers now being made by Fred Offenhauser in the old Miller plant in Los Angeles—had won. The Millers no longer had a serious challenger: The semistocks were unable to win even with the new gasoline and oil restrictions; and the Duesenbergs were now out of racing, August having left the tracks after Fred's death in a highway accident in 1932.

No one had been killed during the race. But two cars had soared over walls, and the clockings showed that the cars were as fast or faster than ever. Death's holiday from the "500" would be a brief one.

Earl Unversaw: Payday

Of his winning ride with Wild Bill, mechanic Earl Unversaw remembered: *He was a pretty wild guy. But he drove a very conservative race. We had one of the smallest engines in the race—220 inches. We used regular pump gasoline and we had plenty of gas left at the end. I got 10 percent of the purse, Bill got 40 percent. At the time, I was making $60 a week as part of the mechanical crew, so it was a real big payday for me.*

(Continued on page 105)

Don Eldredge, Jr.

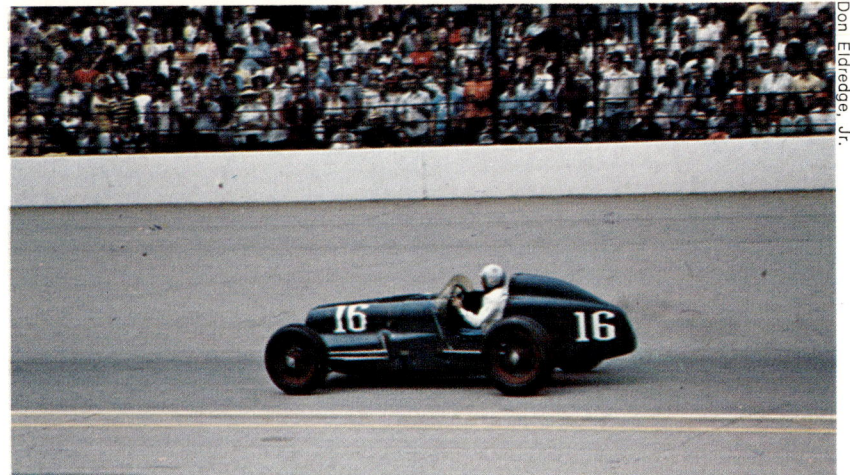

The 1946 winner, the Thorne Engineering Special, hums around the course before the start of the 1976 race. At the wheel is Fred Agabashian, who drove in 11 "500s," from 1947 to 1957. The Thorne averaged 114 miles an hour in winning in 1946. In 1976 the winning average was 148 miles an hour.

Bob Veith, at the wheel of the MG Liquid Suspension Special, prepares for the 1965 race. Powered by a rear-mounted Offy, the car stalled after 145 miles and was placed 24th. (Standing behind the car is Jim Hurtubise, who drove a front-engine Novi that dropped out after a lap.) The suspension of a race car is one of the most critical and sensitive elements in its success or failure. The lightweight racers can be swayed by sudden gusts of wind, bumps, or the air turbulence created by the cars themselves. With a delicate, almost intuitive touch, the chief mechanic sets the suspension system to give an even ride. The proper "set" can add a hundred yards a lap to a car's speed.

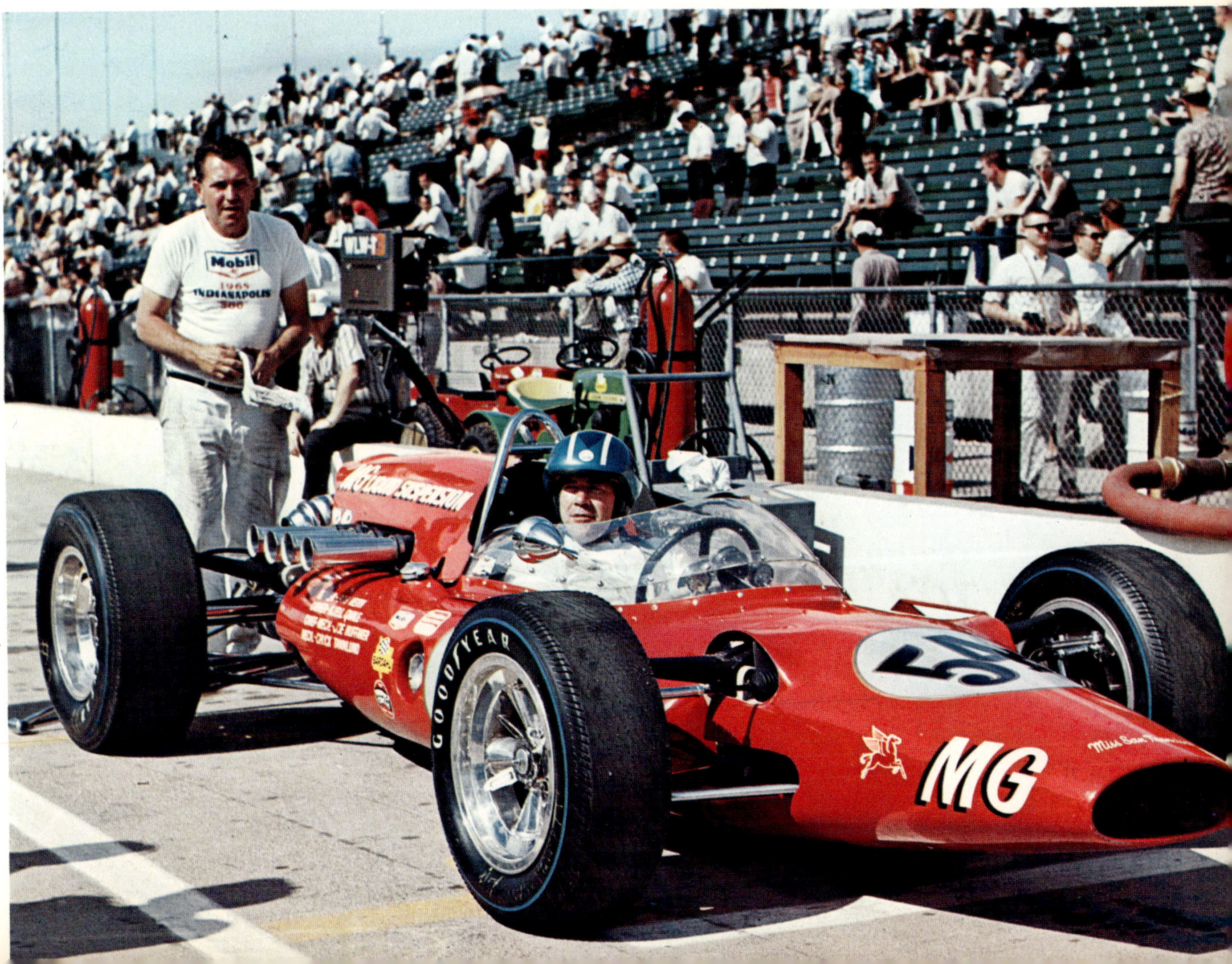

Goodyear

Left: At the start of the 1961 race, Eddie Sachs (No. 12) takes the lead from the pole position. No. 99 is Jim Hurtubise. In this race 32 front-engine roadsters started against one interloper—the rear-engine Cooper-Climax. Driven by Australia's Jack Brabham, it finished ninth. Above: On the pace lap for the 1966 race, 32 rear-engine cars and one roadster go through the first turn. In the front row Mario Andretti, in a Brabham-Ford, is on the pole; Jim Clark, in a Lotus-Ford, is in the middle; and George Snider, in a Coyote-Ford, is on the outside. Minutes later, as the cars began the first lap of the race, they collided (opposite page) in a spectacular smashup that left 11 of the racers disabled or demolished but caused no serious injuries.

Goodyear

Opposite page: Andy Granatelli's rounded profile is in the foreground as he hovers over one of his bright red Novis before the 1965 race. This was the last year of the Novis at Indianapolis. Over a 25-year span, the Novis set many track records during the trials but never won a "500." Above: Mark Donohue's Sunoco McLaren in the pit during the 1972 "500." Donohue averaged 162.962 miles an hour in his winning effort, setting an Indy record that still stands.

Indianapolis Motor Speedway

Goodyear

Opposite page, top: At the start of 1967's race Parnelli Jones in his STP turbocar is in third place and gaining on Gordon Johncock and Mario Andretti. Jones led throughout the race—until the 196th lap, when gearbox failure sent him to the pit. Bottom: Bobby (l.) and Al Unser with their mother, Mary, and father, Jerry, Sr., before the 1967 race. Mom and Pop Unser wear "Goodstone" and "Fireyear" jackets, thus taking no sides while Bobby competes for Goodyear and Al for Firestone. Above: Graham Hill atop Andy Granatelli's turbocar before the 1968 race. It hit the wall and spun out of the race on the 110th lap when "something" gave way in the car. "I lost control," Hill said, but he couldn't explain why—nor could anyone else on the STP team. All three of Granatelli's turbines—the "whoosh" cars that were expected to run away from everyone else—failed to finish. "They failed," noted one unkind reporter, "as all Granatelli cars have failed here since 1946."

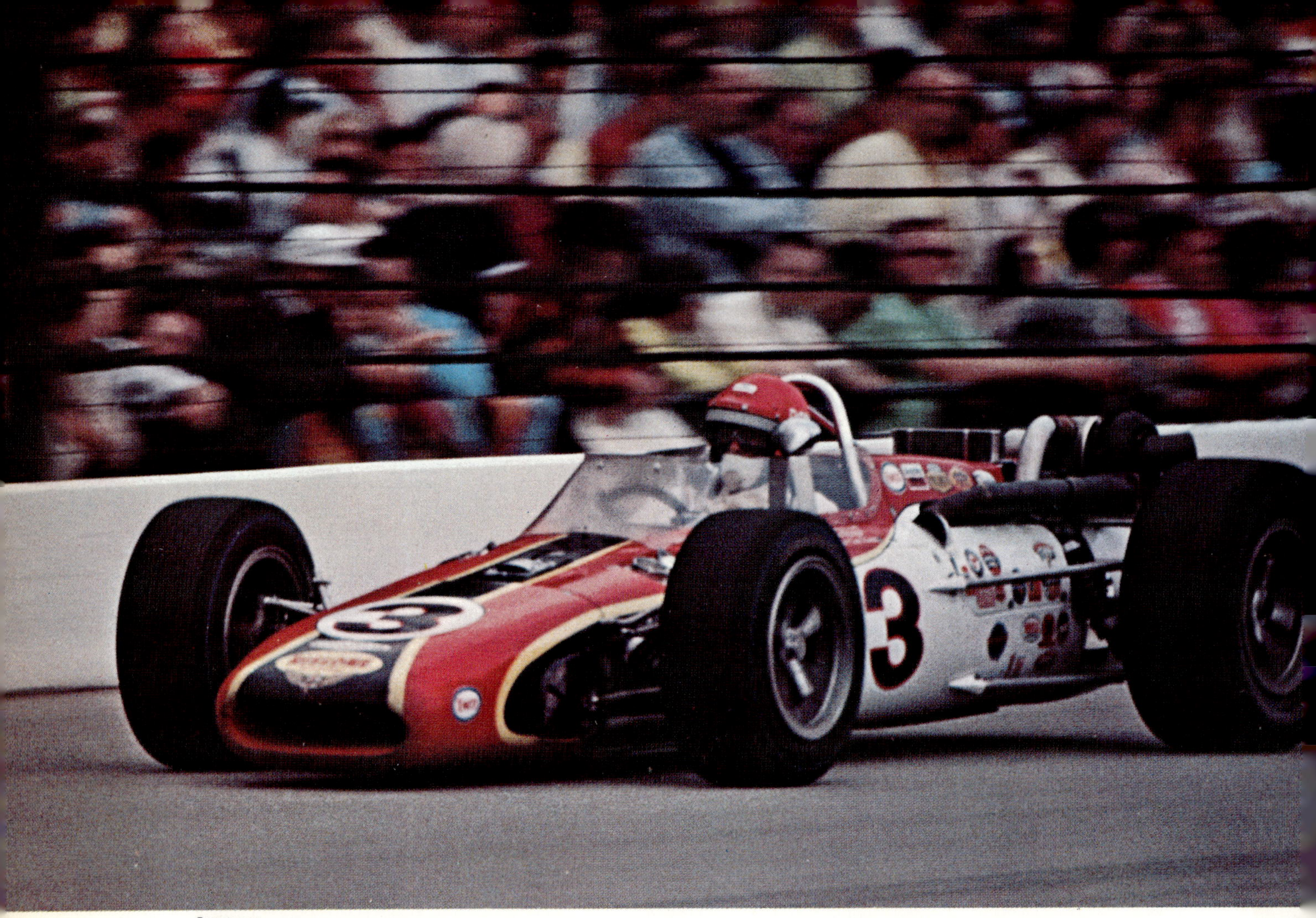

Goodyear

Goodyear

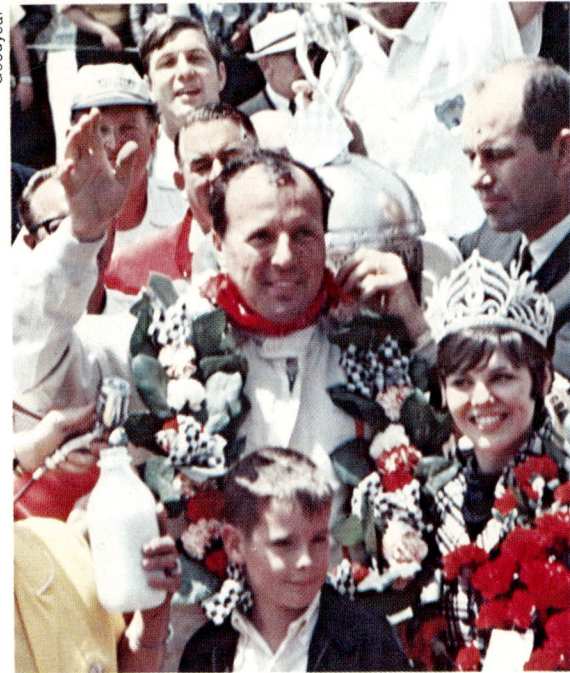

Left: A. J. Foyt in the winner's circle after posting his third "500" victory, in 1967. Above: Bobby Unser hurries his turbocharged Eagle-Offy toward the 1968 checker and a new "500" record of 152.882 miles an hour. A year later he was asked if winning the "500" was worth a million dollars in endorsements and appearances for the driver. "There's no way," he replied. "I think I've made more outside money since winning the race than any previous driver. But I haven't come close to any million dollars. And the cost of living has gone up for me. . . . You wouldn't believe the letters and telephone calls I get from people who want money for something."

Left: Dashing Bill Cummings, sporting crash helmet and goggles, wears a winner's grin. Below: He poses at the wheel of the winning car with his mechanic, Earl Unversaw. In the 1920s, when the lighter single-seated cars raced, the fastest cars often broke down before the finish. But in 1930, when Billy Arnold finished first, noted a magazine, "quite the contrary happened: The fastest car won." And in the 1934 race that also seemed to be true.

1934's TOP TEN

Race open to cars with a piston displacement of 366 cubic inches or less.

NO.	DRIVER	CAR	ENGINE	CYL.	BORE	STROKE	PISTON DISPL.	TIME	MPH	WINNINGS*
7	Bill Cummings	Boyle Products Special	Miller†	4	4.125	4.125	220	4:46:05.20	104.863‡	$20,000
9	Mauri Rose	Duray Special	Miller	4	4.062	4.250	220	4:46:32.43	104.697	10,000
2	Lou Moore	Foreman Axle Shaft Special	Miller	4	4.250	4.500	255	4:52:19.63	102.625	5,000
12	Deacon Litz	Stokely Food Special	Miller	4	4.062	4.250	220	4:57:46.27	100.749	3,500
16	Joe Russo	Duesenberg Special	Duesenberg	8	3.500	3.625	275	5:00:19.21	99.893	3,000
36	Al Miller	Shafer 8 Special	Buick	8	3.125	4.625	286	5:05:18.08	98.264	2,200
22	Cliff Bergere	Floating Power Special	Miller	4	4.062	4.250	220	5:06:41.54	97.818	1,800
10	Russ Snowberger	Russell 8 Special	Studebaker	8	3.500	4.375	336	5:08:20.05	97.297	1,600
32	Frank Brisko	F.W.D. Special	Miller	4	4.250	4.500	255	5:09:57.63	96.787	1,500
24	Herb Ardinger	Lucenti Special	Graham	8	3.250	4.000	265	5:12:42.47	95.936	1,400

* Speedway prizes for winning entries. Total awards in race, $83,775: Speedway prizes, $60,000; accessory prizes, $19,550; lap prizes, $4,225. † Front-drive.
‡ New record.

1935

Shaw Plays the Waiting Game

One hundred miles to go... Wilbur Shaw, wind whistling by his helmet, swung his Pirrung Special out of the No. 4 turn and saw Kelly Petillo's black and white Gilmore Speedway Special curve toward the No. 1 turn, at the bottom of the straightaway. Shaw was in second place, almost a lap and a half behind Petillo. Shaw, a racer here since 1927 but never a winner, made a decision. He knew that Petillo, with his leaden foot, was hard on fuel and cars. Shaw decided to play a waiting game. He would wait for Petillo to come back to him, engine-weary, or catch him as he refueled in the pit. And if Petillo's car stayed sound, there was plenty of time for Shaw to charge. Shaw, usually impetuous, would regret not being true to his nature.

On a cloudy, cool day, the field of 33 had rolled onto a Speedway that now was festooned with traffic lights. Six sets had been hung around the course. Each set had two lights—yellow for telling the drivers to reduce their speed to about 75 miles an hour and to maintain their respective positions, and green for "go."

There were two new safety rules. Drivers had to wear crash helmets, the old linen aviator's helmets consigned to museums and romantic memory. And cars had to go the 500 miles on 42.5 gallons of fuel, down from 45 gallons a year before; this required them to average at least 11.7 miles per gallon, which—the Speedway hoped—would keep feet lighter on throttles. But during a practice run, one of Leon Duray's entries, the Bowes Seal Fast Special, leaped a wall and its driver was killed. In the trials a driver and mechanic died. Slowed not a whit by those bloody crashes, a young California hotshot, Rex Mays, won the pole with a clocking of 120 miles an hour, only 2 miles an hour shy of the record.

Before the race Leon Duray unbent the Bowes Seal Fast in Gasoline Alley. Twenty-four-year-old Clay Weatherly, a rangy former high school athlete, begged to ride the car and Duray gave him the wheel. Early in the race Weatherly hit the northwest wall and was killed—the 11th to die at the Speedway in three years.

Under ominous clouds, Kelly Petillo, a 27-year-old California fruit grower who was driving his own car, rammed his Gilmore Special into the lead at the race's halfway point, a few hundred yards ahead of Rex Mays. Petillo's Gilmore was powered by one of the new four-cylinder engines from Harry Miller's old plant in Los Angeles, now owned by Fred Offenhauser. The new engines were slicker, higher-rpm versions of the Millers; soon they would become affectionately known along Gasoline Alley as Offys.

Harry Miller himself was here. He had built five new racers for Henry Ford, the cars powered by Ford V-8s. The five cars broke down because of a blunder by Miller in the steering design, and none finished the race. This $200,000-plus disaster cooled the ardor of Ford and other Detroit manufacturers for the race, and the number of semistocks—the "junk-formula" cars—would begin to dwindle at the Speedway.

With 150 miles to go in this race, Petillo led with Wilbur Shaw a lap behind. Petillo had to pit and Shaw lunged to the front. But then Shaw had to pit; Petillo zoomed back to see his car's No. 5 posted on the scoreboard as the new leader, ahead by a lap. Shaw played a waiting game until there were 50 miles to go. Then he decided he could wait no longer. He unleashed the Pirrung in a wild dash through lapped cars and closed on Petillo. But rain began to patter down on the

Two of the day's most famous women were at this "500." Top: *Life* photographer Margaret Bourke-White, clowning before the race. Bottom: Flier Amelia Earhart, the race's honorary referee. A woman had applied to drive in the race a few years earlier. She was rejected.

bricks. The yellow lights flashed on for the first time in a "500." The field slowed, the cars locked into their positions. The rain soon stopped, but the yellow lights stayed on while the track dried. To Shaw's white-knuckled frustration, the laps clicked away, closer and closer to the finish, as he sat frozen in second place. When the green lights finally did go on, Shaw did not have the room to catch up. Petillo soared by the checker. Despite the rain and the yellow lights, he set a new record of 106.240 miles an hour. This was the fourth straight year of new records, as drivers and crews combined more efficient engines, new blends of fuel, and sleeker cars to add more speed while at the same time getting more miles per gallon.

A disappointed Shaw—a bridesmaid for the second time in three years—told himself he would never play the waiting game again. But to win he would first have to wait.

Frank DelRoy: "Some instinctive driving"

Frank DelRoy, a riding mechanic with Floyd Roberts, remembered a close call. *Petillo was a wild driver. He and Floyd Roberts bulldozed a car around the track. The real smooth drivers of the time were Ted Horn and Chet Miller. They didn't exert a lot of effort—they were nice and easy with a car. But I'll never forget some instinctive driving by Roberts in one '500.' We came out of the No. 3 turn and slid down the bank. I turned and saw Shorty Cantlon's radiator almost in my lap. He was that close to running over us. It was a kind of mental telepathy, both of the drivers said later. One swung right and the other left, and we just missed each other. In 1933 I was behind Les Spangler and his mechanic when they were killed. I saw them flying back at us. It wasn't very nice.*

1935's TOP TEN

Race open to cars with a piston displacement of 366 cubic inches or less.

NO.	DRIVER	CAR	ENGINE	CYL.	BORE	STROKE	PISTON DISPL.	TIME	MPH	WINNINGS*
5	Kelly Petillo	Gilmore Speedway Special	Offenhauser	4	4.250	4.625	262	4:42:22.71	106.240†	$20,000
14	Wilbur Shaw	Pirrung Special	Offenhauser‡	4	4.062	4.250	220	4:43:02.73	105.990	10,000
1	Bill Cummings	Boyle Products Special	Miller‡	4	4.125	4.125	221	4:46:22.48	104.758	5,000
22	Floyd Roberts	Abels & Fink Special	Miller	4	4.250	4.500	255	4:50:37.05	103.228	3,500
21	Ralph Hepburn	Veedol Special	Miller	8	3.312	3.750	258	4:50:45.73	103.177	3,000
9	Shorty Cantlon	Sullivan & O'Brien Special	Miller	4	4.062	4.250	220	4:56:37.07	101.140	2,200
18	Chet Gardner	Sampson Radio Special	Miller	4	4.062	4.250	220	4:56:39.02	101.129	1,800
16	Deacon Litz	Shaler Rislone Special	Miller	4	4.062	4.250	220	4:57:18.22	100.907	1,600
8	Doc MacKenzie	Pirrung Special	Miller	4	4.062	4.250	220	4:58:13.01	100.598	1,500
34	Chet Miller	Milac Front Drive Special	Miller‡	8	2.625	3.500	151	4:58:35.16	100.474	1,400

* Speedway prizes for winning entries. Total awards in race, $78,575: Speedway prizes, $60,000; accessory prizes, $14,425; lap prizes, $4,150. † New record.
‡ Front-drive.

Opposite page: The winning car holds driver Kelly Petillo (also at far l.) and mechanic Jimmy Dunham. Above: Inside the Gil Pirrung garage, where the Pirrung Special is gussied up for the race, in which it finished ninth. Second from left is driver George (Doc) MacKenzie. Holding the hammer is Egbert (Babe) Stapp, who came in 25th in another car. Right: One of the ill-fated streamlined cars built by Harry Miller for Henry Ford. They were front-drives and slung so low that the driver's elbow hung only 30 inches above the track. The four wheels were independently suspended, the engine a Ford V-8. A steering foul-up put all the cars out of the race, but Miller's newest creations, said *Motor Age* magazine, "have the smoothest exteriors of any race cars ever built anywhere."

The grimy-faced winner, Louis Meyer, stands with his wife, June, next to the Packard pace car, one of his winnings. He also won about $15,000 in lap and accessory prizes along with the $20,000 first prize. In the background, the garages of Gasoline Alley.

1936

To the Place of Milk and Money

Louis Meyer shook his head in disgust and anger. No one could say, of course, that he had been pursued by bad luck at the Indianapolis 500. He'd won in 1928 and 1933, and only he and Tommy Milton had won the race twice. In 1928 he had arrived here broke; now he owned his car, the Ring-Free Special. But this evening, as lights winked on in the garages along Gasoline Alley and mechanics tinkered with the cars that would start in tomorrow's "500," the 31-year-old Meyer had reason to think that all his bad luck had hit him at once.

Like the other drivers and owners, Meyer had worried about the newest limit on fuel: 37.5 gallons for the race, down from 42.5 a year ago, as the Speedway tried again to slow up cars and make the casualty list shorter. Contestants mixed heavy, powerful fuels with lighter, more volatile ones in an effort to squeeze the last inch of mileage out of every gallon. They set and reset carburetors. Perhaps because of too thin a fuel mixture, Meyer had blown three engine blocks during practice runs. He cracked his last Miller only days before his final chance to qualify. A new block was flown in from Los Angeles, and he qualified at 114 miles an hour. But late this afternoon, on a practice whirl, the Miller had chugged in with a damaged piston. Tonight Meyer and his mechanics would rip apart the engine, put it back together, and hope it would stay in place for the 500-mile trip over the bricks.

By dawn they had finished. Meyer napped. By 10 o'clock he sat in his red and white Ring-Free Special with his riding mechanic. The car was back in the next to last row. Up front, on the pole, Rex Mays, a young dirt track racer from California, waited for the start in a Gilmore Special that had qualified at 119 miles an hour. In the third row Wilbur Shaw gripped the wheel of another Gilmore, built and owned by himself. As streamlined as a torpedo, Shaw's car had averaged 15 miles per gallon during his 117-mile-an-hour qualifying run.

Tommy Milton, now retired, stood before the field on this breezy, sunny morning. Milton had consented to drive the pace car, a Packard, provided that the Packard be awarded to the winner of the race. Packard officials agreed, instituting a new prize for "500" winners that has been given every year since.

The 33 drivers looked down from the starting line at a safer No. 1 turn. All the turns, in fact, had been widened and rebuilt to make the track safer. The original turns, with both inside and outside walls, had been like tunnels—and out-of-control cars often ricocheted between the walls like pinballs. Now the inside walls had been lopped off and safety aprons had been added; cars in trouble could dip low, out of the way, onto the aprons. New outside walls had been built at a sharper angle to the track so cars couldn't shoot up them as though they were takeoff ramps. And because most of the accidents in recent years had involved rookie drivers, the Speedway now required new drivers to pass a 100-mile test before they could practice or take part in time trials.

At the start Rex Mays bolted through the first 10 miles at a record 118 miles an hour. Then he swerved in with a faulty throttle and Wilbur Shaw zoomed to the front with an average of 115 miles an hour for the first 100 miles—another record. But as Shaw rushed down a straightaway, rivets

began to pop off his hood. Shaw, cursing whoever had put them on, had to sit in the pit for 17 minutes while the hood was refastened.

The methodical Louis Meyer clipped off car after car as he moved his Ring-Free Special steadily through the pack; by the halfway point he had forged into the lead, his pace a record 111 miles an hour. At 350 miles, following his race plan, Meyer refueled, and Ted Horn, in a Miller-Hartz Special, buzzed into the lead. But Meyer came out to catch Horn, stretch his lead, and become the first driver ever to win three "500s."

Meyer and the next four finishers snapped Kelly Petillo's record of 106.240 miles an hour, set a year earlier; a new race record had been posted now for the fifth straight year. Since restrictions on fuel consumption had not slowed the cars—and with the track now thought safer (there were no serious accidents this year)—the limit on fuel, it was announced, would be erased for next year's race.

Wilbur Shaw finished seventh, but he had covered the 500 miles four minutes faster than Meyer; those 17 minutes for hood repairs had cost him the race. Next year, Shaw promised himself, he would check and recheck every detail. Louis Meyer had become the first to win three "500s," but what Wilbur Shaw was on the eve of doing would make him America's most famous race car driver.

Louis Meyer: "I held my breath"

After a drink of milk in what was now called Victory Lane—the area behind the pits on the way to Gasoline Alley—Meyer told reporters: *Gasoline was my biggest worry. That's why I didn't figure I had the race won until I got the checkered flag. I was sure of the car, but I wasn't sure I had enough gas to finish. We had used up all our fuel on the last pit stop. On the last dozen laps, I kept thinking how terrible it would be to run out of gas on the homestretch. That last lap, I held my breath.*

Opposite page: Cars skim down the short south chute toward the No. 2 turn. Left: Eddie Rickenbacker (l.) and T. E. (Pop) Myers examine new concrete walls on the outside of the turns; the walls slanted inward so cars wouldn't "ramp" up and over them. Below: A driver's view of a Bugatti's instrument panel. The Speedway decided on drivers' tests after noting that rookies had been at the wheel during most of the accidents that had killed nine drivers and six mechanics in the past six years.

Above: Ladies dressed in the fashions of the time stroll the infield. Left and below: Louis Meyer and the winning car, mechanic Lawson Harris seated next to the three-time winner. Opposite page: While press, timers, and judges watch the race from perches in the pagoda, spectators down below loll on the grass, gossip, or stream to and from the refreshment stand. During the race driver Al Miller was flipped from his car. He fractured his left hip. He'd lost part of the leg in a previous accident. "I was lucky," he said later, "I broke my wooden leg."

1936's TOP TEN

Race open to cars with a piston displacement of 366 cubic inches or less.

NO.	DRIVER	CAR	ENGINE	CYL.	BORE	STROKE	PISTON DISPL.	TIME	MPH	WINNINGS*
8	Louis Meyer	Ring-Free Special	Miller	4	4.250	4.500	255	4:35:03.39	109.069†	$20,000
22	Ted Horn	Miller-Hartz Special	Miller‡	8	2.875	3.500	182	4:37:20.54	108.170	10,000
10	Doc MacKenzie	Gilmore Speedway Special	Offenhauser	4	4.250	4.625	262	4:39:10.36	107.460	5,000
36	Mauri Rose	F.W.D. Special	Miller	4	4.250	4.500	255	4:39:39.85	107.272	3,500
18	Chet Miller	Boyle Products Special	Miller‡	8	2.625	3.500	152	4:40:35.17	106.919	3,000
41	Ray Pixley	Fink Auto Special	Miller	4	3.687	4.750	203	4:45:01.58	105.253	2,200
3	Wilbur Shaw	Gilmore Special	Offenhauser	4	4.250	4.500	255	4:47:49.00	104.233	1,800
17	George Barringer	Kennedy Tank Special	Offenhauser	4	4.250	5.000	255	4:52:18.65	102.630	1,600
53	Zeke Meyer	Boyle Products Special	Studebaker‡	8	3.125	4.250	251	4:56:03.57	101.331	1,500
38	George Connor	Marks-Miller Special	Miller	4	4.250	4.500	255	5:03:14.49	98.931	1,400

* Speedway prizes for winning entries. Total awards in race, $82,525: Speedway prizes, $60,000; accessory prizes, $17,025; lap prizes, $5,500.   † New record.
‡ Front-drive.

1937

For the 25th, Bang-Bang

Wilbur Shaw whipped what he called his "pay car" out of the northwest turn. His cream and red Shaw-Gilmore Special blurred down the straightaway past the stands at better than 180 feet per second, then faded from view into the south turns. With only 50 miles to go, Wilbur Shaw seemed to be streaking toward his first "500" victory.

Shaw glanced at his oil-pressure gauge. The needle hung at zero. Shaw winced. Just like last year... he'd been ahead and then the hood had blown off... and now, ahead again, no oil.

He came out of the No. 2 turn onto the backstretch and went down on the throttle. Shaw saw the needle swing away from zero. He might, he thought, be able to pick up the oil pressure on the straightaways so the bearings wouldn't burn out. It was against the rules to stop for oil. As he came by the pits his crew raised a blackboard that told him he led by 114 seconds.

Calculations leaped across Shaw's brain. To conserve his engine, he decided, he could slow about 6 miles an hour on each lap and still come home seconds ahead of that car behind him. Maybe.

He eased back on the throttle. In his Hamilton-Harris Special veteran driver Ralph Hepburn edged nearer and nearer to Shaw... 100 seconds behind, 90 seconds, 80 seconds. The grandstands were filled to overflowing, and the crowd's bellow mixed with the bang-bang bursts of the two cars as they hurtled by.

This was the 25th running of the Indianapolis classic, the race's silver anniversary. So far, estimated Speedway general manager T. E. (Pop) Myers, some 1,200 drivers had tried to win $1.3 million in prizes. Almost three dozen people had died in the effort—a mechanic, a fireman, and an engineer had been killed during practice runs this year.

The qualifying runs had produced "the fastest '500' field ever," according to the newspapers, a claim that had been made on the eve of most every "500" in recent years. But this field unquestionably was the fastest. A former milkman from Chicago, Jimmy Snyder, won the pole with a record 125.287 miles an hour, and three other cars exceeded the old record of 122.391, set in 1928 by Leon Duray. Cars whirled faster through the turns, where the bricks had been covered over with rock asphalt. And there was no fuel limit to keep feet lighter on throttles (but the cars had to use "pump" gasoline, no exotic alcohol-gasoline concoctions allowed).

Early in the race the 34-year-old Shaw snaked through the pack and into the lead in a car he'd wrecked in a Long Island road race the year before. He himself had put the car together again. "It's my pay car," he said with his wide smile. "I'll make money with it as an owner and driver."

Right behind Shaw late in the race hung Ralph Hepburn. A blazing sun and fumes from his engine had overwhelmed Hepburn earlier and he'd been spelled at the wheel by a relief driver. With 33 laps left in the race, he came back and saw that he was closing on a slowed-up Shaw. With only 10 miles to go, Hepburn whizzed out of the northwest turn and saw Shaw dip into the southwest turn, at the bottom of the straight. On each circuit Hepburn edged closer. Minutes later the two cars thundered by the grandstands hubcap to hubcap, the crowd on its feet. And as they zoomed toward the final turn of the 200th lap, Hepburn

An ad for the Speedway features its president. The World War I hero also flew for the U.S. in World War II, then became president of Eastern Air Lines. Below: The LaSalle pace car tows the field through the No. 1 turn, the original bricks on all four turns now smoothed over with asphalt. Cars could rip faster through the asphalt turns, made stickier by the heat, but a total of 70 tires had to be changed.

nudged his Hamilton's red nose in front.

The race had come down to the nose-to-nose finish that Shaw had calculated. His oil pressure showed zero, but Shaw called on his Offy engine for a climactic effort. He stood on the floor and his creamy hood lunged ahead. The crowd screamed as it saw the two dots bob out of the turn at the top of the stretch and blossom toward the finish line, wheel to wheel. At better than 150 miles an hour, Shaw took the checker only two seconds ahead of Hepburn—the closest "500" finish ever.

Shaw had circled the 500 miles more than two hours faster than Ray Harroun 25 years earlier. His average speed, 113.580, was 4 miles an hour faster than Louis Meyer's record of a year before.

Shaw pocketed $33,500 and had, at last, won a "500." He would not stop with one—or even two.

Louis Meyer: "What might have been"

Looking back on his bid for a fourth "500" win, Louis Meyer later recalled: *I remember that race for what might have been. My car—it was a Mike Boyle car—had plenty of speed. And maybe it had more speed than Shaw's car. But the car kept running hot and I had to bring it in four times to the pits. Then we had to wait until it cooled down enough to get water in it. Altogether I was in the pits ten minutes, I guess, probably more . . . but we only finished six or seven minutes behind Shaw.*

Opposite page, top: As thousands cheer, Shaw and his mechanic raise their hands in triumph as they take the checker. Bottom: The winning crew sits in the Gilmore on the straightaway bricks. The handsome Shaw, who fit the Hollywood image of what a race driver should look like, immediately became the darling of admen, his face plastered over newspaper and magazine ads. Right: Two photos catch cars during the race—Ronney Householder (top) finished 12th in a Topping, Billy DeVore 7th in a Miller.

1937's TOP TEN

Race open to cars with a piston displacement of 366 cubic inches or less.

NO.	DRIVER	CAR	ENGINE	CYL.	BORE	STROKE	PISTON DISPL.	TIME	MPH	WINNINGS*
6	Wilbur Shaw	Shaw-Gilmore Special	Offenhauser	4	4.250	4.500	255.0	4:24:07.80	113.580†	$20,000
8	Ralph Hepburn	Hamilton-Harris Special	Offenhauser	4	4.250	4.500	255.0	4:24:09.96	113.565	10,000
3	Ted Horn	Miller-Hartz Special	Miller‡§	8	2.875	3.500	182.0	4:24:28.87	113.434	5,000
2	Louis Meyer	Boyle Products Special	Miller	8	3.375	3.750	268.0	4:30:55.70	110.730	3,500
45	Cliff Bergere	Mid-West Red Lion Special	Offenhauser	4	4.250	4.500	255.0	4:35:23.60	108.935	3,000
16	Bill Cummings	Boyle Products Special	Offenhauser§	4	4.250	4.500	255.0	4:40:03.03	107.124	2,200
28	Billy DeVore	Miller Special	Miller	4	4.250	4.500	255.0	4:40:23.17	106.995	1,800
38	Tony Gulotta	Burd Piston Ring Special	Offenhauser	4	4.250	4.500	255.0	4:45:40.42	105.015	1,600
17	George Connor	Marks-Miller Special	Miller	4	4.250	4.500	255.0	4:48:56.00	103.830	1,500
53	Louis Tomei	Sobonite Plastics Special	Studebaker	8	3.500	4.375	336.7	4:54:37.33	101.825	1,400

* Speedway prizes for winning entries. Total awards in race, $92,135: Speedway prizes, $60,000; accessory prizes, $23,635; lap prizes, $8,500.   † New record.
‡ Supercharged.   § Front-drive.

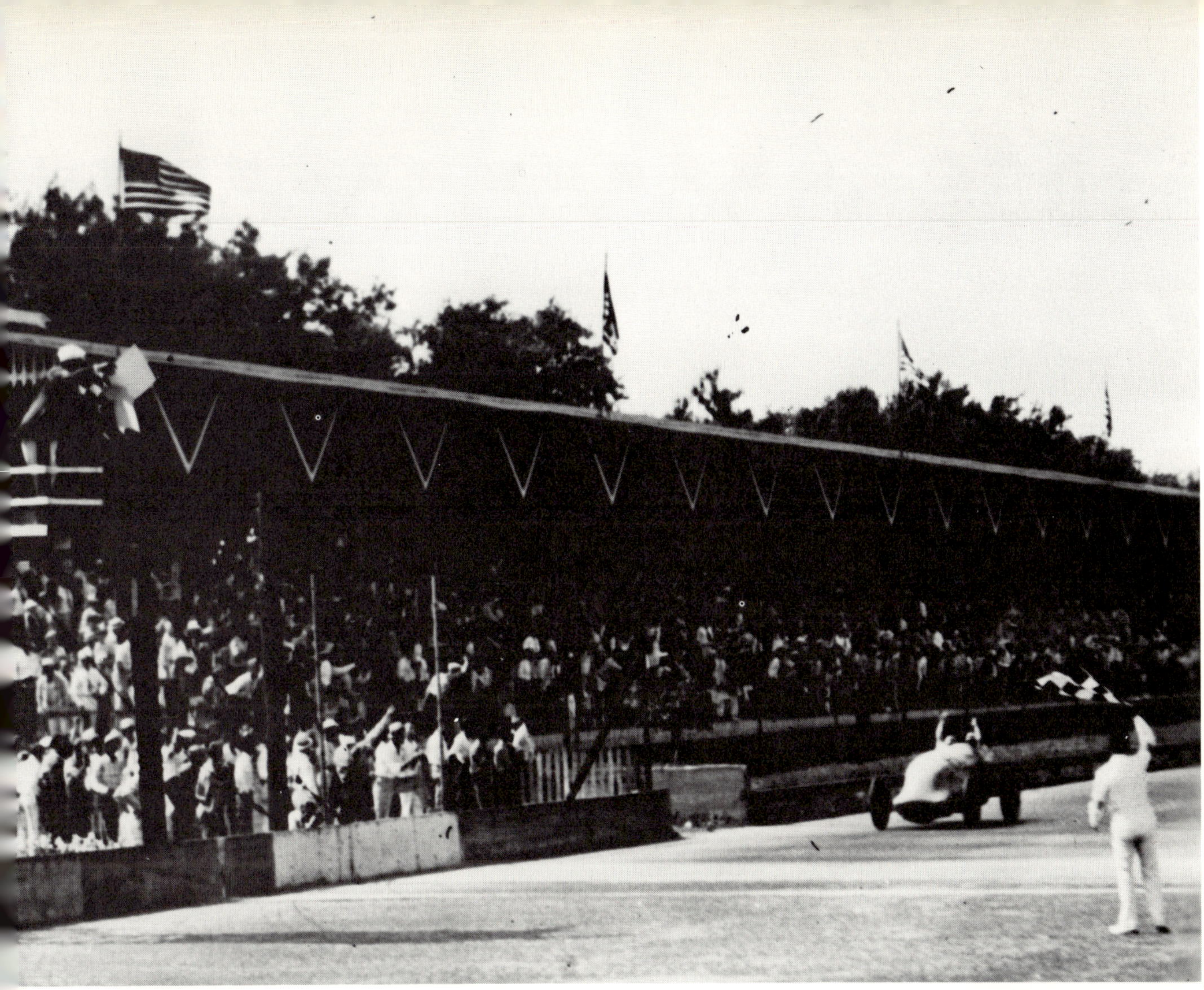

GILMORE
SPECIAL
WINNER
WILBUR SHAW (driver) JIGGER JOHNSON
Indianapolis Motor Speedway
1937

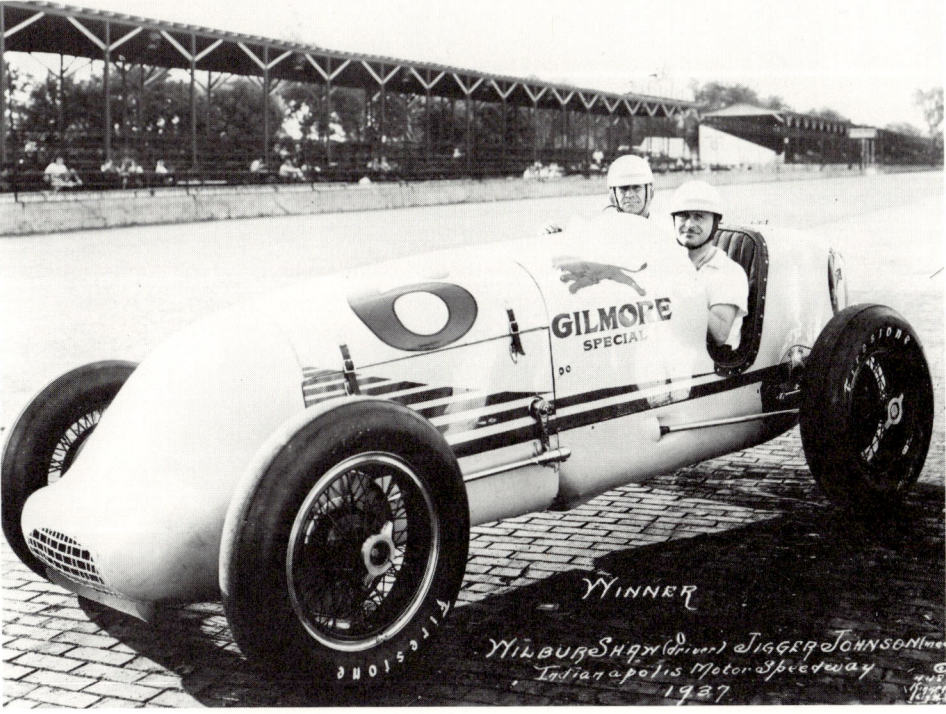

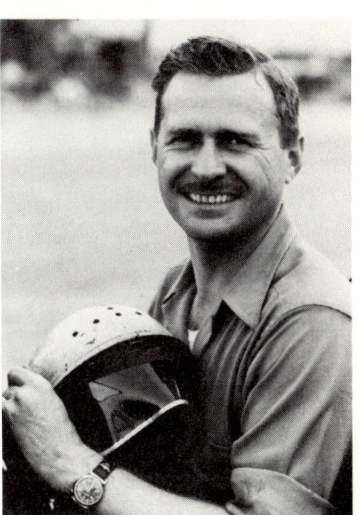

1938

Battle of the Fuels

"The 'Five Hundred Mile Race' this year was not only a battle of drivers and machines but of several schools of engine and car design and types of fuel."

With those words, Speedway timing and scoring director Chester S. Ricker summed up the effects of new rules for the 1938 race. To attract European racers, Speedway president Eddie Rickenbacker accepted a new international formula. It put no restrictions on the kind or amount of fuel and limited engines to 274 cubic inches without superchargers, 183 with superchargers. And single-seat bodies were brought back, ending the era of the riding mechanic.

The new formula detoured the semistocks from the Speedway to tracks and road races where they ran against their own kind. At the Speedway European Maseratis and Alfa Romeos would challenge the Offenhauser-Miller custom racers. On Gasoline Alley drivers and mechanics debated the qualities of gasoline versus alcohol as a fuel. Most chose gasoline. The reason: more miles per gallon. A typical car ran 9 miles on a gallon of gasoline, only 3 miles on a gallon of alcohol.

In the narrower one-man bodies, the driver was perched high in the center straddling the drive shaft and transmission, and the gearbox was often wrapped with sponge so it wouldn't burn his legs. For millionaire driver Joel Thorne, however, designer Art Sparks built a body with the drive shaft running alongside the cockpit, dropping the driver's seat and creating a low-slung racer that was the forerunner of the car later to become famous as the Indianapolis roadster.

On the pole waiting for the start sat the Burd Piston Ring Special, entered by former driver Lou Moore and piloted by Floyd Roberts, who had set a new qualifying record with a speed of 125.681 miles an hour. Roberts, a husky California dirt track racer, had never won a major race in 22 years of trying. "My luck has always run in cycles," he said. "Now it's running good and I'll win."

This year's race would be run on fewer bricks, the track now resurfaced with asphalt on every portion except the middle of both stretches. The cars took the starting flag on a cool morning, rain clouds sweeping over the crowd estimated at 150,000. It had become an Indianapolis habit to say that the "500" was lucky with the weather. The luck held good. Rain did not spatter the track until the end of the race, after the top five finishers had completed 200 laps.

Near the 100th mile a car hit the wall on the southeast turn and tumbled over three times. Driver Emil Andres survived, but a wheel flew off and killed a spectator.

Near the 200-mile point the three leaders were alcohol-fuel cars, trailed by Floyd Roberts and Wilbur Shaw in gasoline cars. Then the alcohol cars had to stop to take on fuel. Roberts rammed his red, black, and silver Burd Piston Ring Special into the lead. At about 300 miles Roberts plunged into the pit to change one Firestone and refuel—the first and only stop he would make. He lost a minute and the lead to an alcohol car driven by Jimmy Snyder, the Flying Milkman from Chicago. But at 375 miles Snyder went in for fuel, his third stop, and Roberts gunned his 270-cubic-inch Miller into the lead. He moved away from Wilbur Shaw, who finished a faraway second, to win with an average speed of better than 117 miles an hour, almost 4 miles an hour faster than Shaw's record of the year before. This was the seventh straight year a new record had been hung up.

The winner turns his car off the track and into what has come to be called Victory Lane. Waiting in the foreground are photographers. For being pictured drinking a bottle of milk, each "500" winner got $100 from a dairy organization.

1938's TOP TEN

Race open to nonstock supercharged engines with a piston displacement of 183.060 cubic inches or less and nonstock nonsupercharged engines with a piston displacement of 274.59 cubic inches or less.

NO.	DRIVER	CAR	ENGINE	CYL.	BORE	STROKE	PISTON DISPL.	TIME	MPH	WINNINGS*
23	Floyd Roberts	Burd Piston Ring Special	Miller	4	4.937	4.625	270.0	4:15:58.40	117.200†	$20,000
1	Wilbur Shaw	Shaw Special	Offenhauser	4	4.000	4.250	256.0	4:19:33.67	115.580	10,000
3	Chet Miller	I.B.E.W. Special	Offenhauser‡	4	4.250	4.500	255.0	4:20:59.51	114.946	5,000
2	Ted Horn	Miller-Hartz Special	Miller‡§	8	2.875	3.500	182.0	4:27:22.39	112.203	3,500
38	Chet Gardner	Burd Piston Ring Special	Offenhauser	4	4.260	4.500	257.0	4:31:57.48	110.311	3,000
54	Herb Ardinger	Offenhauser Special	Offenhauser‡	4	4.250	4.500	255.0	Flagged#	199 laps	2,200
45	Harry McQuinn	Marchese Special	Miller	8	2.875	3.500	151.0	Flagged#	197 laps	1,800
58	Billy DeVore	P.R.&W. Special	Offenhauser	4	4.250	4.500	255.0	Flagged#	185 laps	1,600
22	Joel Thorne	Thorne Engineering Special	Offenhauser‡	4	4.260	4.500	256.0	Flagged#	185 laps	1,500
29	Frank Wearne	Indiana Fur Special	Offenhauser	4	4.260	4.750	270.8	Flagged#	181 laps	1,400

* Speedway prizes for winning entries. Total awards in race, $91,075: Speedway prizes, $63,100; accessory prizes, $21,875; lap prizes, $6,100.   † New record.
‡ Front-drive.   § Supercharged.   # Flagged due to rain.

Roberts went home to Van Nuys, California, with his share of the $38,000 first-prize winnings, the rest going to Lou Moore and the crew. "Floyd has always wanted to retire to a farm as soon as he had enough money," his wife said. "I am hoping he will." Floyd wouldn't—and next year he would find that his luck indeed ran in cycles.

Harry McQuinn: "Sore and bloody"

A driver in ten "500s" in the 1930s and 1940s, Harry McQuinn was later chief steward at the Indianapolis Motor Speedway. *Today's drivers get out of a car at the Speedway and fly off to Europe for a race the next day. In those days a driver got out of a car bruised, beat up, sore, and bloody. You needed a relief driver then; today a relief driver is almost unheard of. The track is smoother now, but the big thing is that today's cars are molded to fit the driver. That began to happen when former drivers like Lou Moore and Harry Hartz became owners. They realized that it made no sense if the driver gave out before the car did. If the driver is comfortable and feeling good in the last laps, that's a tremendous advantage.*

Opposite page: Cars curve into the first turn of the pace lap, Duke Nalon (No. 43) in 33d place seeing what it's like to be the last of the pack. Note the safety apron on the inside of the turn that replaced, in 1936, the concrete wall which made every turn a lethal channel. Right: The pudgy, 38-year-old Floyd Roberts. Below: Roberts at the wheel of his slope-nosed winner. Next to him is owner and former driver Lou Moore.

1939

Promises To Be Kept

"If I don't lead the field home, you won't owe me a cent." That was the promise made by wiry, intense Wilbur Shaw to wealthy Chicagoan Mike Boyle in the summer of 1938. Shaw wanted Boyle to buy an Italian Maserati whose precise steering had astonished Shaw. "I guarantee I'll win the race for you," Shaw promised. Boyle bought the Maserati and told Shaw: "Win, lose, or draw, you get the usual 40 percent."

Readying the Boyle Maserati for the 1939 race, Shaw was delighted by the car's torsion-bar suspension. The Maserati's straight-eight engine, which ran on alcohol, had two Roots superchargers. It accelerated swiftly in first and second gears, although in third it gave away some speed to American cars.

The fastest qualifiers, though, drove American racers—Jimmy Snyder on the pole in a supercharged Thorne Engineering Special, and Louis Meyer, aiming for a fourth "500" crown, next to him in a Bowes Seal Fast Special. This year the trials had been cut back from 10 laps (25 miles) to 4 laps (10 miles), a distance they have remained. Snyder and Meyer both qualified at faster than 130 miles an hour to shatter the old record by almost 5 miles an hour. Most of the 33 qualifiers this year were fueled by alcohol blends that didn't yield as many miles per gallon as gasoline but kept engines cooler.

On a hot Memorial Day, a Tuesday this year, an estimated 100,000 vehicles and 145,000 spectators squeezed through the Speedway gates. The crowd was thought to be the largest ever for a "500" not held on a weekend. (Eddie Rickenbacker, as usual, did not disclose the total number of tickets sold.) This "500" would be run on an even smoother track, for all the bricks were now covered with asphalt except the middle section of the front straightaway.

At straightaway speeds of 150 miles an hour, three glimmering bullets clung together for much of the first half of the race—Louis Meyer in the red Bowes, Wilbur Shaw in the maroon Maserati, Jimmy Snyder in the blue Thorne.

Far behind, Bob Swanson swung the Hamilton-Harris Special into the No. 2 turn and went into a skid. The previous year's winner, Floyd Roberts, saw the nose of the Hamilton-Harris whirl toward him. Roberts jerked his wheel and tried to squeeze between the spinning car and the wall. But his car nicked Swanson's, flipped, and hurtled high over the wall. It hit nose first. Roberts, his neck broken, was pulled from his wrecked car. He was dead—the first driver to find both triumph and death at the Indianapolis Motor Speedway.

Swanson was flung onto the track. Another car roared down on him. Driver Chet Miller swerved, missed Swanson by a foot, hit the inside rail, and overturned; but he and Swanson, though badly injured, survived.

For 30 minutes the yellow lights slowed the field. When the green lights came on, Meyer led Shaw by half a lap. Biting the Maserati low into the turns, Shaw crept toward Meyer and bolted by him on the straightaway, in front of cheering crowds. With 40 miles to go the two cars hurtled

At the field hospital, in the infield, nurses and other medical personnel line up for the photographer. More than a hundred doctors and nurses were on hand. Also available: four pints of blood of four different types. They would be needed.

into the No. 1 turn, Meyer ten feet behind Shaw. Meyer swung above Shaw on the banked turn, skidded, and screeched to a stop, a tire shredded.

Less than a minute later he came out of the pit a lap behind and charged after Shaw—and that fourth "500" victory. He veered too fast into the No. 2 turn, ramming the car against the wall, but jerked safely to a stop. Louis Meyer stepped out of the cockpit, pulled off his helmet, and made a promise he kept: He would find a safer way to make a living.

Shaw toed the Maserati across the finish line for his second "500" victory in three years. For the first year since 1931, the winning speed was not a record, the pace slowed by the yellow lights after Roberts's crash. And for the first time since 1919, a foreign car had won (and for the first time since 1927, a Miller or an Offy hadn't won). Shaw puckered and kissed actress Gene Tierney. In his grinning, cocky way, Wilbur Shaw, too, made a promise: Next year he would be the first to win two "500s" in a row.

Above: Ralph Hepburn looks back at the first rear-engine car to race at the Speedway. The last inspiration of Harry Miller, it had four-wheel drive, an idea that Miller had put into racers earlier in the decade. The six-cylinder, independently sprung Miller dropped out after 47 laps with a broken valve—but would be heard from again. Below: An overview of the Speedway, looking northeast, in the late thirties. The golf course is on the right, the main entrance in the lower left corner. Opposite page: Shaw and the winning Maserati.

Wilbur Shaw: "The way he lived"

After the race Shaw was asked how he felt about winning a race that had cost a life: *I guess every race has its gruesome side. I would just as soon not talk about it other than to say that Floyd Roberts, in going out, died the way he lived, thinking of somebody else. He was avoiding hitting Bob Swanson when he crashed to his death.*

1939's TOP TEN

Race open to nonstock supercharged engines with a piston displacement of 183.060 cubic inches or less and nonstock nonsupercharged engines with a piston displacement of 274.59 cubic inches or less.

NO.	DRIVER	CAR	ENGINE	CYL.	BORE	STROKE	PISTON DISPL.	TIME	MPH	WINNINGS*
2	Wilbur Shaw	Boyle Special	Maserati†	8	2.720	4.000	183.0	4:20:47.39	115.035	$20,000
10	Jimmy Snyder	Thorne Engineering Special	Sparks†	6	3.203	3.750	182.0	4:22:35.61	114.245	10,000
54	Cliff Bergere	Offenhauser Special	Offenhauser‡	4	4.312	4.625	270.0	4:23:51.40	113.698	5,000
4	Ted Horn	Boyle Special	Miller‡	8	3.375	3.750	268.0	4:28:08.82	111.879	3,500
31	Babe Stapp	Alfa Romeo	Alfa Romeo†	8	3.000	3.200	181.0	4:29:42.68	111.230	3,000
41	George Barringer	Bill White Special	Offenhauser	4	4.135	4.250	228.0	4:30:12.60	111.025	2,200
8	Joel Thorne	Thorne Engineering Special	Sparks	6	3.535	4.625	271.8	4:31:42.04	110.416	1,800
16	Mauri Rose	Wheeler's Special	Offenhauser	4	4.260	4.500	256.4	4:33:51.80	109.544	1,600
14	Frank Wearne	Burd Piston Ring Special	Offenhauser	4	4.500	4.250	270.0	4:38:16.65	107.806	1,500
26	Billy DeVore	Leon Duray Barbasol Special	Duray†	4	3.812	4.000	182.0	4:47:43.37	104.267	1,400

* Speedway prizes for winning entries. Total awards in race, $87,050: Speedway prizes, $63,100; accessory prizes, $17,550; lap prizes, $6,400. † Supercharged. ‡ Front-drive.

1940

"Gone Touring"—to Triumph

Wilbur Shaw saw the dark clouds clinging to the north horizon as he bellowed up the backstretch in the maroon Boyle Maserati. Rain—it was coming soon, rain that could lock him into place and cost him a shot at the leader. That was the way Shaw had lost to Kelly Petillo back in 1935. He wasn't going to let it happen to him again.

Shaw's foot came down harder on the throttle. He crept closer to the leader, California leadfoot Rex Mays, at the wheel of a Bowes Seal Fast Special. Shaw knew that most of the fast cars in this race consumed gasoline, while Shaw's Maserati cooked alcohol, which ran the engine faster and considerably cooler. But Shaw would have to stop twice for alcohol, while the gasoline cars would need to stop only once to refuel. Before the race Shaw had decided to set his throttle at 121 miles an hour, fast enough, he had figured, even with two pit stops, to win.

But now his calculations had been scrambled by those lurking clouds. He pushed the Maserati up a notch, to 122 miles an hour, and the ivory back of the Bowes Seal Fast loomed larger and larger in front of him. Shaw shot by Mays, went in for his first pit stop, and came out in fifth place. In rapid-fire order he picked off Joel Thorne, Ted Horn, Mauri Rose, and Mays to pop into the lead again at 250 miles. For the next hundred miles he hurried the Maserati around the course, eyes darting glances at the lowering clouds.

Shaw was streaking toward a triumph achieved by no driver before him—two straight "500" victories. There had been no doubt in Shaw's mind that he could win twice in a row with this Maserati. He'd called the Maserati's steering "velvet" compared to the wrenching needed to pull American racers through the four turns. The Maserati's independent front suspension, plus other features of its springy chassis, said *Automotive Industries* magazine, gave the Maserati driver a racer's edge: "The Maserati can be driven farther and faster without fatigue on the part of the driver than almost any of the American jobs. Even if the engine of the Maserati . . . is not quite as 'hot' as several of our own powerplants."

Now, on this cold and damp afternoon, those hot American engines droned in Shaw's wake as he decided, with 150 miles to go, to refuel. He took on 50 more gallons of alcohol and came out still ahead.

Lightning flashed. Rain pelted the backstretch, on the eastern side of the course. As Shaw passed the 375th mile, the yellow lights flicked on. Cars "went touring," in the parlance of the pits, locked into position at 80 miles an hour. Shaw cruised the remaining 125 miles in his shark-nosed Maserati, his average at the finish a below-the-record 114.277 miles an hour. Over the past four years he had racked up one second and three firsts—an unprecedented streak—and now he and Louis Meyer were the only three-time "500" winners.

After Mays finished second and Mauri Rose third, the other cars were flagged and placed in the order they had been in when the yellow lights went on. This was the first "500" in which the yellow had hobbled the drivers for the last 100 miles when, as Shaw himself said, "the race is won." The obvious question was whether Mays or Rose

Wilbur Shaw is encircled in Victory Lane. His wife, in the white hat, is about to kiss that oil-smeared mouth. Of this winner Speedway historian Al Bloemker wrote: "Most drivers respected Indianapolis—and some feared it. Wilbur loved it."

might have nipped Shaw with their hotter cars in a run to the finish.

The diminutive, pipe-smoking Mauri Rose shrugged when asked that question; there was no way he could answer it. But next year he would get the chance to make that last burst to the finish —and his quarry again would be Shaw.

Emil Andres:
The making of a driver

A driver at the "500" since 1936, Emil Andres finished 12th in 1940, his best finish up to that time. Thirty-six years later he talked about his "500" career. *In the 1938 race the front wheel of my car suddenly collapsed. It flew off and killed a spectator in the infield. But I didn't know anything about that for ten days. My car somersaulted, rolled over three or four times. In that kind of a crash, you don't feel anything, see anything, hear anything. You're just knocked unconscious. When I came to ten days later in the hospital, I just wanted to go racing again. I was a better driver after that—willing to take more chances, maybe. I wasn't really successful in racing until after that accident.*

Above: Boots Shaw kisses her husband. For Shaw (opposite page), the ride was worth about $30,000 in total prizes. Someone asked him if he would quit driving now that he had scored three "500" wins. "Of course not," he said. "I'll be back next year with a hotter car to try to make it four." Below: Proof that even in pre-TV America, some preferred to get it on the set at home.

1940's TOP TEN

Race open to nonstock supercharged engines with a piston displacement of 183.060 cubic inches or less and nonstock nonsupercharged engines with a piston displacement of 274.59 cubic inches or less.

NO.	DRIVER	CAR	ENGINE	CYL.	BORE	STROKE	PISTON DISPL.	TIME	MPH	WINNINGS*
1	Wilbur Shaw	Boyle Special	Maserati†	8	2.718	4.000	179.2	4:22:31.17	114.277	$20,000
33	Rex Mays	Bowes Seal Fast Special	Winfield†	8	2.968	3.250	179.6	4:23:45.31	113.742	10,000
7	Mauri Rose	Elgin Piston Pin Special	Offenhauser	4	4.312	4.625	270.0	4:24:08.96	113.572	5,000
3	Ted Horn	Boyle Special	Miller‡	8	3.375	3.750	268.0	Flagged§	199 laps	3,500
8	Joel Thorne	Thorne-Donnelly Special	Sparks	6	3.531	4.625	271.0	Flagged§	197 laps	3,000
32	Bob Swanson	Sampson Special	Sampson†	16	2.000	3.000	183.0	Flagged§	196 laps	2,200
9	Frank Wearne	Boyle Special	Offenhauser	4	4.625	4.500	257.2	Flagged§	195 laps	1,800
31	Mel Hansen	Hartz Special	Miller†‡	8	2.875	3.500	182.1	Flagged§	194 laps	1,600
16	Frank Brisko	Elgin Piston Pin Special	Brisko‡	6	3.625	4.375	271.0	Flagged§	193 laps	1,500
49	Rene LeBegue	Lucy O'Reilly Schell Special	Maserati†	8	2.145	3.280	183.0	Flagged§	192 laps	1,400

* Speedway prizes for winning entries. Total awards in race, $85,525: Speedway prizes, $63,100; accessory prizes, $14,825; lap prizes, $7,600. † Supercharged. ‡ Front-drive. § Flagged due to rain.

Winner Wilbur Shaw Indianapolis Motor Speedway 1940

His chariot seeming to be poised at respectful attention, a paralyzed Wilbur Shaw is lifted onto a stretcher after the crash that wrecked the Maserati's tail and deflated a tire. "Only God knows why it didn't catch on fire," Shaw said later.

1941

From the Pit a Rose Blooms

Mauri Rose's Elgin Piston Pin Special shuddered as its Maserati engine coughed. Rose veered the car into the pit. The car's owner, Lou Moore, flung open the hood. The diagnosis was quick: Ignition trouble. The prognosis was just as quick: The car was through for the day. Rose snatched his helmet and goggles from the cockpit and told Moore he would try to get a ride as a relief driver in another pit.

"The hell you are," shot back Moore. He glanced toward the track, where his other entry, the Noc-Out Hose Clamp Special, hung amid a splash of colored metal two minutes behind the leader, Wilbur Shaw. In his maroon Boyle Maserati, Shaw was pointing toward his third straight "500" win.

"There's nothing wrong with that car that a little more pressure on the throttle won't cure," Moore snapped. He signaled to the Noc-Out's driver, Floyd Davis, to pit on the 72d lap. He turned to Rose, a small man with a large mustache, and told him to take the car and catch Shaw.

This "500" day had dawned as each of the previous 28 had begun: An aerial bomb exploded at 6:00 A.M., the signal to open the gates and let in the crowd that had assembled outside during the night, thousands sleeping in cars or on the ground. But then, a little after 7 o'clock, as cars and people packed the tunnels that ran under the track to the infield, a tongue of flame had leaped high above Gasoline Alley into the morning's grey drizzle. A welder's torch had ignited gas fumes, and within minutes flames licked at the garages while frantic mechanics pushed a million dollars' worth of racing cars away from the crackling destruction. Fire trucks screamed into the track. After an hour the fire was put out. One row of garages stretched in a blackened, smoking line. But only one starting car had been destroyed.

Wilbur Shaw crunched through his charred, soaked garage. The evening before, he had noticed that one of the 12 spare wheels for his Boyle Maserati seemed improperly balanced. He'd marked the wheel with chalk. But water from the fire hoses had washed off the markings. Shaw couldn't pick out the suspect wheel.

The start of the race was delayed an hour. When the cars bolted by the pacer, Shaw, Mauri Rose, and Rex Mays—the three front-row cars—swept away from the pack to whirl through the first 10 miles at better than 122 miles an hour. When Rose dropped out with ignition trouble in the 60th lap, Shaw began to pull steadily away from Cliff Bergere, now his closest pursuer. Bergere was trying to become the first driver to go 500 miles in a gasoline-driven car without a pit stop (a diesel car had done it in 1931). With only 120 miles to go, Shaw closed on the checker that would mark him as the only man to win three straight "500s" and four in a lifetime. He swung into the No. 1 turn. His right rear wheel—Shaw later swore it was the one he'd marked—tore loose. The car slammed into the wall. Shaw was lifted out of the cockpit, paralyzed, and hurried to a hospital.

Bergere inherited first place. Mauri Rose, meanwhile, had replaced Floyd Davis in the Noc-Out in the 72d lap and had moved up steadily, from 14th place to third, behind Bergere, when he saw Shaw spin into the wall. Rose pressed more speed out of his Offy and began to close on Bergere.

By now Bergere was becoming dizzy and sore after 400 miles of ceaseless pounding in his car. He coughed and gasped, sickened by gas fumes.

His car, also sponsored by Noc-Out, began to fade —it would finish fifth—and Rose overtook him to blast by the checker with the fastest average, 115.117 miles an hour, since 1938. Rose and Floyd Davis became the first co-winners of the race since Joe Boyer and L. L. Corum in 1924.

Ten days after the race, Shaw left the hospital, recovered from his injuries. "Everyone expected me to win," he said, "and I would have won but for that wheel. Next year I'll be back to win that fourth."

But he had run his last Indianapolis race. And "next year" would be a world war away.

Cliff Bergere:
"Sick as a dog"

Thirty-five years later, Cliff Bergere recalled his 500 miles in a gasoline car without a stop, a record grind never since equaled at Indianapolis: *The way it came about, Lou Moore put a big tank on his other car, the one Floyd Davis was driving, and he asked me if I wanted the same tank on mine. I said yes. The idea was, you'd save time by making no pit stops. But there weren't enough louvers in the cowling of the car. I was sick as a dog from gas fumes the last 50 or 60 miles. The other Lou Moore car stopped when they took Davis out and put Mauri Rose in. They refueled the tank during that stop just to be sure, and Mauri went all the rest of the way—about 125 laps—without a stop to catch me and win.*

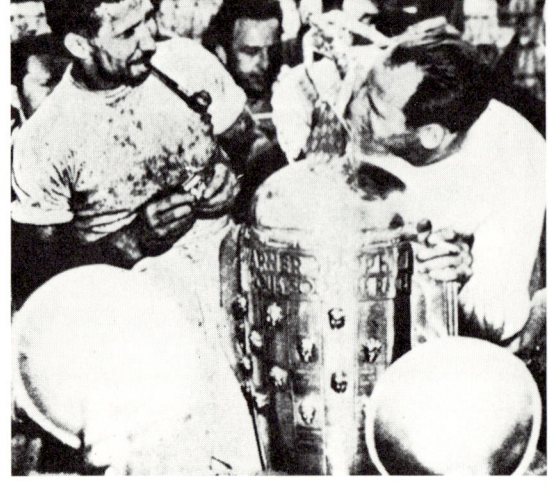

Above: Mauri Rose lights his pipe as he and Floyd Davis admire the Borg-Warner Trophy. First awarded to the winner in 1936, the trophy is four feet tall, weighs 80 pounds, and is made of sterling silver. It was valued in 1941 at $10,000, at about $75,000 now. Sculpted on the cup is the face of each winner since 1911. Left: The drivers, Rose with pipe, get a physical before the race. Opposite page, top: Rose (inset) and Davis with the winning car. Bottom: Rose takes the checker. He and Davis divided the driver's share of the winnings 50-50.

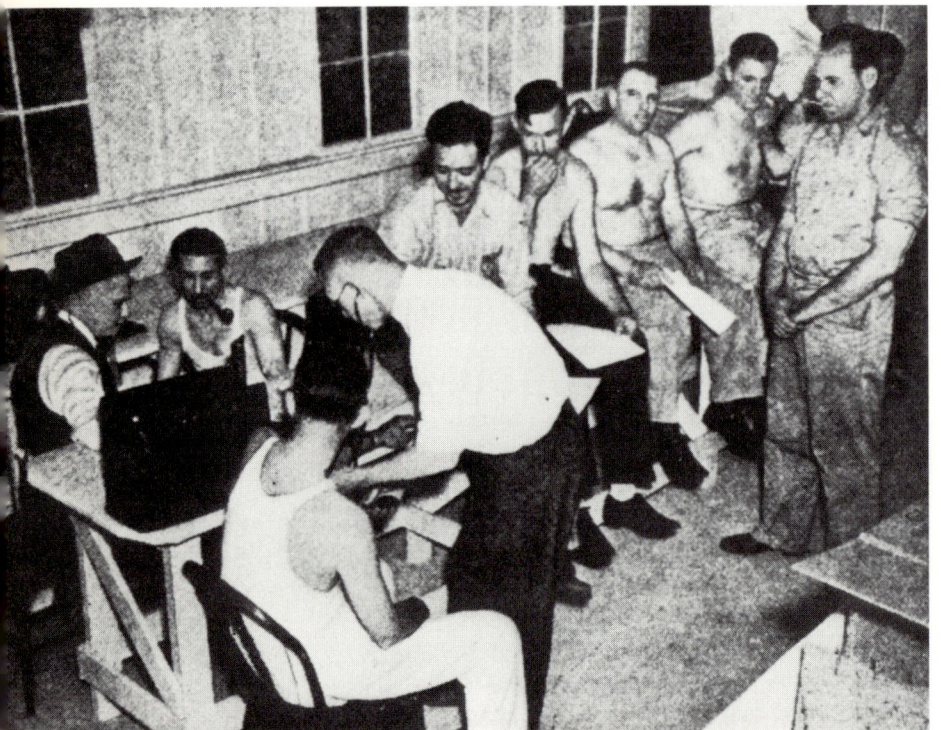

Co-Winners — Mauri Rose & Floyd Davis — Indianapolis Motor Speedway — 1941.

1941's TOP TEN

Race open to nonstock supercharged engines with a piston displacement of 183.060 cubic inches or less and nonstock nonsupercharged engines with a piston displacement of 274.59 cubic inches or less.

NO.	DRIVER	CAR	ENGINE	CYL.	BORE	STROKE	PISTON DISPL.	TIME	MPH	WINNINGS*
16	Floyd Davis and Mauri Rose	Noc-Out Hose Clamp Special	Offenhauser	4	4.312	4.625	270.0	4:20:36.24	115.117	$20,000
1	Rex Mays	Bowes Seal Fast Special	Winfield†	8	2.968	3.250	179.8	4:22:06.19	114.459	10,000
4	Ted Horn	T.E.C. Special	Sparks†	6	3.204	3.750	181.4	4:23:28.39	113.864	5,000
54	Ralph Hepburn	Bowes Seal Fast Special	Novi†	8	3.125	2.937	180.1	4:24:00.79	113.631	3,500
34	Cliff Bergere	Noc-Out Hose Clamp Special	Offenhauser	4	4.312	4.625	270.0	4:24:15.10	113.528	3,000
41	Chet Miller	Boyle Special	Miller‡	8	3.375	3.750	268.0	4:28:02.75	111.921	2,200
15	Harry McQuinn	Ziffrin Special	Alfa Romeo†	8	3.010	3.200	181.0	4:28:20.96	111.795	1,800
7	Frank Wearne	Bill Holabird Special	Offenhauser	4	4.250	4.350	255.0	4:30:42.92	110.818	1,600
45	Paul Russo	Leader Card Special	Miller†	8	2.480	3.500	137.0	4:44:00.88	105.628	1,500
29	Tommy Hinnershitz	Marks Special	Offenhauser‡	4	4.312	4.625	270.0	4:45:18.05	105.152	1,400

* Speedway prizes for winning entries. Total awards in race, $90,925: Speedway prizes, $63,100; accessory prizes, $18,425; lap prizes, $9,400. † Supercharged. ‡ Front-drive.

The shapes and sounds of cars to come were seen in this race. Above: Ralph Hepburn sits in the car that came in fourth. It held a howling, supercharged V-8 brute of an engine that would enthrall fans —the Novi. Left: A Miller-Gulf, one of Harry Miller's rear-engine, four-wheel-drive creatures, is tended in the pits and checked (below) by Miller (l.) and a driver. Two Miller-Gulfs qualified for the 1941 race. But on the morning of the race, gas fumes seeped from the Miller-Gulf garage to where a blowtorch hissed. Boom! Fire roared through Gasoline Alley (opposite page). One Miller-Gulf was destroyed. The other— No. 12 at left—finished only 28th, but this car was the forerunner of the rear-engine "funny cars" of the 1960s.

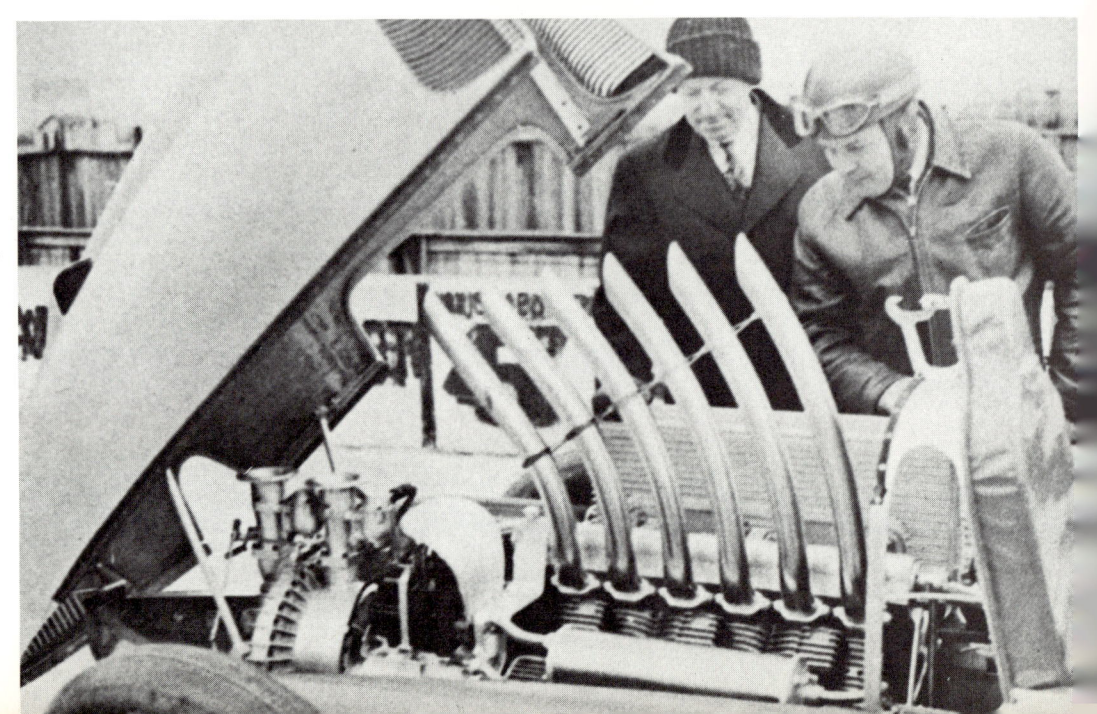

1946

Changing of the Guard

Wilbur Shaw stared, dismayed by these wounds to a loved one. He saw yawning cracks on the asphalt turns and grass bunched thick between the bricks on the straightaway. The 37-year-old wooden grandstands seemed to tremble in the wind. Everywhere he looked on this day at the Speedway early in 1945, Shaw saw encroaching decay. For four years the gates had been padlocked, summer heat and winter winds the Speedway's only occupants during the years of World War II.

Shaw had come here to test Firestone tires. He left Indianapolis worried about the future of the racetrack where he had achieved the three greatest triumphs of his life. He talked with Eddie Rickenbacker, now the president of Eastern Air Lines. Rickenbacker told Shaw he preferred to sell the Speedway rather than invest money in restoring it. In September of 1945 Shaw, after conferring with many potential investors, talked with Anton (Tony) Hulman, a Terre Haute, Indiana, millionaire and former Yale athlete. Hulman accepted the challenge of restoring the dilapidated racing facility and on November 14, 1945, bought the Speedway for $750,000. Shaw was named president and general manager, and T. E. (Pop) Myers stayed on as vice-president. Carpenters bolstered and patched seven of the eight grandstands. Grandstand G, built in 1915, was razed and a new, double-decked, steel-and-concrete grandstand rose in its place. The 2.5-mile ribbon of brick and asphalt was smoothed for racing.

On a hot Memorial Day in 1946 the "500" came back to the Indianapolis Motor Speedway. The crowd of better than 150,000 saw several prewar favorites: Mauri Rose, Ted Horn (who had finished in the top four in the previous six races), and 50-year-old Ralph Hepburn, another veteran who, like Horn, had never ridden up Victory Lane.

This year Hepburn was favored. He was driving the Novi Governor Special, a front-drive car with a supercharged eight-cylinder engine that had finished fourth in 1941. The car was financed by Lew Welch, of Novi, Michigan, a town that got its name because it was near highway tollgate No. VI. The Novi's V-8 engine was made up of two four-cylinder Offys joined with a common crankcase. Now sporting a new, streamlined chassis, the ponderous, 2,000-pound Novi slammed through the 4-lap trials in record-breaking time, turning in a single-lap speed of 134.499 miles an hour (which broke the 1939 record by nearly 4 miles an hour) and averaging an astonishing 133.944 for the 4 laps. Many fans in the grandstands were betting that they would see the first "500" to be run in under four hours.

Its supercharger's scream piercing the flatulent din of the other engines, Hepburn's Novi flashed over the first 140 miles of the race in 71 minutes. Lap after lap it pulled away from a pack that dwindled steadily, the "tired iron" of the old prewar cars broken down by the heat and the Novi's searing pace. But the Novi had to pit for fuel and hydraulic-brake adjustments. Nine minutes later it peeled out of the pit, in 13th place. Hepburn put his foot to the floor and the Novi howled by cars to leap into fourth. Then Hepburn heard a loud grinding. The Novi shuddered and slowed. It had

On the 40th lap Mauri Rose's Blue Crown spins into the wall on the No. 3 turn, rides down the wall wheels high, then slams into the stalled car of Henry Banks, who had left the cockpit. Rose went to the hospital with a fractured hip while his wreck was towed off the track.

139

gulped a valve and was through for the day—and years of anguish and frustration for Novi owners, drivers, and fans had begun.

Two young drivers battled wheel to wheel for the lead. In his nine-year-old, blue and white Thorne Engineering Special, 24-year-old George Robson, a California dirt track driver, glanced at his fuel gauge. Though he was using a low-miles-per-gallon alcohol blend, Robson was carrying a huge tank and so far had stopped only once to refuel. With 100 miles to go he swept by Jimmy Jackson's green and gold Jackson Special. Jackson clung close to Robson but could not catch him. As Jackson whipped out of the No. 4 turn on the 200th lap, he saw Robson's blue and white Thorne shoot by the checker. Robson won by 34 seconds with a time that was almost six minutes slower than Floyd Roberts's 1938 record. Robson's victory behind an Art Sparks engine was the first by an American engine that wasn't an Offy or Miller since 1927.

Early in the race Mauri Rose had spun, hitting another car; Rose, his hip fractured, heard about the finish in a hospital. In the next two races he would be much, much closer at the finish.

Emil Andres: Three steaks a day

Of the first postwar "500," Emil Andres, who finished fourth, recalled: *I drove a ten-year-old Maserati. It had been a Grand Prix car in 1936. All of the cars were old and a lot of them fell apart. In that race I broke a supercharger, an axle, and the clutch slipped, but I nursed it home fourth. In those days, even before the war, there would be only one or two new cars in each year's race. Today it's the other way around—all the cars are new each year except maybe one or two. That's why the costs are so prohibitive—one reason anyway. They say it costs $7,000 or $8,000 a week to keep a crew at Indianapolis. Hell, we went there with $150 and stayed a month. Today they got to eat steaks three times a day.*

The new management (l. to r.): Tony Hulman, who brought money; Wilbur Shaw, who brought glamor; and T. E. (Pop) Myers, who brought expertise.

1946's TOP TEN

Race open to nonstock supercharged engines with a piston displacement of 183.060 cubic inches or less and nonstock nonsupercharged engines with a piston displacement of 274.59 cubic inches or less.

NO.	DRIVER	CAR	ENGINE	CYL.	BORE	STROKE	PISTON DISPL.	TIME	MPH	WINNINGS*
16	George Robson	Thorne Engineering Special	Sparks†	6	3.205	3.750	183.0	4:21:26.70	114.820	$20,000
61	Jimmy Jackson	Jackson Special	Offenhauser‡	4	4.275	4.500	255.0	4:22:00.74	114.498	10,000
29	Ted Horn	Boyle Maserati Special	Maserati†	8	2.718	4.000	179.2	4:33:19.60	109.819	5,000
18	Emil Andres	Elgin Piston Pin Special	Maserati†	8	2.702	4.000	183.0	4:35:28.65	108.902	3,500
24	Joie Chitwood	Noc-Out Hose Clamp Special	Offenhauser	4	4.412	4.625	270.0	4:36:45.30	108.399	3,000
33	Louis Durant	Alfa Romeo Special	Alfa Romeo†	8	2.716	3.937	182.0	4:45:30.88	105.073	2,200
52	Gigi Villoresi	Maserati Special	Maserati†	8	3.070	3.070	181.7	4:57:40.23	100.783	1,800
7	Frank Wearne	Wolfe-Tulsa Special	Offenhauser	4	4.375	4.500	271.0	Flagged	197 laps	1,600
39	Bill Sheffler	Jack Maurer Special	Offenhauser	4	4.250	4.500	255.0	Flagged	139 laps	1,500
17	Billy DeVore	Schoof Special	Offenhauser	4	4.250	4.250	255.0	Out	167 laps	1,400

* Speedway prizes for winning entries. Total awards in race, $115,450: Speedway prizes, $75,350; accessory prizes, $20,100; lap prizes, $20,000. † Supercharged. ‡ Front-drive.

Above: Tony Bettenhausen noses through a practice lap. He drove a different car in the race, dropping out with gear ailments after 79 laps. Only seven cars were running at the end—the fewest to finish in the race's 30 runnings. Left: George Robson, a dirt track racer for 15 years, who won $13,800 in lap prizes plus $5,000 in accessory prizes to go with the $20,000 first prize. His car (below) made only one 30-second stop. Three months later Robson wrecked a car on a track in Atlanta and was killed.

1947

For Bill It Wasn't "OK"

```
16  27  1  9  54
 0   0  2  3   4
```

Glancing at those numbers as he buzzed by the scoreboard at the 400-mile mark, the 39-year-old Bill Holland, here for his first "500" ride, could see his No. 16 posted as the leader. And he saw that No. 27, his teammate Mauri Rose in another Blue Crown Spark Plug Special, was in second place. The day before, most of the drivers had attended a meeting at which the scoreboard markings were explained. But Holland had missed the meeting. Now, after a glance at that scoreboard, he thought he led Rose by a lap. Actually, with Rose about 2 miles behind, Holland and Rose were on the same lap, as the zero indicated.

From his pit the Blue Crown owner, Lou Moore, saw Holland thunder by, then Rose. With only 100 miles left in the race, Moore knew that his $60,000 investment in the two Blue Crowns could pay off in a one-two finish. But he feared a duel for first that might end with one or both cars plastered against a wall. Moore grabbed a blackboard. As both drivers zoomed by again, they saw the "E-Z" sign. Holland nodded and slowed a couple of miles an hour. But Mauri Rose, eager for a second "500" victory, kept his foot down. Lap by lap he bit into the lead of the rookie. With 7 laps to go, Rose swept by Holland on the backstretch. Holland waved as Rose shot by, thinking he now led by a little less than a lap.

Lou Moore saw Rose come down the straightaway; Moore flashed a "P-1" sign to Rose, telling him he was in first. A few seconds later Holland swept past; to him Moore gave the "OK" sign. Holland waved back. Again Moore hoped there would be no disastrous last-minute smashup.

Moore's front-drive Blue Crowns had been the prerace co-favorites with the supercharged, front-drive Novis. The Novis' V-8s, it was said, packed 500 horsepower under their hoods, while the unblown Blue Crowns got little more than 250 horses from their four-cylinder Offys. But the 270-cubic-inch Offys had qualities that the Novis had yet to show: reliability and endurance.

Early in the race Cliff Bergere had led in one of the Novis, but a supercharger conked out and it was through. Holland had jammed his Blue Crown into the lead. Near the 100-mile point he skidded on the southwest turn. The veteran William (Shorty) Cantlon swerved to miss him, slammed into the wall, and was crushed to death. He was the first to die at the Speedway since Floyd Roberts in 1939.

Holland had held the lead until Rose popped by with 20 miles to go and Holland waved him on, thinking he was still a lap in front. Rose flashed by the checker 32 seconds ahead of Holland, who, reassured by Moore's "OK" signs, came home still thinking he was the winner—and was enraged at Moore when he found out he was second.

Roland Free hops out of his car after it spun around to face the field. Out of the race after 87 laps, he placed 17th. Before the race, unhappy drivers, organized into a union, "struck" for 40 percent of Speedway gate receipts. The strike crumbled after Wilbur Shaw promised a boost in prize money.

Holland's anger was cooled by $14,000 in lap prizes plus $10,000 in second-place money (he kept 40 percent of the winnings, the rest going to owner Moore). Rose, with only $3,500 in lap money, won about the same amount of money as the rookie—but Rose got his name and face on the Borg-Warner Trophy, a kiss from actress Carole Landis, and his second "500" victory. Both of those "500" triumphs, though, had been dimmed by someone else's shadow: He'd shared the ride with Floyd Davis in 1941 and this time he was accused of stealing the race from Holland. Just ahead, however, was untarnished triumph for little Mauri—and for Holland, revenge.

Bill Holland: "The lousiest deal"

In the pits after the race Bill Holland could not suppress his anger: *After I got the 'E-Z' signal I was going into the turns at only 90 miles an hour. I thought I had it in the bag. I could have won by a lap and a half. The first time I knew I didn't win the race was when I pulled into the pits and I heard the man on the loudspeaker say Holland was second. My wife had come down from the stands to kiss me. It's the lousiest deal I ever got.*

1947's TOP TEN

Race open to nonstock supercharged engines with a piston displacement of 183.060 cubic inches or less and nonstock nonsupercharged engines with a piston displacement of 274.59 cubic inches or less.

NO.	DRIVER	CAR	ENGINE	CYL.	BORE	STROKE	PISTON DISPL.	TIME	MPH	WINNINGS*
27	Mauri Rose	Blue Crown Spark Plug Special	Offenhauser†	4	4.312	4.625	270.0	4:17:52.17	116.338	$20,000
16	Bill Holland	Blue Crown Spark Plug Special	Offenhauser†	4	4.312	4.625	270.0	4:18:24.29	116.097	10,000
1	Ted Horn	Bennett Brothers Special	Maserati‡	8	68.9mm	101.6mm	179.2	4:20:52.55	114.997	5,000
54	Herb Ardinger	Novi Governor Mobil Special	Novi†‡	8	3.125	2.937	181.0	4:24:32.52	113.404	3,500
7	Jimmy Jackson	Jim Hussey Special	Offenhauser†	4	4.275	4.500	258.3	4:25:52.65	112.834	3,000
9	Rex Mays	Bowes Seal Fast Special	Winfield‡	8	2.968	3.250	179.6	4:30:08.05	111.056	2,200
33	Walt Brown	Permafuse Special	Alfa Romeo‡	8	69mm	100mm	183.0	4:54:51.47	101.744	1,800
34	Cy Marshall	Tattersfield Special	Alfa Romeo‡	8	3.010	3.200	182.1	Flagged	197 laps	1,600
41	Fred Agabashian	Ross Page Special	Duray‡	4	3.812	4.000	183.0	Flagged	191 laps	1,500
10	Duke Dinsmore	Schoof Special	Offenhauser	4	4.312	4.625	270.0	Flagged	167 laps	1,400

* Speedway prizes for winning entries. Total awards in race, $137,425; Speedway prizes, $98,350; accessory prizes, $19,075; lap prizes, $20,000. † Front-drive. ‡ Supercharged.

Humming over the bricks, a car rolls by grandstand C, the wooden structure erected in 1911. It was typical of the tottery state of the Speedway when Tony Hulman took over. From 1946 to 1950 Hulman built four new steel-and-concrete grandstands. But old grandstand C was not replaced until 1963. Opposite page: Mauri Rose, winner of his second "500." During the postwar years, with returning GIs anxious to watch fast-paced sports, Rose became to auto racing what Joe DiMaggio was to baseball and Sammy Baugh to pro football. America's best-known race car driver, Rose was featured on magazine covers when stories were done on the "500" or other races.

1948

Closer and Closer and Then—Oops!

Crash helmet strapped under his chin, 52-year-old Ralph Hepburn hunched in the seat of the quivering white arrow as it howled by the empty grandstands. Hep had taken the wheel of this big Novi after Cliff Bergere had spun in the car and quit, calling the Novi too much car for the track. But Hep liked the Novi. In 1941 he'd driven the first one to appear at Indianapolis to a fourth-place finish. And in 1946 he'd blasted a Novi around the 4-lap trials at better than 133 miles an hour, a record that still stood.

Now, warming up the car for the 1948 trials, he shot it along the backstretch. As the Novi approached the No. 3 turn, the howl of its supercharger faded a moment, then whined higher as Hep added power. The Novi spun out of control. Tires screeched and steel screamed against concrete as the Novi hit the wall nose first. The impact broke Hepburn's neck; he was dead when rescuers reached him.

Hep's death shook Chet Miller, who was to drive the other Novi in this race, and he quit the team. He was replaced by Duke Nalon, who blithely steered the brute through the trials at 131.603 miles an hour, fastest of the qualifiers. The 33-car field would be pursuing the biggest purse yet offered at the Speedway. Including lap and accessory prizes, the drivers would rush toward $171,000 in awards—almost double the 1941 total.

The race was held on May 31, Memorial Day celebrated on a Monday this year. More than 150,000 fans crowded into the Speedway, and millions of others listened to periodic broadcasts from the race on a Mutual radio network of 500 stations. The day before the race three-time winner Wilbur Shaw had told the assembled drivers:

"Just remember that a foolhardy driver never gets to be an old driver. The race is not won in the first 100 laps but in the last 100 laps."

Duke Nalon heeded that advice and during the first half of the race snuggled his Novi within striking distance of the leader, Ted Horn, who was at the wheel of a Maserati. Horn had finished fourth or higher in eight straight "500s" but had never won. Hanging right behind Nalon's Novi were Mauri Rose and Bill Holland in their blue and white Blue Crown Spark Plug Specials, the front-drive Offys that had run one-two in the previous year's controversial finish. Near the 250-mile point, Nalon's Novi howled by Horn's Maserati. Mauri Rose, seeing Nalon take off, clung with him and also passed the Maserati. Minutes later Rose surged past Nalon to take the lead.

Both cars had to pit for fuel. When they came out Rose still led, Nalon was glued right behind him, and Bill Holland moved his Blue Crown up to third place.

Aiming for his third "500" win, the swarthy Rose, an Indianapolis engineer, swooped through the turns in the front-drive. But the supercharged Novi was faster on the straightaways. Lap by lap the cigar-shaped Novi snapped closer. Then, as the crowd let out a roar of astonishment, the Novi —with only 50 miles to go—suddenly rolled into the pit.

Again the Novi jinx had struck. During the last refueling, there had been air bubbles in the tank and the Novi hadn't taken on a full load of alcohol. Now, as he refueled, Duke Nalon watched grimly as Bill Holland's Blue Crown streaked into second place. Nalon came out too late to catch either of the Blue Crowns, and Rose zoomed by the checker to win his third "500," joining Louis

Duane Carter, Sr., walks away from his beached car. His rear axle snapped and he lost his rear wheels. In the foreground is one wheel and the axle, which spun into the infield. Nosing into view is the Novi driven by Duke Nalon.

Meyer and Wilbur Shaw as the only three-time winners. Rose had covered the 200 laps faster than any previous driver, his time just ten minutes over four hours and his average speed of 119.814 miles an hour breaking Floyd Roberts's record of 117.200, set ten years earlier.

This year there were no arguments—Rose was the clear-cut winner. But in their "family" dispute, Mauri had not heard the last from teammate Bill Holland.

Harry McQuinn: Run to the ground

Former driver Harry McQuinn—he finished 33d in 1948—commented on the Novi's record-breaking runs in trials and its failures in races: *I think Lew Welch, who owned the Novis, was anxious to set records. But you can run a car only so hard. The harder you run it, the more likely it is to break up. You can set records and you can win '500s,' but it's often hard to do both without running the car into the ground.*

Opposite page: Rose takes the checker to win his second straight "500" and the third of his life. Bottom: Duke Nalon's pursuing Novi; the distinctive wail of its supercharger had by now made it a crowd-pleaser. Left and above: Little Mauri and his winning Blue Crown. After the race he announced his engagement. A troubleshooting engineer, Rose later worked for General Motors.

1948's TOP TEN

Race open to nonstock supercharged engines with a piston displacement of 183.060 cubic inches or less and nonstock nonsupercharged engines with a piston displacement of 274.59 cubic inches or less.

NO.	DRIVER	CAR	ENGINE	CYL.	BORE	STROKE	PISTON DISPL.	TIME	MPH	WINNINGS*
3	Mauri Rose	Blue Crown Spark Plug Special	Offenhauser†	4	4.312	4.625	270.0	4:10:23.33	119.814‡	$20,000
2	Bill Holland	Blue Crown Spark Plug Special	Offenhauser†	4	4.312	4.625	270.0	4:11:47.40	119.147	10,000
54	Duke Nalon	Novi Grooved Piston Special	Novi†§	8	3.125	2.937	181.0	4:14:09.78	118.034	5,000
1	Ted Horn	Bennett Brothers Special	Maserati§	8	2.718	4.000	179.2	4:14:34.47	117.844	3,500
35	Mac Hellings	Don Lee Special	Offenhauser	4	4.132	4.625	270.0	4:24:38.52	113.361	3,000
63	Hal Cole	City of Tacoma Special	Offenhauser	4	4.125	4.625	247.0	4:28:50.86	111.587	2,200
91	Lee Wallard	Iddings Special	Offenhauser	4	4.062	4.500	233.0	4:34:47.00	109.177	1,800
33	John Mauro	Phil Kraft Special	Alfa Romeo§	8	69mm	100mm	183.0	Flagged	198 laps	1,600
7	Tommy Hinnershitz	Kurtis-Kraft Special	Offenhauser	4	4.312	4.625	270.0	Flagged	198 laps	1,500
61	Jimmy Jackson	Howard Keck Special	Offenhauser†	4	4.312	4.625	270.0	Out	193 laps	1,400

* Speedway prizes for winning entries. Total awards in race, $171,075: Speedway prizes, $123,900; accessory prizes, $27,175; lap prizes, $20,000.   † Front-drive.   ‡ New record.   § Supercharged.

1949

The Duke's Wall of Fire

Duke Nalon feathered the throttle as his white Novi hurtled toward the No. 3 turn. Only a few hundred feet behind him, the howl of his supercharger piercing the wind, hung Rex Mays in another of Lew Welch's screaming Novis. The Novis had won the No. 1 and No. 2 starting positions in the time trials; together they had shot by starter Seth Klein's green flag, setting a string of lap records as they looped the track for the first 60 miles.

Nalon swung through the northeast turn on his 24th lap. He jabbed at the throttle as the front-drive car hugged the bank. On this turn Ralph Hepburn had died a year earlier in a Novi. Now an axle snapped in Nalon's Novi. The car spun and slammed into the wall tail first. Sparks showered the car. The fuel tank ruptured, spilling alcohol, and an eight-foot-high wall of flame flashed across the track. Nalon leaped from the car; he was badly burned but would survive. A half-dozen other drivers had to burst through the flames or dodge around them.

For some 20 minutes the yellow lights glowed while the track was cleared. When the green lights came on, the leader was Rex Mays in the surviving Novi. But poised within striking distance were Mauri Rose and Bill Holland in their blue and white Blue Crown Spark Plug Specials, the cars that had finished one-two in the last two "500s."

The question most frequently asked before this race probably had been: Could Mauri Rose become the first to win a fourth "500" and three in a row? The second most frequent question may have been: Would Bill Holland, after two straight second-place finishes, finally beat his teammate Rose? And a third must have been: Could the powerful Novis finish ahead of their front-drive rivals, the Offy-driven Blue Crowns?

But now the jinx that had crippled the Novis so often in the past had knocked Nalon's car out of the race. Twenty-five laps later the jinx struck again. Rex Mays was leading when a magneto failed and the big Novi shuddered to a stop. Mays watched Holland roar by, Rose on his tail. Once more—for the third successive year—the "500" had become a private duel between Lou Moore's two front-drives and their pilots, 43-year-old Rose and 41-year-old Holland.

Holland bit daringly into the turns and began to pull away from Rose. With 50 miles to go Holland had almost lapped Rose. He swung in behind his teammate so he could keep him in sight, careful not to make a mistake like the one that had cost him victory in 1947. But with 20 miles to go Rose's Blue Crown slowed and stopped, out of the race with a broken magneto strap. Holland swept by the checker with a 121.327-mile-an-hour speed record, almost 2 miles an hour faster than Rose's record of a year ago. With cash prizes now approaching $200,000 as the Speedway tied the awards to gate receipts (according to a formula that has never been disclosed), Holland won for himself and Moore the fattest first prize yet—about $60,000 including lap and accessory awards.

For the third straight year a front-drive car—the inspiration of Jimmy Murphy some 25 years earlier—had won at Indianapolis. And this year an Offy had been under the hood of each of the

Duke Nalon's Novi spins and throws a wheel (l.) as Mauri Rose approaches. Rose goes by as Nalon's flaming car hits the wall, two wheels flying. Bill Holland cuts through the wall of flame. With Nalon escaped, the Novi is its own smoking pyre.

1949's TOP TEN

Race open to nonstock supercharged engines with a piston displacement of 183.060 cubic inches or less, nonstock nonsupercharged engines with a piston displacement of 274.59 cubic inches or less, and diesel engines with a piston displacement of 402.68 cubic inches or less.

NO.	DRIVER	CAR	ENGINE	CYL.	BORE	STROKE	PISTON DISPL.	TIME	MPH	WINNINGS*
7	Bill Holland	Blue Crown Spark Plug Special	Offenhauser†	4	4.312	4.625	270	4:07:15.97	121.327‡	$20,000
12	Johnnie Parsons	Kurtis-Kraft Special	Offenhauser	4	4.312	4.625	270	4:10:26.97	119.785	10,000
22	George Connor	Blue Crown Spark Plug Special	Offenhauser	4	4.312	4.625	270	4:10:50.78	119.595	5,000
2	Myron Fohr	Marchese Special	Offenhauser	4	4.312	4.625	270	4:12:32.65	118.791	3,500
77	Joie Chitwood	Wolfe Special	Offenhauser	4	4.312	4.625	270	4:12:36.97	118.757	3,000
61	Jimmy Jackson	Howard Keck Special	Offenhauser†	4	4.312	4.625	270	4:14:31.00	117.870	2,200
98	Johnny Mantz	Agajanian Special	Offenhauser	4	4.312	4.625	270	4:16:06.01	117.601	1,800
19	Paul Russo	Tuffy's Offy Special	Offenhauser	4	4.312	4.625	270	4:28:11.28	111.862	1,600
9	Emil Andres	Tuffy's Offy Special	Offenhauser	4	4.312	4.625	270	Flagged	197 laps	1,500
51	Norman Houser	Troy Oil Co. Special	Offenhauser	4	4.125	4.500	243	Flagged	181 laps	1,400

* Speedway prizes for winning entries. Total awards in race, $179,050; Speedway prizes, $136,300; accessory prizes, $22,750; lap prizes, $20,000. † Front-drive. ‡ New record.

top ten finishers. The Offy would continue to rule at the Speedway, but the reign of the nose-heavy front-drives was near an end. Some young California chargers and a man named Frank Kurtis would see to that.

Tony Hulman: "Did we get letters!"

The man who bought the Speedway in 1945, Tony Hulman has intoned, "Gentlemen, start your engines," to begin every "500" since 1955. But from 1946 to 1954 Wilbur Shaw delivered the command and Hulman was only a spectator at the Speedway he owned. *I didn't mind at all having Wilbur deliver the command, which seems to have begun way back in auto racing, no one knows when, but Shaw made it world famous. I still have trouble pronouncing 'your'—I pronounce it 'yaw'—and I carry the words around in my pocket for a week before the race, practicing, so I won't forget them. The race I remember best was 1946. We weren't sure that too many people would come to the race, it being the first after the war, and we had only a couple of gates open. There was a tremendous traffic jam outside, people trying to get in. I went with some friends in their car, and we got caught in the jam and almost missed the start. We just did get in. Oh, did we get letters about that from people who missed the race. It was the most letters we've ever gotten.*

Opposite page: Mauri Rose sits forlornly, his Blue Crown stopped on the track with a broken magneto strap. He was placed 13th, having gone 192 laps, only 8 short of winning the $10,000 second prize. Above: Bill Cantrell skids out of the race on the 95th lap with a damaged drive shaft. The race's new chief steward was former winner Tommy Milton. The cheapest tickets cost $3, for the infield; the most expensive cost $30, for the best grandstand seats. Twenty-nine spectators were hurt when an old section of grandstand collapsed. Left: Bill Holland, a winner at last; he owned a roller-skating rink in Reading, Pennsylvania. Below: Holland and his winning Blue Crown. During practice, a driver was killed in a crash. According to a tally kept by the *Indianapolis News*, he was the 29th driver or mechanic to die at the Speedway since 1911.

1950

From California Here They Come

An amiable young driver from the midget tracks of California, Johnnie Parsons long ago had learned to grin at bad news. But there was no grin on his face when he heard this bad news an hour before the start of the 1950 Indy 500. A crack had been discovered in the engine block of his yellow and silver Wynn's Friction Proofing Special. "She could pour out her guts at any time during the race," his mechanic told Parsons.

"I'll go flat out," Parsons said, "and hope she holds together while I win all the lap prizes I can."

Under rain-heavy dark clouds, a crowd estimated at 160,000 jammed the stands. A new double-decker grandstand loomed at the No. 1 turn. Missing from the field were the crowd-pleasing Novis. Both of Lew Welch's big screamers had broken down in the trials. Bill Holland had qualified the front-drive Blue Crown Spark Plug Special that he'd driven to victory a year ago; and Mauri Rose, no longer driving for Lou Moore, sat at the wheel of an Offenhauser Special. Between them, Holland and Rose had won the last three "500s."

Here to challenge these two veterans, both in their mid-40s, was a flock of young drivers from California's midget, dirt, and hot-rod tracks. One of them, Johnnie Parsons, had hummed home second in 1949, behind Holland; attracted by his success, young drivers like Bob Sweikert, Troy Ruttman, Walt Faulkner, and Bill Vukovich came to Indianapolis seeking the sudden fame and riches that Parsons had won. They drove these big cars as they drove hot rods and midgets—foot down from start to finish—and Gasoline Alley soon dubbed them the "young chargers."

The chargers came to Indianapolis boasting of a new device that had blown their hot rods around tracks. It was called a fuel injector. The injector replaced the old carburetor; it sprayed the fuel directly into the intake ports of the cylinders. Offys with carburetors developed 300 horsepower on alcohol-base fuels. Offys with injectors produced up to 360 horses on pure methanol (wood alcohol). That didn't match the 500 horsepower of supercharged Novis, but the unblown Offys accelerated more quickly off the turns and were less likely to come apart during a 500-mile race. Almost immediately the fuel injector made the carburetor old-fashioned along trendy Gasoline Alley.

Also new from California were lighter cars (the Speedway had erased its minimum weight limit of 1,750 pounds). Parsons's second-place finish the year before in a light chassis built by Frank Kurtis had turned the eyes of other owners to Kurtis-Kraft bodies. During the trials Walt Faulkner had whisked a rear-drive Kurtis-Kraft 2000 through the 4 qualifying laps at 134.343 miles an hour to break the record held by the big front-drive Novi. "In a lighter and smaller car—with fewer horses under the hood," wrote Al Bloemker in his Speedway history, *500 Miles to Go,* Faulkner had "shattered the Novi's most prized records and at the same time sounded the death knell for all cars of front-drive design."

With the clouds low and dark, the 33 qualifiers exploded by starter Seth Klein's green flag. On the 34th lap Parsons pushed the nose of his rear-

The field bellows through the first turn. Most cars had Offenhauser engines. Retired driver Louis Meyer and Dale Drake had purchased the former Miller plant in Los Angeles from Fred Offenhauser. The Offy engines were also called Meyer-Drakes.

drive Kurtis-Kraft to the front. He was chased by Bill Holland and Mauri Rose in their front-drives. Lap after lap Parsons pulled down the $50, $100, and $150 lap prizes. At 250 miles he led the pack by 30 seconds. He and the other leaders stopped to refuel, but Parsons came out still ahead. A half-dozen drivers, Rose and Holland among them, strained to catch him.

A cloudburst suddenly drilled rain onto the No. 4 turn, at the north rim of the track. The Speedway's chief steward, Tommy Milton, flicked on the yellow lights. The rain streamed down, the sky darkened. Milton made a decision. He gave the checker to Parsons as he came by the 345-mile point, and all the other cars were placed as they had stood when the yellow went on. It was the shortest Indianapolis race since 1916 and the first abbreviated by rain since 1926.

Parsons's rear-drive Offy engine had held together for as long as he'd needed it. His average of 124 miles an hour, faster than any previous winner's, was not posted as a record because he had not gone the 500 miles. For the fourth straight year, Bill Holland and Mauri Rose were among the top three finishers. But the front-drives were rolling down their last miles at Indianapolis, and Holland and Rose had made their last stops in the winner's circle. The rear-drive Offys, installed in Frank Kurtis's chassis, were on their way to the top. And one of those young and hungry California chargers—though he'd failed to qualify for this year's race—would soon become as famous as Wilbur Shaw, Mauri Rose, or any other driver before him. His name was Bill Vukovich; on Gasoline Alley they would call him the Mad Russian.

Johnnie Parsons: Quit? Who me?

In the winner's circle a reporter asked Johnnie Parsons if he would quit after winning the big one. *Quit? Are you kidding? Look, I've only run in this race twice—and once I was second and this time first. The way I look at it, I just got here.*

Opposite page, top (from l.): Wilbur Shaw and Tony Hulman welcome Clark Gable and Jack Benny to the Speedway for the race. Gable was filming a movie about "500" racing, *To Please a Lady*. Bottom left: Shaw introduces Eddie (Rochester) Anderson, Benny's sidekick, to the cockpit of a car that isn't a Maxwell. Bottom right: Former driver Egbert (Babe) Stapp (r.) is among the helpers fixing "500" earrings onto Barbara Stanwyck, the co-star of *To Please a Lady*. Left: TV camera and crew focus on the race. It was telecast the first time a year before by WFBM-TV to some 3,000 local sets. An unprecedented number of drivers, 21, took the rookie test this year. Among them were Bill Vukovich and Bob Sweikert.

1950's TOP TEN

Race open to nonstock supercharged engines with a piston displacement of 183.060 cubic inches or less, nonstock nonsupercharged engines with a piston displacement of 274.59 cubic inches or less, and diesel engines with a piston displacement of 402.68 cubic inches or less.

NO.	DRIVER	CAR	ENGINE	CYL.	BORE	STROKE	PISTON DISPL.	TIME*	MPH	WINNINGS†
1	Johnnie Parsons	Wynn's Friction Proofing Special	Offenhauser	4	4.312	4.625	270	2:46:55.97 (138)	124.002	$57,458
3	Bill Holland	Blue Crown Spark Plug Special	Offenhauser‡	4	4.312	4.625	270	2:47:33.97 (137)	122.638	21,898
31	Mauri Rose	Offenhauser Special	Offenhauser‡	4	4.312	4.625	270	2:48:44.96 (137)	121.778	15,268
54	Cecil Green	John Zink Special	Offenhauser	4	4.312	4.625	270	2:48:45.97 (137)	121.766	10,963
17	Joie Chitwood	Wolfe Special	Offenhauser	4	4.312	4.625	270	2:47:32.99 (136)	121.755	8,788
8	Lee Wallard	Blue Crown Spark Plug Special	Offenhauser	4	4.312	4.625	270	2:48:34.97 (136)	121.009	6,763
98	Walt Faulkner	Grant Piston Ring Special	Offenhauser	4	4.312	4.625	270	2:47:13.55 (135)	121.094	7,663
5	George Connor	Blue Crown Spark Plug Special	Offenhauser	4	4.312	4.625	270	2:47:14.25 (135)	121.086	4,938
7	Paul Russo	Russo-Nickels Special	Offenhauser	4	4.312	4.625	270	2:48:48.32 (135)	119.961	4,988
59	Pat Flaherty	Granatelli-Sabourin Special	Offenhauser	4	4.312	4.625	270	2:48:49.02 (135)	119.952	4,638

* Race stopped at 345 miles due to rain; figures in parentheses show number of laps run.   † Total prizes for winning entries. Total awards in race, $201,035: Speedway prizes, $154,900; accessory prizes, $26,125; lap prizes, $20,000.   ‡ Front-drive.

Opposite page: The 25-year-old pagoda eyes the action as the cars fly down the front stretch; the original bricks remain only in the middle part of the stretch. The cars have formed a "groove," the dark portion of the grey ribbon of asphalt. The groove is laid down by tire rubber and is the path most drivers have found to be the fastest way around the track. At Indy the groove is low toward the grass on the turns, swinging high toward the wall on the straightaways. Those swings, almost kissing the wall, are the waltzes with death that melt the stomachs of fans and test the nerves of drivers. Above: A fire in the pits is extinguished. Left: Winner Johnnie Parsons. Below: Parsons in the winning Kurtis-Kraft-Offy. He raced in eight more "500s" before he retired in 1958.

1951

Faster and Faster, Fewer and Fewer

"Whatever it costs," Lew Welch had told his crew in the summer of 1950, "I want them ready to win next year's race."

"Them" were two of Welch's speed beasts—the powerful, 2,000-pound Novis that were record-breakers in trials, broken-down losers in races. During the 1951 trials Welch's two supercharged Novis seemed to shriek their mastery over the speedway that had frustrated them since 1941. Duke Nalon rammed one of the Novis, the Purelube Special, through the 4 laps at an average of 136.498 miles an hour to grasp once more the qualifying record the Novis had lost a year earlier.

Two days later the old record holder, Walt Faulkner, arrived at the Speedway. He had towed from California a low, light, fuel-injected racer built for owner J. C. Agajanian. Again Faulkner snatched the record away from the Novis as he slammed the car through the 4 laps at a new record speed of 136.872.

On a sun-drenched Memorial Day, the fastest field yet assembled for a "500" formed at the starting line. The average speed of the qualifiers was 133 miles an hour, compared to 131 a year earlier. Drivers raved about the new Firestone tires with treads that made for tighter gripping on the turns.

Five new grandstands had been erected since Tony Hulman's takeover of the track. Attendance this year was estimated at more than 175,000. In the infield, truck owners sold "seats"—the tops of their cabs—for as much as $30.

Again the favorites were the front-drive Novis. But early in the race Jack McGrath, one of the young chargers, rammed his light rear-drive Hinkle Special into the lead. At straightaway speeds of close to 150, he averaged 128 miles an hour for the first 25 miles—a record. At 50 miles McGrath was passed by Lee Wallard, a 40-year-old Florida driver who had raced here three times and twice finished in the top ten. Wallard shot his blue and gold Belanger Motors Special, its lightweight body (1,350 pounds) built by Frank Kurtis and its rear-drive engine the usual Offy, by the 50-mile point with an average speed of 129—another record. And his average for 100 miles, still 129, was yet another record.

At these speeds the heavy Novis began to shred tires; both broke down and neither finished the race. Wallard lost the lead, then regained it, and zoomed by the 250-mile point with an average of 126 miles an hour, another new mark. Engines, cars, and even men began to come apart, strained by speeds never before seen for so long a stretch in this 42-year-old brickyard. Bill Vukovich ran out of oil. Walt Faulkner snapped a crankshaft. Johnnie Parsons blew a magneto. Jack McGrath had to be replaced by a relief driver. In his Belanger a grim-faced Wallard battled the wheel, his nerves, bones, and muscles strained as the car bucked over the track on a broken shock absorber.

His worried crew signaled to Wallard that Johnnie Parsons could come to his relief. But Wallard saw a chance to strengthen his hold on first when the second-place car, driven by Mike Nazaruk, swung to the pits for new tires. Wallard pushed the Belanger out to a lead of almost a lap, then slowed to 123 to spare himself and the banging car. Only eight of the 33 starters were still running as Wallard blew by the checker. Wallard's winning average of 126.244 miles an hour was almost 5 miles an hour faster than Bill Holland's 1949 record. And for the first time ever, a car had gone the 500 miles in under four hours.

Action in the pits. Top left: A car is refueled while a front tire is changed. Top right: A fire is extinguished in Walt Brown's car. Bottom: Andy Linden, who finished fourth, has words with his crew. Note the bald state of his rear tire.

The Novis and their front-drive kin were through—although Lew Welch would go on spending money on Novis, potentially the fastest things on four wheels but destined never to be winners. What would win at the Speedway . . . and win and win and win . . . was a new car with an old-fashioned name—the Indianapolis roadster.

Fred Agabashian: "Wait till next year"

A "500" driver from 1947 to 1957, Fred Agabashian never won a "500" and led for only one lap—in 1954. *It should have been 2 laps at least, and I always thought we should have won that 1951 '500.' In those days we only changed right-side tires. The cars used to drop a lot of oil and they'd leave a groove of oil. We'd run the left-side tires in the oil and the right-side tires on the dry track, except through the corners, where we'd run all four tires through the oil. That way you got longer wear. We'd make one stop about halfway, for fuel and right-side tires. Jimmy Davies was leading, but just after my stop I passed him on the north chute to take the lead. But as I went into turn four, Rodger Ward—who was lapped—came wide and almost nailed me to the wall. I had to back off, drop back, and Davies went by underneath me to retake the lead. So, since I didn't cross the finish line for the lap, it wasn't official that I'd led. Then a few laps later the clutch went. So we parked it, got some chicken and milk, and said wait till next year.*

Above: On the northeast (No. 3) turn, Mauri Rose's car spins out of control and crashes. Rose stepped out of the car and, minutes later, retired from racing. Right and below: Lee Wallard and his winning No. 99. Opposite page: His wife hugs him in Victory Lane while Loretta Young and the Borg-Warner Trophy glisten and glow. This was Wallard's last "500"; in the three previous years he placed 7th, 23d, and 6th. He died in 1963. By 29 cubic inches, his Offy was the smallest unblown engine among the top ten finishers.

1951's TOP TEN

Race open to nonstock supercharged engines with a piston displacement of 183.060 cubic inches or less, nonstock nonsupercharged engines with a piston displacement of 274.59 cubic inches or less, and diesel engines with a piston displacement of 402.68 cubic inches or less.

NO.	DRIVER	CAR	ENGINE	CYL.	BORE	STROKE	PISTON DISPL.	TIME	MPH	WINNINGS*
99	Lee Wallard	Belanger Motors Special	Offenhauser	4	4.250	4.250	241	3:57:38.05	126.244†	$63,612
83	Mike Nazaruk	Jim Robbins Special	Offenhauser	4	4.312	4.625	270	3:59:25.31	125.302	21,362
9	Jack McGrath	Hinkle Special	Offenhauser	4	4.312	4.625	270	4:00:29.42	124.745	14,962
57	Andy Linden	Leitenberger Special	Offenhauser	4	4.312	4.625	270	4:02:18.06	123.812	10,012
52	Bobby Ball	Blakely Special	Offenhauser	4	4.312	4.625	270	4:02:30.27	123.709	8,612
1	Henry Banks	Blue Crown Spark Plug Special	Offenhauser	4	4.312	4.625	270	4:03:18.02	123.304	6,962
68	Carl Forberg	Auto Shippers Special	Offenhauser	4	4.312	4.625	270	Flagged	193 laps	5,862
27	Duane Carter	Mobilgas Special	Offenhauser‡	4	4.322	4.625	272	Flagged	180 laps	5,482
5	Tony Bettenhausen	Mobilgas Special	Offenhauser‡	4	4.312	4.625	270	Out	178 laps	5,162
18	Duke Nalon	Novi Purelube Special	Novi‡§	8	3.187	2.840	181	Out	151 laps	5,062

* Total prizes for winning entries. Total awards in race, $207,650: Speedway prizes, $154,700; accessory prizes, $32,950; lap prizes, $20,000. † New record.
‡ Front-drive. § Supercharged.

1952

Screeches, Sparks, and Curses

Sitting in the garage, the two veteran drivers were ticking off the names of great drivers who had never won at the Speedway, wheelmasters like Ted Horn and Cliff Bergere and, way back, Roscoe Sarles and Bennett Hill. Listening was 31-year-old Bill Vukovich, the nation's champion midget-car driver, here for his second "500."

Suddenly he stood up, bored by what he had heard. "All you have to do to win here," he snapped, "is keep your foot on the throttle and turn left."

In one sentence Vukovich had capsuled his brazen self-confidence. Even among his fellow California chargers, the Mad Russian, as they called him, was respected for his get-out-of-my-way dashes through a pack to snatch the lead. Off the track he had the same attitude, bulling through interviewers and fans to hide moodily behind locked garage doors.

For the 1952 race Vukovich had been given the wheel of a new car built by body designer Frank Kurtis for oilman Howard Keck. The engine, a fuel-injected Offy, was offset in the frame so that the drive shaft ran alongside the driver instead of below him—the same idea used by Art Sparks in 1938. With the driver's seat placed only five inches above the track, the car had a low center of gravity. And with the cockpit planted to one side, the low-slung car had the look of a two-seater. On Gasoline Alley it was immediately dubbed the "roadster."

The Mad Russian slammed the roadster around the 4-lap trials at an average of better than 138 miles an hour to set a new record. A Novi, driven by Chet Miller, regained the record with a 139-mile-an-hour performance a few days later. But the pole had already been won by a monstrous, 2,500-pound, diesel-powered car piloted by Fred Agabashian. Built by Cummins Diesel, the same people whose diesel had whirled around the 200 laps without a stop in 1931, this diesel seemed unbeatable: It could go 500 miles at 130 miles an hour or better and didn't have to stop for fuel. But its hulking weight destroyed rubber at high speeds. It failed to finish this year and never raced again.

For much of the first 400 miles of the race two of the California chargers, Vukovich and 22-year-old Troy Ruttman, his 220-pound body squeezed into a red Agajanian Special, jockeyed for the lead. With 100 miles to go the Mad Russian moved out to almost a lap lead over Ruttman. But in the pits Ruttman's crew noticed that Vukovich was wrestling with his wheel on the turns. The word was signaled to Ruttman: Vukie's got steering trouble. *Go!*

Ruttman stood down hard on the floor and closed on Vukovich. With 25 miles to go Ruttman swung out of the No. 4 turn and saw the yellow dot that was Vukovich's Fuel Injection Engineering Special blur toward the No. 1 turn, at the bottom of the stretch. At 150 miles an hour Ruttman thundered down the stretch and, a minute later, swept into the No. 3 turn. He saw Vukovich's yellow roadster skid toward the wall, brush the wall in a shower of sparks, and screech to a stop. A pivot pin had cracked and Vukovich's car was

164

Troy Ruttman, a former heavyweight boxer and the son of a race driver, is engulfed in smoke as his crew sprays foam on flames that broke out during his only pit stop. Though his arm was burned, Ruttman swung the Agajanian Special back into the race.

through. The Mad Russian hopped out, uninjured, and threw a flurry of curses at the crumpled roadster.

Minutes later Ruttman—the youngest "500" winner ever—pulled his fullback's frame out of the Agajanian Special after taking the checker with a speed of almost 129 miles an hour, 2 miles an hour faster than Lee Wallard's record the year before. Ruttman won over $61,000 for himself and owner J. C. Agajanian.

Still steaming, the Mad Russian stalked to his garage. To his crew he shouted, "That Ruttman never won an easier one. You can be damn sure I won't let it happen again next year."

"Seldom," Speedway historian Al Bloemker later wrote, "has one fulfilled a more difficult promise so convincingly."

Ray Harroun: "A far cry"

At Indianapolis for the 36th running of the "500" was the race's first winner, Ray Harroun. He was asked how the race had changed. *Well, it's a far cry from the old days. Then we'd loaf through the front half and let some of the cars wear out and then make our move. But now the trick seems to be to get out in front and hang on. And I see them go through those corners. It's the same corners we went through, and I don't see how they get through them at those speeds. We skidded on them at 60 miles an hour, and even with the better tires they got today, I am amazed to see them go through those corners at close to a hundred miles an hour as pretty as you please.*

Opposite page: A Studebaker leads the field through the pace lap. In the background, part of the crowd estimated at 175,000. Most of the cars had identical 270-cubic-inch, nonsupercharged Offys. "The race," wrote a critic, "has become just a playground for the Meyer-Drake Offys." Top: Jimmy Bryan gestures with seeming unhappiness during a stop, but he came in sixth. Above: A dice between a roadster (No. 93) driven by Bob Scott and the old-fashioned front-drive Novi (No. 21) driven by Chet Miller. Both cars dropped out of the race early. A year later, during practice, Miller rode another Novi into a wall at the Speedway. The car whirled 300 feet, crashed again, and Miller, a veteran of 16 "500s," was killed.

Opposite page: Actress Arlene Dahl wipes the grease off Troy Ruttman's face before her kiss. The Borg-Warner Trophy looms behind Ruttman. An official in the foreground holds the cup that the winner kept (today the cup is a replica of the Borg-Warner). Left: The 22-year-old, 6-foot-4-inch Ruttman. Below: He sits in his winner, owner J. C. Agajanian in the background, wearing the cowboy hat. The orange Cummins Diesel caused most of the prerace excitement. Cummins was reported to have spent a half-million dollars to win the "500" and boost diesel sales. Its body by Kurtis, the car was cigar-shaped and set so low that even if it were upside down, its tires would have touched the ground. It was equipped with a turbosupercharger. Cummins hoped the car could go the full 500 miles at a steady 130 without a stop except for tires. But in the race its turbosupercharger swallowed flying rubber; it smoked out after 71 laps and never raced again.

1952's TOP TEN

Race open to nonstock supercharged engines with a piston displacement of 183.060 cubic inches or less, nonstock nonsupercharged engines with a piston displacement of 274.59 cubic inches or less, and diesel engines with a piston displacement of 402.68 cubic inches or less.

NO.	DRIVER	CAR	ENGINE	CYL.	BORE	STROKE	PISTON DISPL.	TIME	MPH	WINNINGS*
98	Troy Ruttman	Agajanian Special	Offenhauser	4	4.322	4.500	264	3:52:41.88	128.922†	$61,743
59	Jim Rathmann	Grancor-Wynn Special	Offenhauser	4	4.312	4.625	270	3:56:44.24	126.723	24,368
18	Sam Hanks	Bardahl Special	Offenhauser	4	4.312	4.625	270	3:58:53.48	125.580	14,768
1	Duane Carter	Belanger Motors Special	Offenhauser	4	4.323	4.500	264	3:59:30.21	125.259	11,815
33	Art Cross	Bowes Seal Fast Special	Offenhauser	4	4.312	4.625	270	4:01:22.08	124.292	9,218
77	Jimmy Bryan	Peter Schmidt Special	Offenhauser	4	4.312	4.625	270	4:02:06.23	123.914	7,463
37	Jimmy Reece	John Zink Special	Offenhauser	4	4.312	4.625	270	4:03:17.15	123.312	6,368
54	George Connor	Federal Engineering, Detroit Special	Offenhauser	4	4.312	4.625	270	4:04:42.50	122.595	6,118
22	Cliff Griffith	Tom Sarafoff Special	Offenhauser	4	4.372	4.500	270	4:05:05.65	122.402	5,763
5	Johnnie Parsons	Jim Robbins Special	Offenhauser	4	4.352	4.500	270	4:06:19.71	121.789	5,518

* Total prizes for winning entries. Total awards in race, $230,100: Speedway prizes, $169,300; accessory prizes, $40,800; lap prizes, $20,000. † New record.

1953

Water on the Neck

The red and yellow roadster harrumphed down the straightaway on the final lap of its qualifying run. In the cockpit, track whooshing beneath him, Bill Vukovich, the Mad Russian, could see black clouds extending to the horizon. He rammed his Fuel Injection Engineering Special through the south turns, flashed north on the backstretch. As Vukovich twisted into the north turns, thick rain tattooed the track and splashed his goggles. But Vukovich's foot stayed on the floor. He roared blindly through the rain and past the finish line. He took the flag with an average speed of better than 138 miles an hour, fastest time of the first-day qualifiers, to win the pole.

The day of the race dawned dry, still, and hot, the sun scarlet over the plains. Three Purdue majorettes fainted during the prerace parade. A Firestone official held a thermometer to the bricks and saw the mercury touch 130. In the grandstands and on the baking infield, sweating spectators guzzled drinks, wiped their brows, and talked of the luck of the Speedway with the temperamental Indiana weather.

On the pole, Vukovich squinted into the heat waves undulating off the track. He sat in a roadster that was identical, except for its paint job, with about half the other cars in the field. Eighteen were Kurtis-Kraft, fuel-injected Offys, their engines off-center, their drivers low to the ground. All told, 32 of the cars were powered by Offys, the 33d by a Novi (another Novi had crashed in the trials, killing driver Chet Miller).

Vukovich's Offy roadster jumped into the lead from the start. On loop after loop he swiveled the red and yellow rear-drive around lapped cars to lead by a mile . . . 2 miles . . . 3 miles. "He doesn't know how to run anywhere else except in front," wrote an admiring reporter. In the Mad Russian's wake, drivers tapped their helmets as they zoomed by the pits to signal they wanted relief drivers. In the postwar years, relief drivers had become more and more a rarity as rides became smoother on fatter tires and a resurfaced track. There had been only one relief driver in the past two years. But in this heat-baked "500," there were 14 relief drivers, and some cars had as many as three drivers.

When Vukovich pitted a second time, his crew asked him if he wanted relief. The Mad Russian glared, grabbed a cup of cold water, dashed it on the back of his neck, and stormed back into the heat and traffic.

Far behind was 38-year-old Carl Scarborough, a former midget-car racer. His crew saw him swaying at the wheel and signaled him in. He was pulled, gasping, from the cockpit. Minutes later he was dead of heat exhaustion.

Vukovich rammed his red and yellow roadster through the dwindling field—only eight cars were still running at the end—and ignored his crew's signals to ease up. He came by the finish 8 miles in front, his time only a shade off Troy Ruttman's record of a year earlier. From the record purse of nearly a quarter of a million dollars, the Mad Russian collected the biggest first prize to date—$89,496.

The Mad Russian had led for 195 of the 200

Starter Seth Klein waves the checker at his 15th consecutive "500," going back to 1935. He also started the 1925 and 1926 races. After this race he was succeeded by W. H. Vandewater and then Pat Vidan, who started all the races from 1962 through 1976.

laps, a pit stop having cost him the lead for the other 5 laps. In his three years of "500" racing, he had led for 353 of the 420 laps he was on the track. This year his Fuel Injection Special had finished far ahead of identical Kurtis roadsters with identical four-cylinder, 270-cubic-inch Offys. Before the following year's race the Mad Russian would see some drivers conferring and would ask, "Are you guys trying to decide who's going to finish second?"

Nothing could beat him, he was saying, and for a while he was right.

Esther Vukovich: "He's the boss"

Her white dress smeared after she and actress Jane Greer kissed her husband in the winner's circle, Esther Vukovich was asked if she wanted their nine-year-old son, Billy, Jr., to be a race car driver. *Definitely not. I can't stop Bill, Sr., from racing. This is what he has always wanted to do, he loves it, and he wants to be the best there is at it. And now he is. I couldn't stop him if I wanted to. He's the boss in the family. But Billy, Jr., never.*

Above: The Mad Russian, Bill Vukovich. Actually he was of Slavic ancestry. After the race an official shouted at him, "You've made the biggest purse anyone ever thought of making." Vukie stared. "I can't hear a damn thing," he said. The crowd was estimated at 155,000 and, with added double-decker grandstands, 75,000 of them were in the seats. Opposite page, top: Vukie in the Kurtis-Offy, the first of a long line of roadsters that would win at Indianapolis. Bottom: Esther Vukovich waits to greet her husband in Victory Lane.

1953's TOP TEN

Race open to nonstock supercharged engines with a piston displacement of 183.060 cubic inches or less; nonstock nonsupercharged engines with a piston displacement of 274.59 cubic inches or less; diesel engines with a piston displacement of 402.68 cubic inches or less; and turbine engines, no size limitation.

NO.	DRIVER	CAR	ENGINE	CYL.	BORE	STROKE	PISTON DISPL.	TIME	MPH	WINNINGS*
14	Bill Vukovich	Fuel Injection Engineering Special	Offenhauser	4	4.375	4.500	270	3:53:01.69	128.740	$89,496
16	Art Cross	Springfield Welding's Clay Smith Special	Offenhauser	4	4.312	4.500	263	3:56:32.56	126.827	27,296
3	Sam Hanks	Bardahl Special	Offenhauser	4	3.375	3.500	270	3:57:13.24	126.465	16,241
59	Fred Agabashian	Grancor-Elgin Piston Pin Special	Offenhauser	4	4.375	4.500	270	3:57:40.91	126.219	12,946
5	Jack McGrath	Hinkle Special	Offenhauser	4	4.312	4.625	270	4:00:51.33	124.556	10,621
48	Jimmy Daywalt	Sumar Special	Offenhauser	4	4.312	4.625	270	4:01:11.88	124.379	7,696
2	Jim Rathmann	Travelon Trailer Special	Offenhauser	4	4.375	4.500	270	4:01:47.65	124.072	6,846
12	Ernie McCoy	Chapman Special	Offenhauser	4	4.312	4.625	270	4:03:06.23	123.404	5,946
98	Tony Bettenhausen	Agajanian Special	Offenhauser	4	4.312	4.500	263	Out	196 laps	5,646
53	Jimmy Davies	Pat Clancy Special	Offenhauser	4	4.312	4.500	274	Flagged	193 laps	5,546

* Total prizes for winning entries. Total awards in race, $246,300: Speedway prizes, $176,900; accessory prizes, $39,400; lap prizes, $30,000.

WINNER
Bill Vukovich

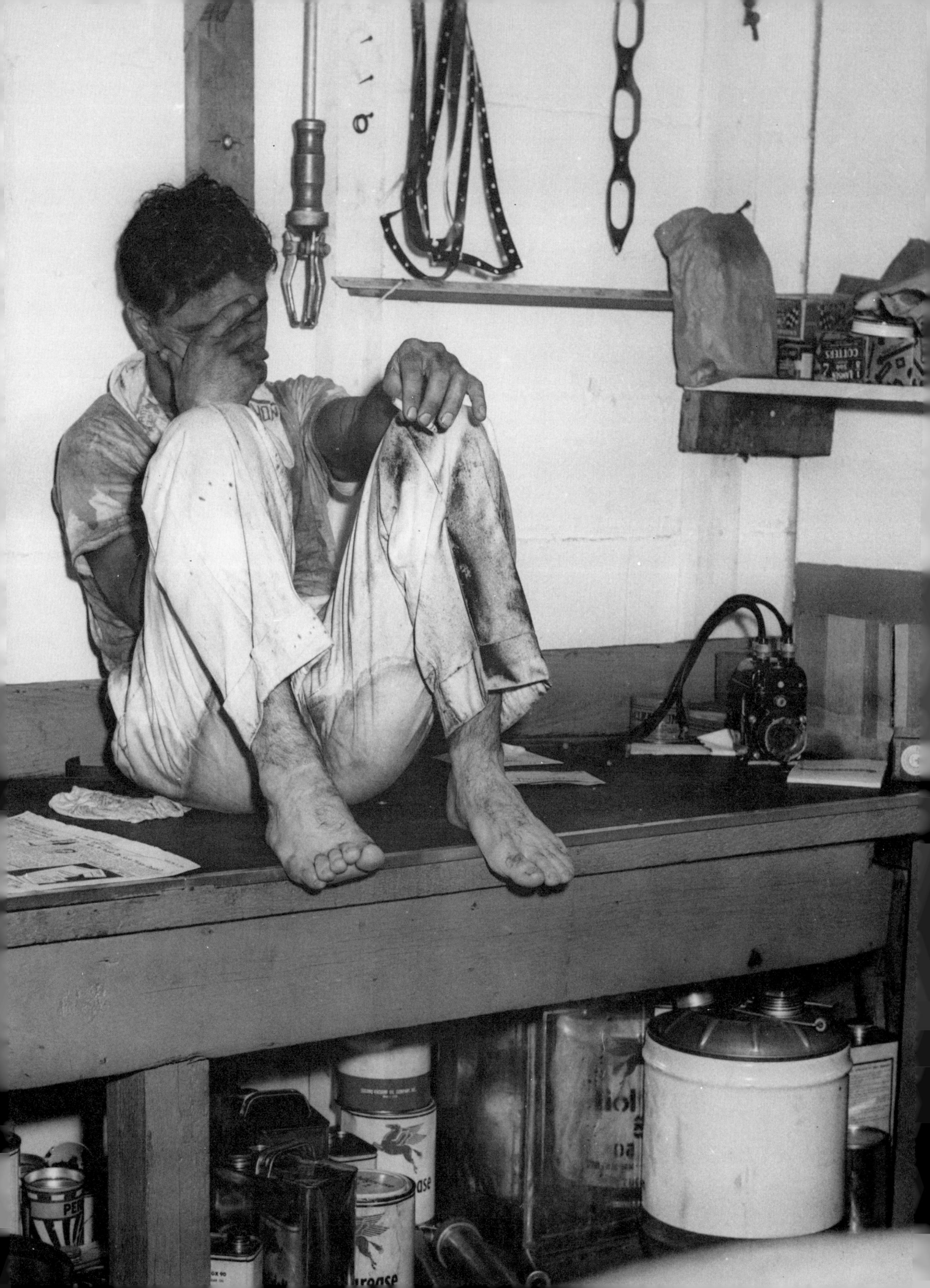

1954

Weaving and Dipping from Way Back

Bill Vukovich, the Mad Russian, folded his 5-foot 8-inch, 145-pound frame into the cockpit of Howard Keck's Fuel Injection Engineering Special. Only two years old, the red and yellow roadster was "tired iron" by now. One "500" grind, mechanics estimated, was the equivalent of 50,000 miles of highway driving. For three days the car, 1953's winner, had grumbled and groaned, unable to qualify. Today was the last day for qualifying. A grim Vukovich put his foot to the car and it shot around the 4 laps at 138 miles an hour to win a place in the seventh row, 18 cars stacked ahead of it.

On the pole sat Jack McGrath, a shrewd dirt track racer who had qualified at a record 141.033 miles an hour. He became the first driver ever to qualify at better than 140. It was indicative of the ever increasing speed at the "500" that Walt Faulkner's 1950 qualifying record, 134.343, would not have been fast enough to get him into this year's race: The slowest of the 33 cars qualified at over 137 miles an hour.

Favored in a poll of the drivers was McGrath. "Vukovich," said one, "can't get through all those hot cars in front of him." Most of those cars were twins of the Mad Russian's roadster—body by Kurtis, fuel-injected engine by Offy. Two of every three qualifiers, in fact, sat in Kurtis-Kraft roadsters, and every engine in the race was an unblown Offy.

Vukovich was jauntily confident. "If they offered me second place right now," he said on the eve of the race, "I'd refuse." He told friends he would become the third driver—Wilbur Shaw and Mauri Rose were the others—to win "500s" back to back.

On a cool, gusty, overcast Memorial Day, an estimated 200,000 fans—many seated in the new double-decked grandstands built since 1946—watched the 33 cars line up in formation. Sitting in the Dodge pace car was Ralph DePalma, the honorary referee. Lap prizes had been boosted to $150 a lap; they enticed cars in the front row to rush out and grab the early lead. From the pole Jack McGrath zoomed ahead to pull down $150 every 70 seconds, his speed a record-breaking 139 miles an hour.

By the 50-mile point, weaving through stragglers and dipping dangerously low into the banked turns, Vukovich had snaked into sixth place. By 100 miles he had crept to fifth and by 150 he had moved into third, behind McGrath and Art Cross.

McGrath and Cross pitted for tires. The Mad Russian bolted into the lead, then went in for tires, and came out in second place, behind McGrath. At 300 miles he slipped by McGrath on the backstretch and edged away to a lead of half a lap. As he swerved to the pits one last time, the car scraped against the pit wall. The inside tires could not be changed without losing time. Vukovich and his crew decided to risk going the rest of the way on the worn tires. He veered onto the track in pursuit of a new leader, Jimmy Bryan. With 125 miles to go Vukovich swooped by Bryan and moved away to lead by half a lap. Then, eyeing those inside tires, he slowed slightly but still rode home ahead of the other 18 finishers with a new record speed—130.840 miles an hour. The Mad Russian got a kiss from actress Marie Wilson ("It was greasy but nice," she said) and picked up 40 percent of the $74,934 first-prize money. He had joined Rose and Shaw as the only men to win two

The exhausted winner slumps in his garage after the race. "I'm about half deaf...and half blind," he said. With rain in the air, the American Automobile Association ruled that a "500" stopped at any point after a minimum of 101 laps would be considered an official "500"—an edict that still stands.

175

Above: Pat O'Connor spins off the No. 1 turn and onto the infield, out of the race 19 laps from the finish. He placed 21st. Left: Driver Len Duncan is engulfed by smoke during a pit fire. Below: First at the 200th lap is Bill Vukovich (in car at r.) as he passes a lapped car and—waving—sees the checker for a second straight year. Opposite page, left: He is interviewed in the winner's circle in front of the Borg-Warner Trophy. On the car's hood is a trophy for him, filled with water. Far right: He poses in the winner. It is spotted with decals from companies that paid thousands of dollars to have their names ride on what they hoped would be a spotlighted winner.

"500s" in a row. Next year, he told people, he would become the fourth driver to win three "500s" and the following year the first to win four. "Then I'll retire," he said, "to the farm in Fresno." But like Floyd Roberts before him, the Mad Russian would wait too long to retire.

Bill Vukovich: Deaf and blind

How did he come from so far back in the pack? Bill Vukovich was asked in the winner's circle. *I just pushed down on it and kept going. It was a tough road to hoe from that far back in the pack but what else could you do but stamp on it? It was a lot easier from the front last year, sure, but the heat wasn't as tough this time. Even so, like last year when I finished, I'm about half deaf from the noise and half blind from oil.*

1954's TOP TEN

Race open to nonstock supercharged engines with a piston displacement of 183.060 cubic inches or less; nonstock nonsupercharged engines with a piston displacement of 274.59 cubic inches or less; diesel engines with a piston displacement of 402.68 cubic inches or less; and turbine engines, no size limitation.

NO.	DRIVER	CAR	ENGINE	CYL.	BORE	STROKE	PISTON DISPL.	TIME	MPH	WINNINGS*
14	Bill Vukovich	Fuel Injection Engineering Special	Offenhauser	4	4.375	4.500	271	3:49:17.27	130.840†	$74,934
9	Jimmy Bryan	Dean Van Lines Special	Offenhauser	4	4.312	4.500	263	3:50:27.26	130.178	35,884
2	Jack McGrath	Hinkle Special	Offenhauser	4	4.312	4.625	270	3:50:36.97	130.086	26,909
34	Troy Ruttman	Automobile Shippers Special	Offenhauser	4	4.375	4.500	271	3:52:09.90	129.218	12,709
73	Mike Nazaruk	McNamara Special	Offenhauser	4	4.375	4.500	271	3:52:41.85	128.923	10,934
77	Fred Agabashian	Merz Engineering Special	Offenhauser	4	4.385	4.500	272	3:53:04.83	128.711	8,034
7	Don Freeland	Bob Estes Special	Offenhauser	4	4.375	4.500	271	3:53:30.65	128.474	6,884
5	Paul Russo	Ansted Rotary Engineering Special	Offenhauser	4	4.375	4.500	271	3:54:18.39	128.037	6,259
28	Larry Crockett	Federal Engineering, Detroit Special	Offenhauser	4	4.312	4.625	270	3:56:24.56	126.899	6,484
24	Cal Niday	Jim Robbins Special	Offenhauser	4	4.375	4.500	271	3:56:24.93	126.895	6,309

* Total prizes for winning entries. Total awards in race, $269,375: Speedway prizes, $199,200; accessory prizes, $40,175; lap prizes, $30,000. † New record.

1955

The Jinx Waited on the Backstretch

The blue and red Hopkins Special arrowed down the 3,300 feet of straightaway past the rows of double-decked grandstands. In a seat near the finish line Esther Vukovich watched her husband's roadster disappear into the No. 1 turn. There were more than 350 miles to go, but with his fastest challenger in the pits, Bill Vukovich seemed on his way toward becoming the first man to win three straight "500s."

"I've got the best car I've ever driven," Vukovich had told reporters before the race. His previous sponsor, Howard Keck, had withdrawn from racing. A wealthy Floridian, Lindsey Hopkins, had bought a new $25,000 roadster for the Mad Russian—a shiny Kurtis-Kraft 500C powered by a fuel-injected, 270-cubic-inch Offy. Of the Kurtis-Kraft roadsters, *Sports Illustrated* commented: "Bred for the 500 . . . the car has just one purpose: to win at Indianapolis." There would be 21 of them among this year's 33 starters, as alike, noted the magazine, "as a row of peas."

A familiar face was gone from the Speedway—the mustached, grinning Wilbur Shaw had been killed in an airplane crash the previous fall. His command to the drivers, "Gentlemen, start your engines!" had become a tradition during the postwar years. In his place at the microphone to give the command today stood Speedway owner Tony Hulman.

In the front row waited Jack McGrath, as daring a charger as Vukovich. Vukovich, in the second row, was the favorite despite the jinx that had struck Wilbur Shaw and Mauri Rose when they tried to win three in a row; both had failed to finish.

At the start McGrath rushed to the head of the pack, but on the 3d lap Vukovich swung out of the No. 4 turn and blasted into the lead. Nose to nose the two cars winged through two of the fastest laps in "500" history—better than 140 miles an hour. On the 25th lap McGrath pushed his Hinkle Special in front, but Vukovich brought the grandstand crowd up and cheering as he tore off a new race lap record of 141.354 miles an hour to shoot back into the lead.

By now Vukovich and McGrath had lapped most of the field. Near the 125-mile mark McGrath's Hinkle began to growl and he swung it into the pits for ignition repairs. Vukovich flashed by the crowd and disappeared around the No. 1 turn toward the backstretch. He had taken McGrath's best speed and had sent him to the pit.

The crowd waited for Vukovich's blue and red dot to blossom toward them out of the No. 4 turn, at the top of the stretch. Cars bellowed by, but no Hopkins Special. A murmur swept the stands, and Esther Vukovich heard it . . . "Where's Vukovich?" It was then that spectators saw black smoke pluming out of the backstretch.

The cars had swept down the backstretch toward the No. 3 turn. Vukovich veered to pass three lapped cars. An axle snapped on Rodger Ward's car and suddenly there was a blurred mass of spinning, twisting metal in front of Vukovich. He could have swung toward the infield but chose a faster route, a patch of daylight six feet wide between the wall and Ward's spinning wreck. Vukovich yanked the wheel—and the door shut as Johnny Boyd's car was knocked into his path. At 150 miles an hour Vukovich's front wheel hit

Jimmy Bryan's Dean Van Lines Special—it finished second in 1954—smokes out of the race with a bad fuel pump. A typical Kurtis roadster, it weighed 1,800 pounds, less than an MG. The aluminum, 522-pound Offy engine produced 330 horsepower at 5,500 rpm running on methanol fuel.

Opposite page, top: At the start the 33 cars hit the bricks. The day was one of the chilliest ever for a "500"— 54 degrees at race time. Dinah Shore sang "Back Home in Indiana," then waited to kiss the winner. Bottom: With Vukovich pinned underneath, his Hopkins Special burns before rows of spectators on the backstretch. A dirt track racer at 14, he managed a gas station in Fresno when he wasn't on the race circuit. Below: Jim Rathmann (No. 33), Jimmy Bryan (No. 1), and Keith Andrews (No. 31) fly past the pit area and into the No. 1 turn.

the other car. His Hopkins Special soared over Boyd's car, rolled once in midair, crashed nose first, bounced high, hit again with an awful roar, and belched flame and smoke. The Mad Russian was pinned in the cockpit of the upside-down car.

In the grandstand Esther Vukovich and the wives of the other three drivers in the crash were asked to come to the field hospital. Three wives got good news: Their husbands had survived. Esther Vukovich learned that her husband and the father of their two children was dead. He had left $7,500 in lap prizes.

The crowd, hearing of Vukovich's death, seemed to sag, and it watched with muted enthusiasm as Bob Sweikert, a driver from the California midget tracks, nosed into the lead at 400 miles and pulled away to win by 2 laps. His average speed was below the previous year's record; the yellow lights had slowed the race for 30

1955's TOP TEN

Race open to nonstock supercharged engines with a piston displacement of 183.060 cubic inches or less; nonstock nonsupercharged engines with a piston displacement of 274.59 cubic inches or less; diesel engines with a piston displacement of 335.57 cubic inches or less; and turbine engines, no size limitation.

NO.	DRIVER	CAR	ENGINE	CYL.	BORE	STROKE	PISTON DISPL.	TIME	MPH	WINNINGS*
6	Bob Sweikert	John Zink Special	Offenhauser	4	4.312	4.625	270	3:53:59.13	128.209	$76,138
10	Tony Bettenhausen	Chapman Special	Offenhauser	4	4.375	4.500	270	3:56:43.11	126.733	30,088
15	Jimmy Davies	Bardahl Special	Offenhauser	4	4.375	4.500	270	3:57:31.89	126.299	16,988
44	Johnny Thomson	Schmidt Special	Offenhauser	4	4.312	4.625	270	3:57:38.44	126.241	12,888
77	Walt Faulkner	Merz Engineering Special	Offenhauser	4	4.375	4.500	270	3:59:16.66	125.377	10,763
19	Andy Linden	Massaglia Special	Offenhauser	4	4.375	4.500	270	3:59:57.47	125.022	8,513
71	Al Herman	Martin Brothers Special	Offenhauser	4	4.312	4.625	270	4:00:23.81	124.794	7,063
29	Pat O'Connor	Ansted-Rotary Special	Offenhauser	4	4.312	4.625	270	4:00:41.09	124.644	6,413
48	Jimmy Daywalt	Sumar Special	Offenhauser	4	4.375	4.500	270	4:01:09.39	124.401	6,413
89	Pat Flaherty	Dunn Engineering Special	Offenhauser	4	4.332	4.625	272	4:01:46.05	124.086	6,113

* Total prizes for winning entries. Total awards in race $270,400: Speedway prizes, $199,900; accessory prizes, $40,500; lap prizes, $30,000.

minutes after Vukovich's crash and two other accidents.

According to records kept by the *Indianapolis News,* Vukovich was the 40th person—driver, mechanic, or spectator—to die during the 39 runnings of the "500." Editorialists again hammered for an end to the annual Memorial Day "massacre" at Indianapolis. Tony Hulman rose to defend the race and almost immediately felt the rug being pulled out from under him.

Johnnie Parsons: Heartbreak stop

The 1950 winner talked of his frustration in the 1955 race: *I started 26th and I worked my way all the way up to second at about 300 miles. Sweikert was ahead of me. I had already made my pit stop and had a full tank to go all the way. He was about two-thirds of the front stretch ahead of me, so I could read his pit boards telling him he had to come in to refuel. He had to stop. But on the backstretch I had to stop permanently when a magneto quit. Two laps later Sweikert stopped to refuel. If that mag hadn't quit, I would have been first, and there was no way I could lose. To come all the way from 26th to second and know you are going to take the lead, and then the car quits ... talk about heartbreak.*

Left: Flanked by Tony Hulman and Dinah Shore, winner Bob Sweikert displays a late edition of the *Indianapolis News,* flown to the track by helicopter, that proclaims his victory—and shows a photo of Vukovich's flaming wreck. Below: The winner. "This is the first time I've ever finished the race, let alone won it," Sweikert said. "The race was tough because of the stiff wind. The car jumped six feet." He finished sixth in the 1956 race, then went to a track at Salem, Indiana, where he was killed.

Tony Bettenhausen's Belanger Motors Special slams into the southwest wall, its rear tire flying loose. The car skidded out of control after blowing a tire. Bettenhausen walked away from the wreck with a broken collarbone —lucky this time.

1956

The Wearing of the Green

Chunky, tanned Paul Russo, a grandfather at 42, gripped the wheel of the blood-red Novi as it flitted by the double-decked grandstands at better than 150 miles an hour. The whine of its supercharger hung in the humid air even after the Novi had vanished around the No. 1 turn. Chasing the Novi, the cars only ten seconds apart, was Pat Flaherty in a pink and white John Zink Special, its Offy engine leaving in its wake a full-throated rumble.

Russo's Novi was a brand-new one built by Frank Kurtis, the roadster designer. Knee-high and with a long nose, it looked like a surfboard on wheels. No longer was the Novi a front-drive car; like the roadster's, its drive shaft ran alongside the driver to the rear wheels. But its engine was a brute V-8 similar to that of earlier Novis. It was said to crank out 600 horsepower, about 200 more than the Offys. With a trailing dorsal fin, the Novi had a futuristic, car-of-tomorrow look next to the peas-in-a-pod roadsters and, as usual, was the popular favorite.

One of the newer roadsters was the John Zink Special, built for Oklahoma businessman John Zink by crewcut, 32-year-old A. J. Watson in his Glendale, California, shop. The car was lower, narrower, and 200 pounds lighter than the 1,800-pound Kurtis-Kraft roadsters that had won the past three "500s." In it Pat Flaherty, a California dirt track racer and a Chicago pub owner, won the pole with a record-breaking speed of 145.596 miles an hour.

The faster speeds had been expected. Nearly three-quarters of the track had been resurfaced with asphalt, which now covered all the old bricks except a sentimental stretch in front of the grandstands. An all-day rain the day before the race, however, created lakes in the infield, flooded tunnels, and left part of the track under water. Maintenance crews worked feverishly through the night to ready the track and tunnels. Race day was cloudy but dry. At noon the 33 racers waited on a dry track for Tony Hulman to tell them to start their engines.

Since 1911 the "500"—and races at other speedways—had been supervised by the Contest Board of the American Automobile Association (AAA). The AAA, concerned about its image as a safety-conscious organization, had been appalled by a series of racing disasters in 1955, including the one that had killed Bill Vukovich. Shortly after the 1955 race, Speedway owner Tony Hulman and the rest of the racing world were stunned when the AAA announced its withdrawal from racing. A new sanctioning body was quickly organized by owners, drivers, and the Speedway. It was named the United States Auto Club (USAC).

This first USAC-sponsored "500" was a record-breaker from the start. Russo blasted the Novi through the first 50 miles at an average of 141 miles an hour, 3 miles an hour above the old record. With Flaherty growling behind him in the John Zink, Russo's Novi howled into its 21st lap. As it neared the No. 1 turn, a tire blew. The car spun, hit a low wall, and ricocheted, flaming now, into the center of the turn, where Russo skidded it to a stop. He hopped from the burning car and ran to safety. Two cars spun as drivers stomped on their brakes to avoid the wreck. A third car whirled into the pits, scattering mechanics and hitting several; but the worst injury was a broken leg.

The Novi was out of the race, seemingly jinxed

again (Russo had never blown a tire in nine previous "500s"). Pat Flaherty thrust the John Zink into the lead. In his Ansted Rotary Special, another Kurtis-Offy roadster, Pat O'Connor dueled with Flaherty for the lead. Behind them five other cars spun, blew tires, or hit walls as they tried to keep up on the newly asphalted track, which may have been too abrasive for the tires at those speeds.

Near the race's halfway mark Flaherty—wearing a shamrock on his helmet in defiance of the driver superstition that green is bad luck—began to pull ahead. With more crack-ups behind him, he led the rest of the way to win by 21 seconds, about half a mile. Though the race had been slowed by the yellow lights, which were on for an hour and 11 minutes, Flaherty's average speed was still a highly respectable 128.490 miles an hour.

Flaherty shared with John Zink and A. J. Watson a record purse of $93,819. In second place was Sam Hanks. Steady Sam had raced here since 1940 but had never won. Coming up for Sam was an even fatter purse—and a final checker.

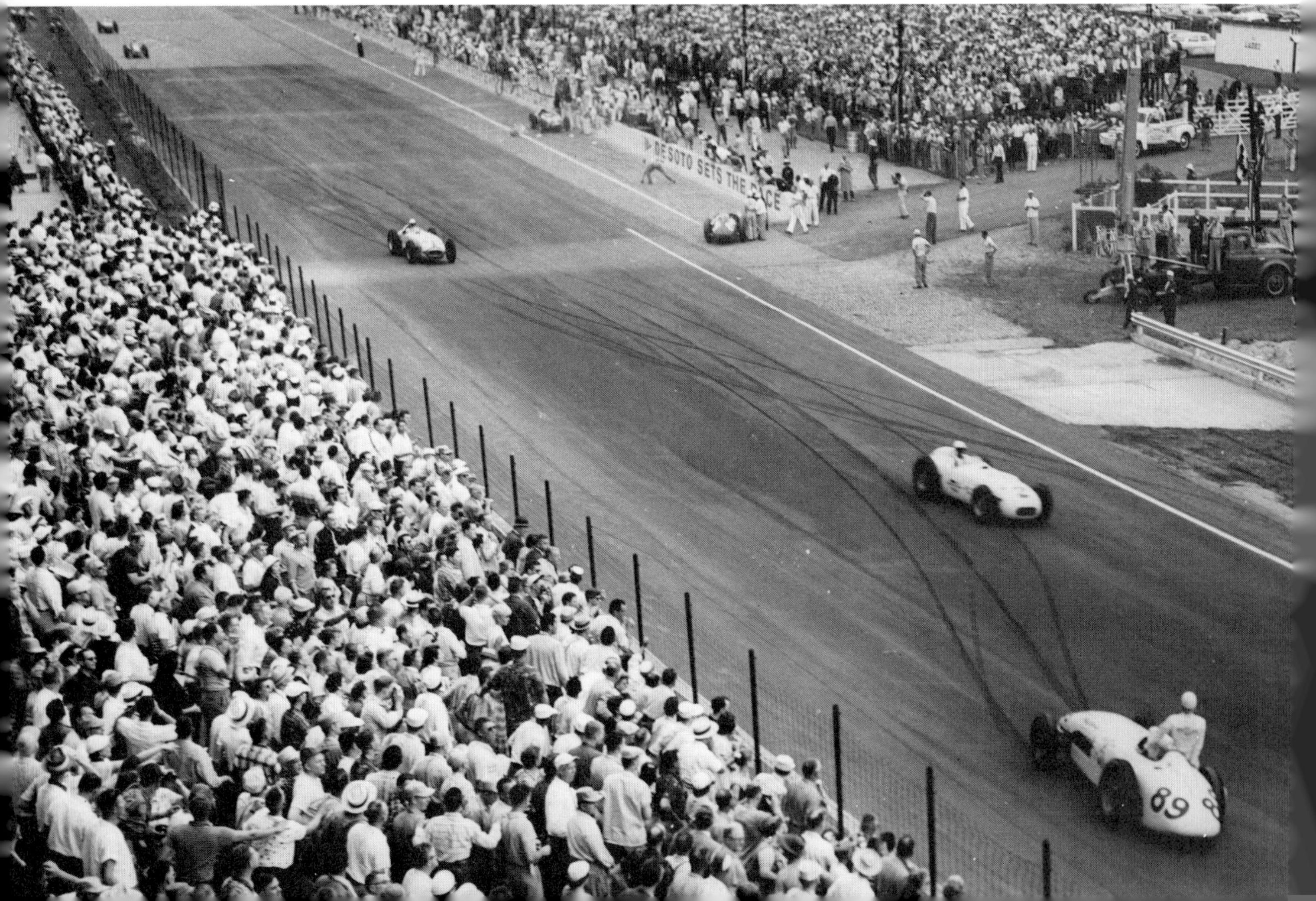

Opposite page, top: In his spinning Novi, Paul Russo (No. 29) faces in the direction of an oncoming horde of speeding steel. Pat O'Connor (r.) ducks inside and passes safely. But Sam Hanks and Keith Andrews tangled wheels and spun. Dodging whirling cars, Johnny Thomson skidded into the pits and broke a mechanic's leg. Bottom: On lap 94 Keith Andrews leaves his No. 89 after a spin turned him the wrong way. Jimmy Bryan (No. 2) goes by. Right: Pat Flaherty and his winning car. Most of the cars were driven by 270-inch unblown Offys, their power, durability, and reliability preferred to the smaller supercharged engines.

Pat Flaherty: Luck o' the Irish

With a freckle-faced smile and flashing his helmet with the shamrock, Pat Flaherty talked about luck in the winner's circle: *I was lucky. And my luck held right to the end—well, just about. I was on my way here to the winner's circle after doing those last two safety laps and I broke a throttle rod. If it had happened a couple of minutes earlier, it would have cost me the race. After I got the lead I was only concerned about sticking to the pace we had planned and keeping distance between myself and the second car. I knew I'd win if my luck held, because the guys behind me had to take chances, press their luck, and get into trouble. And that's what happened. My luck held—just barely.*

1956's TOP TEN

Race open to nonstock supercharged engines with a piston displacement of 183.060 cubic inches or less; nonstock nonsupercharged engines with a piston displacement of 274.59 cubic inches or less; diesel engines with a piston displacement of 335.57 cubic inches or less; and turbine engines, no size limitation.

NO.	DRIVER	CAR	ENGINE	CYL.	BORE	STROKE	PISTON DISPL.	TIME	MPH	WINNINGS*
8	Pat Flaherty	John Zink Special	Offenhauser	4	4.312	4.625	270	3:53:28.84	128.490	$93,819
4	Sam Hanks	Jones & Maley Special	Offenhauser	4	4.312	4.625	270	3:53:49.30	128.303	32,919
16	Don Freeland	Bob Estes Special	Offenhauser	4	4.312	4.625	270	3:54:59.07	127.668	20,490
98	Johnnie Parsons	Agajanian Special	Offenhauser	4	4.250	4.125	270	3:56:54.48	126.631	15,769
73	Dick Rathmann	McNamara Special	Offenhauser	4	4.312	4.625	270	3:57:50.65	126.133	10,744
1	Bob Sweikert	D-A Lubricant Special	Offenhauser	4	4.500	4.375	270	3:59:03.83	125.489	7,594
14	Bob Veith	Federal Engineering, Detroit Special	Offenhauser	4	4.312	4.625	270	3:59:54.50	125.048	7,494
19	Rodger Ward	Filter Queen Special	Offenhauser	4	4.312	4.625	270	4:00:01.15	124.990	6,294
26	Jimmy Reece	Massaglia Hotels Special	Offenhauser	4	4.312	4.625	270	4:00:07.11	124.938	6,044
27	Cliff Griffith	Jim Robbins Special	Offenhauser	4	4.312	4.625	270	4:01:45.48	123.471	6,194

* Total prizes for winning entries. Total awards in race, $282,052: Speedway prizes, $205,002; accessory prizes, $47,050; lap prizes, $30,000.

1957

The Coming of the Sidewinder

Checkbook in hand, the man walked around the yellow car—for what George Salih would later swear was the 300th time in two days. The man suddenly jammed the checkbook into his pocket. Right about then George made up his mind: He would enter the car in the "500" himself.

Salih was a foreman at the Meyer-Drake factory in Los Angeles, makers of the Offy engines that had won every "500" since 1947. To beat an Offy with an Offy, George reasoned, he needed a chassis more streamlined than anyone else's. He tilted an Offy so that it lay almost flat on its side. With the engine no longer upright, Salih could shape his roadster so that its nose would point like a needle into the wind. Salih built the car in his home workshop for $18,000, his life's savings; but sponsors hesitated to buy the funny-looking car. Finally, desperate to recoup his investment, Salih entered the car himself with the help of $5,000 from the Belond Muffler Company in payment for having the car carry the company's name. Gasoline Alley habitués took one look at the tilted engine and called the yellow racer the "sidewinder."

The Speedway wore a new look for the 1957 race. The old landmark pagoda, nerve center of the race for press and timers since 1913, had been torn down and replaced by a glass-and-steel control tower as tall as a seven-story building. It was surrounded by 14,000 new Tower Terrace seats. A new pit area, a fifth of a mile long, was set back behind a concrete wall.

Again, as they had done so often in the past, race officials tried to slow the cars by reducing engine size—to 170 cubic inches for supercharged engines, 256 for nonsupercharged engines. But Paul Russo rocketed his howling Novi down the straightaways at 180 miles an hour to post the fastest qualifying speed, 144.817 miles an hour, only a fraction off the record. The slowest of the 33 qualifiers averaged just shy of 140, a speed that would have been a record for the bigger engines of only five years earlier.

Waiting for the start of the race in the fourth row, veteran Sam Hanks—a driver here since 1940, but never a winner—hunched down in Salih's yellow sidewinder. Sam had decided to hang back in the early part of the race—"to get acquainted with this little beauty," he told Salih. With the snap of the green flag, Russo rocketed his Novi into first place. Near the 90th mile Hanks nosed into second behind the Novi. Coming off the No. 2 turn, Hanks booted the quicker-accelerating sidewinder by the Novi. On the backstretch Russo nudged the faster Novi even with the yellow sidewinder, but he couldn't fight by. He slowed for the No. 3 turn. The low-slung sidewinder bit into the north turns and came down the straightaway ahead by a gap that the Novi, though dragging faster on the stretches, could not close.

Hanks's sidewinder cut so tightly through the turns that it increased its lead by about 70 feet on each lap. Then Hanks had to take the sidewinder into the pits. His crew fumbled, and he came out 43 seconds later in second place, behind Jim Rathmann's blue Chiropractic Special.

By now Russo's Novi had faded, unable to keep up with the quicker-cornering Offy roadsters. Hanks ripped the sidewinder around the turns and at the 340-mile mark forged ahead of Rathmann. With 125 miles to go, the sidewinder led by 40 seconds. Hanks decided to risk a third pit stop to be sure of his rubber (he had plenty of fuel in a

188

The "500" Queen and her court perch on their float for the first "500" Festival Parade. Organized by Indianapolis businessmen, the parade each year wends its way through packed downtown streets on the day before the race.

1957's TOP TEN

Race open to nonstock supercharged engines with a piston displacement of 170.856 cubic inches or less; nonstock nonsupercharged engines with a piston displacement of 256.284 cubic inches or less; diesel engines with a piston displacement of 335.57 cubic inches or less; and turbine engines, no size limitation.

NO.	DRIVER	CAR	ENGINE	CYL.	BORE	STROKE	PISTON DISPL.	TIME	MPH	WINNINGS*
9	Sam Hanks	Belond Exhaust Special	Offenhauser	4	4.156	4.625	250.0	3:41:14.25	135.601†	$103,844
26	Jim Rathmann	Chiropractic Special	Offenhauser	4	4.312	4.375	255.0	3:41:35.75	135.382	38,494
1	Jimmy Bryan	Dean Van Lines Special	Offenhauser	4	4.218	4.500	251.6	3:43:28.25	134.246	21,794
54	Paul Russo	Novi Automotive Air Conditioning Special	Novi‡	8	3.200	2.625	168.6	3:44:11.10	133.818	19,369
73	Andy Linden	McNamara-Veedol Special	Offenhauser	4	4.250	4.500	255.3	3:44:28.55	133.645	11,094
6	Johnny Boyd	Bowes Seal Fast Special	Offenhauser	4	4.218	4.500	251.6	3:45:49.55	132.846	8,194
48	Marshall Teague	Sumar Special	Offenhauser	4	4.250	4.500	255.3	3:45:59.85	132.745	6,819
12	Pat O'Connor	Sumar Special	Offenhauser	4	4.250	4.500	255.3	3:46:47.35	132.281	8,669
7	Bob Veith	Bob Estes Special	Offenhauser	4	4.250	4.500	255.3	3:47:31.35	131.855	5,969
22	Gene Hartley	Massaglia Hotels Special	Offenhauser	4	4.218	4.500	251.6	3:48:24.40	131.345	5,844

* Total prizes for winning entries. Total awards in race, $300,252; Speedway prizes, $218,052; accessory prizes, $52,200; lap prizes, $30,000.   † New record.
‡ Supercharged.

Right: Winner Sam Hanks. Below: Steady Sam in the pointy-nosed sidewinder that set a new "500" speed record. In fact, the first 11 finishers all broke Bill Vukovich's 130.840-mile-an-hour record, set in 1954. Opposite page, top: Al Keller skids on the No. 1 turn. He hit the wall but was not hurt. Far right: The new control tower and the Tower Terrace seats in front of it look down on the new pit area, separated from the track by a concrete wall.

huge 83-gallon tank in the tail). This time he got out onto the track in 34 seconds, ahead by five seconds, and crept away from Rathmann to win by 21 seconds. His average speed was a new record—better than 135 miles an hour.

In the winner's circle a tearful Sam announced his retirement. "I have done everything now," he said. He was the first driver to win the "500" and quit since Ray Harroun, in 1911. Hanks and Salih split a record first prize of $103,844. With his 60 percent share, Salih had won his $18,000 investment and more. Now all he had to do was prove the sidewinder was not a flash in the pan.

Sam Hanks:
"A baby doll"

Of his sidewinder's swoops around the track, Sam Hanks later said: *I never had a car run so sweet for so long. I went by 'em on the straights and on the turns. I went over 'em and under 'em on the corners and between 'em if I had to on the straights. It just went like a baby doll.*

1958

Carnage on the No. 3 Turn

"Don't bother to sit down for the first 20 laps," driver Eddie Sachs told a reporter on the eve of the 1958 race. "It's going to be a sizzler right from the start to see who gets out there first."

What got out there first was death and destruction.

Crouched in cockpits along the first row were three young and eager chargers—Ed Elisian, Jimmy Reece, and Dick Rathmann. Rathmann had won the pole with a record-busting run of 145.974 miles an hour for the 4 qualifying laps, and Reece had taken the outside spot with a 145.513. In the middle was chunky Ed Elisian, who had set a one-lap record of 146.508. Elisian's idol was the Mad Russian, Bill Vukovich. "He has Vukovich's guts," one driver said of Elisian, "but not Vukovich's skill."

All three sat in the cockpits of "upright" roadsters built by A. J. Watson. The previous year's race had been won by George Salih's sidewinder, with its Offy engine placed almost flat on its side. But Watson insisted that his upright-engine cars could go through the turns as swiftly as the tilted-engine sidewinders. And three of his uprights in the first row seemed to prove he was right.

During the past five years Tony Hulman had spent, by Speedway estimate, more than a million dollars to make the "500" the jewel of auto racing. By now there were other 500-mile races—the Race of Two Worlds at Monza, Italy, for instance—for the big Indianapolis cars, as well as a 500-mile race at Trenton, New Jersey, for stock cars. And cults of sports car fanciers were racing lightly sprung MGs and Jaguars on tracks from Connecticut to California. They looked down their noses at the heavy-axled, only-turn-left Indy roadsters. But the "500," it was said proudly in Indianapolis, was the World Series of auto racing. And with the Speedway offering seats for 120,000 spectators and space for at least 75,000 others on the huge infield, the "500" still drew—as it had in 1911—more people than any other one-day sports event in America.

A longer pit area had been unveiled for the 1957 race, and along with this had come a new procedure for starting the race. Cars filed out of the pits to form 11 rows of three cars each behind the pace car during a parade lap. Then they swept behind the pacer for the pace lap before seeing the green flag for the traditional flying start.

On this year's parade lap, however, the three eager front-row drivers—Rathmann, Elisian, and Reece—leaped ahead of the pace car. Confusion reigned during the parade and pace laps, and an additional lap, run under the yellow flag, was required before the three weaved through the slowed-up pack and regained their positions at the head of the field. The starter snapped the green flag, and the three charged down the straightaway. Foot down, Rathmann whirled out of the south turns and onto the backstretch with Elisian hanging to his tailpipe and Reece snapping at their heels. The three cars surged like a wave up the backstretch, toward the No. 3 turn. Rathmann and Elisian kept their feet down, neither willing to back off. Rathmann flashed low into the turn. Elisian tried to drive through—on Rathmann's inside—at perhaps 130 miles an hour. Elisian's car lost its grip and slid up the banked turn. The cars banged together and Rathmann was batted against the wall. Reece braked to dodge Elisian and was smashed from behind by Bob Veith. Reece's car skittered into the path of the personable, 31-year-old Pat O'Connor, at the

192

Pat O'Connor, in No. 4, climbs over Jimmy Reece (No. 16) and Bob Veith (No. 14) on his way to a fiery death. On the top of the turn, Ed Elisian pins Dick Rathmann against the wall. In the ensuing tangle, Jerry Unser hit a car and skied over the wall. Rookie A. J. Foyt escaped this first-lap disaster but spun out of the race after 148 laps.

Right (from l.): Tony Hulman and Raymond Firestone are interviewed by one of the day's major television personalities: Dave Garroway. Below: Eddie Sachs (l.) and Johnny Tolan dice through the No. 2 turn. At the wheel of the pace car for this race was 1957's winner, Sam Hanks.

wheel of a streaking Sumar Special. The Sumar soared, belly-rolled, crashed upside down, then bounced and landed upright, billowing flames.

Twenty-eight speeding bullets thundered toward the wrecks. The previous year's winning sidewinder, now called the Belond AP Special, was steered this year by Jimmy Bryan, who had replaced the retired Sam Hanks, and he weaved through the tangle. But behind him A. J. Foyt spun and more cars ripped into each other.

Within seconds 15 cars—an estimated million dollars' worth of machinery—had been damaged or destroyed. A half-dozen drivers limped away, injured, but Pat O'Connor was dead. The yellow lights stayed on for half an hour while the track was swept clear. When the green lights flashed, Tony Bettenhausen, George Amick, and Jimmy Bryan each led, lost the lead, regained it—the lead switching 13 times. By the 400-mile point, Bryan led by half a lap in the Belond, and he pulled away for the sidewinder's second straight "500" victory. Despite some 30 minutes at 80 miles an hour because of yellow lights, this year's race was the second fastest "500" yet run.

In three races (it had finished second at Monza), George Salih's sidewinder had won more than $200,000. But A. J. Watson insisted stubbornly that one of his uprights would have won if any of them had escaped the carnage on the No. 3 turn. While other builders assembled more pointy-nosed sidewinders, A. J. went back to his uprights.

Ed Elisian:
"It sure wasn't intentional"

Generally blamed for the 15-car pileup on the third turn—he was suspended after the race by the United States Auto Club—Ed Elisian conceded he'd wanted badly to win to pay $30,000 in debts. *I tried to go under Rathmann on the turn. I don't know why I lost it* [the car]. *I had driven that third corner faster. I have had those hot dogs spin in front of me and run me through the wall on other tracks. But it sure wasn't intentional. I liked Pat O'Connor as well as anybody.*

Jimmy Bryan sits at the wheel of the sidewinder that had now won two straight "500s." Both the total purse —more than $300,000—and Bryan's first-prize share— over $105,000—were records. The 6-1, 200-pound Bryan (r.), a cowboy from Tucson, said, "I missed the wrecks by this much," holding his hands inches apart. On this Memorial Day there was also a 500-mile stock-car race at Trenton, New Jersey. It was won by Glenn (Fireball) Roberts in a 1957 Chevy at an average of 84 miles an hour. Total prizes were $26,900.

1958's TOP TEN

Race open to nonstock supercharged engines with a piston displacement of 170.856 cubic inches or less; nonstock nonsupercharged engines with a piston displacement of 256.284 cubic inches or less; diesel engines with a piston displacement of 335.57 cubic inches or less; and turbine engines, no size limitation.

NO.	DRIVER	CAR	ENGINE	CYL.	BORE	STROKE	PISTON DISPL.	TIME	MPH	WINNINGS*
1	Jimmy Bryan	Belond AP Special	Offenhauser	4	4.176	4.625	252.0	3:44:13.80	133.791	$105,574
99	George Amick	Demler Special	Offenhauser	4	4.250	4.500	255.3	3:44:41.45	133.517	37,370
9	Johnny Boyd	Bowes Seal Fast Special	Offenhauser	4	4.218	4.500	251.6	3:45:23.75	133.099	24,999
33	Tony Bettenhausen	Jones & Maley Special	Offenhauser	4	4.218	4.500	251.6	3:45:45.60	132.855	17,199
2	Jim Rathmann	Leader Card "500" Roadster	Offenhauser	4	4.281	4.375	251.9	3:45:49.45	132.847	11,399
16	Jimmy Reece	John Zink Special	Offenhauser	4	4.281	4.375	251.9	3:46:30.75	132.443	8,690
26	Don Freeland	Bob Estes Special	Offenhauser	4	4.218	4.500	251.6	3:46:34.85	132.403	6,990
44	Jud Larson	John Zink Special	Offenhauser	4	4.281	4.375	251.9	3:49:47.85	130.550	7,049
61	Eddie Johnson	Bryant Heating and Cooling Special	Offenhauser	4	4.156	4.625	250.9	3:50:29.58	130.156	5,999
54	Bill Cheesbourg	Novi Automotive Air Conditioning Special	Novi†	8	3.200	2.625	168.6	3:52:17.35	129.149	6,390

* Total prizes for winning entries. Total awards in race, $305,217: Speedway prizes, $221,667; accessory prizes, $53,550; lap prizes, $30,000. † Supercharged.

1959

A Swig and a Kiss

Rodger Ward whirled the red and blue Leader Card "500" Roadster out of the No. 2 turn and nosed it through the half mile of backstretch at better than 160 miles an hour. As he neared the 250-mile point of this "500," Ward led Johnny Thomson by 2 miles and Jim Rathmann by almost 3 miles. On his eighth "500" ride, the pudgy-faced Rodger Ward barreled closer to his first trip down Victory Lane.

From the pits crewcut, greying A. J. Watson watched the leaders zoom by. Ward and Rathmann were piloting cars Watson had built for this year's race, their upright Offy engines his retort to the trend toward the horizontal-engine sidewinders. Sidewinders had won the previous two "500s," and 16 had been entered in this race, including Johnny Thomson's Racing Associates Special, which was now running in second place, behind Ward.

"In going through the corners," Watson had said, "proper weight distribution is the important factor. And I believe that can be obtained as easily with an upright engine as with a horizontal engine." For even better weight distribution on the left-handed Indy turns, Watson mounted the chassis slightly to the left on the axles. But basically his two new roadsters were lighter (1,625 pounds) versions of the roadster that Frank Kurtis had brought to the "500" in the early 1950s. What made Watson roadsters popular among owners were the same qualities that had made the Offy engine so endearing: speed and stamina. (An Offy was under the hood of every car in this race.)

One of the new Watson cars had been bought by a Milwaukee playing card manufacturer. He named it the Leader Card "500" Roadster and put Rodger Ward behind the wheel. Watson sold the other car to Lindsey Hopkins, the Florida owner, who called it the Simoniz Special. Hopkins hired driver Jim Rathmann, the pencil-thin 6-footer from Los Angeles who'd finished second at Indianapolis in 1952 and 1957.

Rathmann had earned a starting spot in the first row, Ward in the second row. Well back in the pack was the previous year's winner, George Salih's sidewinder, and it flopped out of the race on the first lap with a faulty clutch. Early in the race Ward had whisked ahead to take the lead, then lost it to the sidewinder driven by Johnny Thomson. Around the 225-mile mark, Ward blasted through 11 laps at an average of 142 miles an hour to lead Thomson by 2 miles and Rathmann, in the other Watson roadster, by 3 with 250 miles to go.

Two drivers—Jerry Unser and Bob Cortner—had been killed in smashups during practice. In the 46th lap of the race, Mike Magill's No. 77 flopped on a turn and cartwheeled along for a thousand feet, bouncing his helmeted head along the track. Magill survived, his life probably saved by new mandatory roll bars behind the cockpit (but fireproof uniforms, also mandatory, hadn't saved Jerry Unser, who died of burns).

Well ahead, Ward ducked into the pits twice and came out—after stops of 23 and 25 seconds—still leading. Rathmann trailed by half a lap and Thomson, who'd made a fourth pit stop for tires, was a lap behind when Ward took the checker with a new record average of better than 135 miles an hour.

In Victory Lane, behind the pit area, Ward

Top to bottom: Chuck Weyant (No. 47) spins into Mike Magill, flipping Magill's car against the wall. Magill's car tumbles end over end as others race by. Weyant spins to a stop with his wheels crumpled. The worst injury was Magill's burned neck.

took the traditional swig from a quart of milk and got the traditional victory kiss, from actress Erin O'Brien. Then he took the traditional ride around the track—in the Buick pacer he now owned—to be saluted by the throng. Watching him, A. J. Watson said: "On most tracks it's all in the car, but winning is 75 to 80 percent the driver on this track."

Watson, though, had made his point: The upright engine could more than hold its own against the sidewinder. But Johnny Thomson and his sidewinder would be back for one more run at Victory Lane.

Eddie Sachs: "Lying in his teeth"

In this race Eddie Sachs, a Pennsylvania tavern owner as well as a popular driver, took his third "500" ride and finished 17th, his car breaking down after 182 laps. Had he been nervous before the race? *It's the last 24 hours of waiting that gets you. There's nothing more to do but waiting and thinking about all the things that can go wrong—with the car and with other cars. Sitting around, you know, it gets to you, and if any driver ever tells you he isn't scared, he's lying in his teeth.*

1959's TOP TEN

Race open to nonstock supercharged engines with a piston displacement of 170.856 cubic inches or less; nonstock nonsupercharged engines with a piston displacement of 256.284 cubic inches or less; diesel engines with a piston displacement of 335.57 cubic inches or less; and turbine engines, no size limitation.

NO.	DRIVER	CAR	ENGINE	CYL.	BORE	STROKE	PISTON DISPL.	TIME	MPH	WINNINGS*
5	Rodger Ward	Leader Card "500" Roadster	Offenhauser	4	4.281	4.375	251.9	3:40:49.20	135.857†	$106,850
16	Jim Rathmann	Simoniz Special	Offenhauser	4	4.281	4.375	251.9	3:41:12.47	135.619	39,800
3	Johnny Thomson	Racing Associates Special	Offenhauser	4	4.281	4.375	251.9	3:41:39.85	135.340	32,425
1	Tony Bettenhausen	Hoover Motor Express Special	Offenhauser	4	4.281	4.375	251.9	3:42:36.25	134.768	15,475
99	Paul Goldsmith	Demler Special	Offenhauser	4	4.250	4.500	255.3	3:42:55.60	134.573	11,975
33	Johnny Boyd	Bowes Seal Fast Special	Offenhauser	4	4.281	4.375	251.9	3:44:06.23	133.867	2,200
37	Duane Carter	Smokey's Reverse Torque Special	Offenhauser	4	4.281	4.375	251.9	3:44:59.15	133.342	1,800
19	Eddie Johnson	Bryant Heating and Cooling Special	Offenhauser	4	4.156	4.625	250.9	3:44:59.69	133.336	1,600
45	Paul Russo	Bardahl Special	Offenhauser	4	4.218	4.500	251.6	3:45:00.24	133.331	1,500
10	A. J. Foyt	Dean Van Lines Special	Offenhauser	4	4.218	4.500	251.6	3:45:03.65	133.297	1,400

* Total prizes for top five finishers; Speedway winnings for sixth- through tenth-place finishers. Total awards in race, $338,100: Speedway prizes, $250,500; accessory prizes, $57,600; lap prizes, $30,000. † New record.

Left: Rodger Ward. Below: Ward at the wheel of his roadster. Note that the nose is pointier than the noses of upright-engine roadsters of a few years earlier, part of the trend toward the "doorstop" noses of today. Opposite page: Ward steers the winning No. 5 into Victory Circle, trailed by well-wishers, one of whom hoists the Borg-Warner Trophy. "The last 5 laps were the worst," said Ward, a former Army pilot. "I was worried everything would go wrong."

During the parade lap, a 30-foot-high scaffold tips over and crashes onto fans below, tangling together about a hundred screaming spectators. Two were killed, as many as 70 hurt. The scaffold was built with pipes and boards by an entrepreneur who charged people $5 and $10 to watch the race from it.

1960

Down on Their Heels

Rodger Ward glanced over his shoulder as pit mechanics tightened the nuts on three new wheels. A pneumatic jack, built into the side of the Leader Card "500" Roadster, let down the car. As the wheels bumped the pavement, Ward let out the clutch. The engine stalled. A mechanic grabbed an electric starter and thrust it into the nose of the roadster to restart it. Ward zoomed out onto the track as Jim Rathmann boomed toward the No. 1 turn. Rathmann was the new leader, and Ward cursed the wasted seconds that had cost him the lead.

The 31-year-old Rathmann was called the Bridesmaid of Indianapolis—second in 1952, 1957, and 1959, never a winner. This year he was riding for two wealthy Texans in a brand-new car built by A. J. Watson—the Ken-Paul Special. It was 15 feet long, five feet wide, only 44 inches high.

More than a dozen of the 33 qualifiers were new or old Watson-built cars. "Simplicity personified," said driver Fred Agabashian of the Watson roadsters. Here also were 12 sidewinders, engines flopped almost flat in their sleek noses. In the battle between sidewinders and upright Watsons, newspapers had predicted, speed records would be shattered. And in the trials rookie driver Jim Hurtubise posted a new 4-lap record—149.056 miles an hour—in a Watson upright.

For the first 100 miles of the race Rodger Ward and Jim Rathmann—one-two finishers in 1959—had fought nose to nose for the lead in their Watsons. Then Ward went in for a routine pit stop—routine, that is, until his engine stalled. He came out nearly a full minute later, chasing Johnny Thomson's pink sidewinder and Rathmann's Ken-Paul Special. At straightaway speeds of better than 160 miles an hour, Ward fled by Thomson and closed track on Rathmann with 250 miles to go.

For the next 40 laps Rathmann and Ward zoomed together, never more than a hundred feet between them, their exhausts trailing a sustained bellow as they came by the mass of faces in the grandstands.

With about 125 miles to go, both pitted. The rival crews scrambled over the cars, knowing that one fumble could cost the first prize of better than $100,000. Ward's wheels swung onto the track as Rathmann's wheels began to roll. With 70 miles to go, Thomson's sidewinder joined the chase, and the three colored blobs blurred around the oval no more than a hundred yards apart.

Now there were 50 miles to go. Ward led, Rathmann was second, and Thomson was in the pits repairing a ripped cylinder. Ward saw that his tires were worn. He eased back to 141 miles an hour. Rathmann stormed by to take the lead.

Ward knew he had the faster car. He could hang back and save his tires for a final lunge to the checker. But suppose there was a crash and the yellow lights went on? That would freeze him in place. "I wouldn't have been able to live with myself," Ward said, "giving the race away when I had the faster car."

He unleashed his Leader Card and sprinted into the lead. With 25 miles to go, Rathmann burst off the No. 4 turn to sway ahead. Ward put down his foot, and the two cars shot around the track at higher and higher velocities, ticking off laps at 143 miles an hour, 144, then 145. Rathmann had the lead, Ward had the lead, then Rathmann, who blasted through a lap at 146.128 —the fastest yet posted during a "500." As

Above: Kay and Jim Rathmann leave Victory Circle, followed by Sam Hanks (l.) and Tony Hulman, for a triumphant lap around the track in the pace car Jim now owned. Like the drink of milk, the victory lap had become a "500" tradition. At right: Rathmann and the winning roadster. He retired in 1963.

1960's TOP TEN

Race open to nonstock supercharged engines with a piston displacement of 170.856 cubic inches or less; nonstock nonsupercharged engines with a piston displacement of 256.284 cubic inches or less; diesel engines with a piston displacement of 335.61 cubic inches or less; and turbine engines, no size limitation.

NO.	DRIVER	CAR	ENGINE	CYL.	BORE	STROKE	PISTON DISPL.	TIME	MPH	WINNINGS*
4	Jim Rathmann	Ken-Paul Special	Offenhauser	4	4.281	4.375	251.9	3:36:11.36	138.767†	$110,000
1	Rodger Ward	Leader Card "500" Roadster	Offenhauser	4	4.281	4.375	251.9	3:36:24.03	138.631	48,025
99	Paul Goldsmith	Demler Special	Offenhauser	4	4.281	4.500	255.3	3:39:18.58	136.792	24,350
7	Don Branson	Bob Estes Special	Offenhauser	4	4.281	4.375	251.9	3:39:19.28	136.785	15,475
3	Johnny Thomson	Adams Quarter Horse Farm Special	Offenhauser	4	4.281	4.375	251.9	3:39:22.65	136.750	15,100
22	Eddie Johnson	Jim Robbins Special	Offenhauser	4	4.281	4.375	251.9	3:40:21.88	136.137	9,200
98	Lloyd Ruby	Agajanian Special	Offenhauser	4	4.218	4.500	251.6	3:40:36.88	135.983	7,800
44	Bob Veith	Schmidt Special	Offenhauser	4	4.281	4.375	251.9	3:41:28.78	135.452	7,850
18	Bud Tingelstad	Jim Robbins Special	Offenhauser	4	4.281	4.375	251.9	3:44:21.17	133.717	6,900
38	Bob Christie	Federal Engineering, Detroit Special	Offenhauser	4	4.186	4.625	254.6	3:44:51.54	133.416	6,700

* Total prizes for winning entries. Total awards in race, $369,150: Speedway prizes, $274,850; accessory prizes, $64,300; lap prizes, $30,000.   † New record.

Ward went into the 198th lap he saw a warning strip break out across his right front tire. At any moment the tire could blow. Ward slowed. Second prize, he decided, was better than a hospital bed and no prize at all.

Thirty seconds later Rathmann saw the same strip on his right rear tire. He, too, slowed. To his relief he saw that Ward, only a few hundred yards behind, did not gain on him. Rathmann won by 13 seconds, the closest finish since Wilbur Shaw came home two seconds ahead in 1937. Rathmann's average speed was a record 138.767 miles an hour.

Again the Watson uprights had shown their heels to the sidewinders. The sidewinder was on its way to extinction; George Salih's inspiration never again won a "500." Also on its way to extinction was that rugged beast that now reigned triumphant at Indianapolis—the roadster.

Wayne Weiler, running ninth on the 103d lap, skids (top l.), then hits the southeast wall (top r.). He leaps from his car (above l.) and stands on the wall while a mechanic checks for the fire that Weiler feared. Out of the race, he was placed 24th. The rookie of the year award, begun in 1952, was won by Jim Hurtubise, who set a new qualifying record.

Jim Rathmann: "The rubber was gone"

In the winner's circle after three second-place finishes, Jim Rathmann said: *Ward's car was faster than mine and he could pass me whenever he wanted to. I had to make up for it on the turns and by cutting in front of traffic. I knew my tires were bad and I was wondering when they would give out. At the end the rubber was gone from the right rear. I couldn't have lasted another two laps.*

1961

The British Are Coming

It came like a cold breeze onto the spine to make Indianapolis roadster owners shiver. It was a purebred sports car, the kind that slithered through hairpin turns in Grand Prix races in Europe. Here from England for an American road race, it weaved around the Speedway track on a fall afternoon in 1960 at 144 miles an hour, an astonishing speed for an engine that turned up only 252 horsepower (compared to the Offy's 400-plus). The car weighed about 1,000 pounds, compared to the beefy Indianapolis roadster's 1,600, it had independent suspension over all four wheels for tight cornering, and its engine was mounted in the rear. It wasn't the first rear-engine car to be seen at Indianapolis—Harry Miller had raced a rear-engine Miller-Gulf in the 1939 "500." But the engine in the rear struck some as funny and the car was soon called the "funny car."

Its official name was the Cooper-Climax, and Indianapolis owners saw the ghostly grey road racer as a threat to their roadsters. Nothing radically new had influenced big-car racer design since 1952, when Frank Kurtis had dropped the driver alongside the drive shaft instead of above it. Horizontal and upright engines had each had their proponents over the intervening years, but no one challenged the roadster's superiority at Indianapolis—designers simply focused on building a better roadster. The roadster, however, did have its detractors. One critic called it merely "a refinement of the prewar passenger car, solid axles and all." Another sneered: "The roadster was built to do only one thing: run at Indianapolis."

American sports car enthusiasts long had looked down their noses at the "500" and its stiffly sprung Indianapolis "dinosaurs." One sports car owner, wealthy Jim Kimberly, gave the Cooper-Climax's owner, John Cooper, $30,000 to refit the car for the 1961 "500." Its engine was stretched to 167 cubic inches and tipped to the left for the left-handed turns. And its wheels were fitted with tires made for the "500" by England's Dunlop factory.

By now crowds of 100,000 and more regularly paid their way into the Speedway on weekends to see the qualifying trials. This year they saw Eddie Sachs win the pole with a 147-mile-an-hour clocking. The Cooper-Climax, driven by world Grand Prix champion Jack Brabham, from Australia, whirled around the course at an average of 145 to take the inside spot in the fifth row. Against the big workhorse Offys, the ponylike Cooper-Climax did not seem likely to become the first foreign car to win here since Wilbur Shaw's Maserati in 1940.

But roadster owners were concerned. "I have put ten years of investment, hard work, heartache, and tears into this plant," said Lindsey Hopkins, who owned two of the cars in this year's field. "If it now develops that our cars are obsolete, some of us would seriously have to consider quitting the sport."

But others welcomed the invasion by the Cooper. "I'm glad it's here," said A. J. Watson, builder of three of the last five Indy winners.

On the front straight, before thousands jammed into double-decked grandstands, Jack Turner's car pinwheels down the track—the last act in a chain of smashes that began when Don Davis spun, stumbled from his car, and other drivers, dodging him, collided.

"For years we've been scared to try anything new. Now we are simply going to have to."

From the start of the race, the Cooper showed it lacked the power to stick with the bigger American roadsters. By the 50-mile point the British car hung well back in tenth place, in a line of cars strung out behind Jim Rathmann, driving the previous year's winning car. But at 120 miles a magneto failed and Rathmann's car was through.

The new leader was A. J. Foyt, a burly, crew-cut, 26-year-old Texan, who'd grown up in Houston tinkering with hot rods. In 1960 he'd been the United States Auto Club's national champion, winning enough points at other races to make up for having won none in the big one here at Indianapolis. In his Bowes Seal Fast Special, an A. J. Watson car, Foyt battled Eddie Sachs, driving a Dean Van Lines Special, for lap after lap in one of the longest and fiercest duels ever seen at Indianapolis. Most of the race's last 300 miles was a nose-to-tail dice, the two drivers switching back and forth as the pursued and the pursuer. With the grandstand crowd in a frenzy, Foyt zoomed by with 10 miles to go, Sachs only 100 feet behind him. But Foyt suddenly swung into the pit. On his last stop a nozzle had been defective and he'd received insufficient fuel. That malfunction seemed to have won the race for the veteran Sachs, who bolted for the finish line, only 8 miles away. But as Sachs streaked down the stretch of the 197th lap, he saw a warning strip break out on a tire; he had to pit to avoid a blow-out on the last 7 miles. A wheel was hurriedly snapped on as a startled Foyt zipped by to take the lead. Sachs shot off after him, but Foyt came by the checker eight seconds ahead—a bang-bang finish for the second year in a row. Despite two crack-ups, one of them a spectacular five-car

tangle, no one had been killed in this fast-paced "500." Foyt's winning average set a new record—a little better than 139 miles an hour.

For the third straight year an A. J. Watson roadster had won the "500." The Cooper-Climax had come home ninth, but its performance against the bigger Offys had been impressive. Indianapolis would see more rear-engine funny cars, coming here to try to slay the dinosaur.

A stunned Jack Turner is helped off the track after his end-over-end crash, shown on the preceding page. Not so lucky was Tony Bettenhausen, killed during practice while test-driving Paul Russo's car. Top: Jack Brabham in the Cooper-Climax, which had won the British Grand Prix road race in 1959 and 1960. Most Grand Prix racers were now rear-engine cars.

1961's TOP TEN

Race open to nonstock supercharged engines with a piston displacement of 170.856 cubic inches or less; nonstock nonsupercharged engines with a piston displacement of 256.284 cubic inches or less; diesel engines with a piston displacement of 335.61 cubic inches or less; and turbine engines, no size limitation.

NO.	DRIVER	CAR	ENGINE	CYL.	BORE	STROKE	PISTON DISPL.	TIME	MPH	WINNINGS*
1	A. J. Foyt	Bowes Seal Fast Special	Offenhauser	4	4.281	4.375	251.9	3:35:37.49	139.130†	$117,975
12	Eddie Sachs	Dean Van Lines Special	Offenhauser	4	4.281	4.375	251.9	3:35:45.77	139.041	53,400
2	Rodger Ward	Del Webb's Sun City Special	Offenhauser	4	4.281	4.375	251.9	3:36:32.68	138.539	26,500
7	Shorty Templeman	Bill Forbes Racing Team Special	Offenhauser	4	4.281	4.375	251.9	3:39:10.84	136.873	16,025
19	Al Keller	Konstant Hot Special	Offenhauser	4	4.291	4.375	253.0	3:40:31.94	136.034	10,600
18	Chuck Stevenson	Metal-Cal Special	Offenhauser	4	4.281	4.375	251.9	3:41:00.45	135.742	9,875
31	Bobby Marshman	Hoover Motor Express Special	Offenhauser	4	4.281	4.375	251.9	3:41:20.77	135.534	9,050
5	Lloyd Ruby	Autolite Special	Offenhauser	4	4.301	4.375	254.0	3:42:27.14	134.860	8,750
17	Jack Brabham	Cooper-Climax Special	Climax‡	4	3.780	3.740	167.6	3:43:41.22	134.116	7,250
34	Norm Hall	Federal Engineering, Detroit Special	Offenhauser	4	4.186	4.625	254.6	3:43:42.39	134.104	8,250

* Total prizes for winning entries. Total awards in race, $400,000: Speedway prizes, $301,675; accessory prizes, $68,325; lap prizes, $30,000.   † New record.
‡ Rear-engine.

Left: Actress Jayne Mansfield waves to the crowd during a prerace parade of celebrities. As the Soaring Sixties began, Americans watched another race— the space race between American and Russian astronauts. Below: A. J. Foyt takes the checker for his first "500" win. Opposite page, top: Foyt kisses his wife, with the festival queen on his left, the Borg-Warner Trophy behind him, a quart of milk awaiting him. Opposite page, bottom: Anthony Joseph Foyt in his Watson roadster. Impressed by the Cooper-Climax, Watson talked of an independently sprung roadster for next year.

Jack Brabham: "I could have walked faster"

Despite its impressive performance the Cooper-Climax could have done better, its driver, Jack Brabham, maintained: *We gave the car a number of handicaps. Our Dunlop crew took at least twice the time to change wheels as the more experienced American pit crews. Then we decided to slow to 135 or so in the middle portions of the race to save on tires so we'd need only two pit stops instead of three. But it turned out we had to make three. We should have decided on three stops and gone fast all the way. And we'd hoped to gain on the American cars on the corners, where we were faster, but I got boxed in on the corners by roadsters going so slow that I could have walked faster.*

WINNER

View of the garages along Gasoline Alley. No women were allowed through its gates. With four huge stands built in the last three years, "500" attendance was now estimated at over 250,000.

1962

Two of a Kind

At better than 170 miles an hour, Parnelli Jones cometed by the grandstands in the Agajanian's Willard Battery Special. Spectators swiveled their heads to look toward the top of the stretch. They saw Rodger Ward's Leader Card "500" Roadster appear, a sun-splashed blue dot, as Jones's car vanished around the first turn. Jones and Ward were running one-two after 150 miles of this 46th "500."

They were running on a track whose original 3 million bricks had nearly all vanished. The straightaway in front of the stands—the last bricked portion of the track—had been covered by asphalt. Now the only bricks left on the track were a yard-wide strip at the starting line, for those who wished remembrance of races past.

Again, as in all of the races of the past ten years, nearly all the 33 cars were, except for their colors, virtually the same—roadster bodies by Frank Kurtis or A. J. Watson, four-cylinder Offys under their hoods. The "dinosaur," as some critics called the solid-axled, $25,000 roadster, had won every race here since 1953 and the Offy every "500" but three since 1934.

This year, as last year, there was one interloper among the roadsters. Like the British Cooper-Climax that had finished ninth in 1961, this car had its engine in the rear and it, too, was an independently sprung Grand Prix type sports car. But it had, of all things, a Buick V-8 engine buzzing in its tail. Not since 1947, when a Ford V-8 powered car came in 12th, had a stock engine qualified for the "500." The car, built by California hot-rodder Mickey Thompson (he owned the unofficial world speed record of 406 miles an hour), was driven by Dan Gurney. A Grand Prix road racer, Gurney had never raced at the Speedway oval. But he qualified with a speed of 147.886 miles an hour to land a place in the third row. One sports car fan proclaimed: "It's the handwriting on the wall—the age of the dinosaur is over."

Running on the resurfaced track and wearing tighter-gripping tires from Firestone, cars bolted to new records in the trials. Before a weekend crowd of 150,000, four cars topped the old qualifying record of 149.056 miles an hour; and one, driven by 28-year-old Parnelli Jones, shot over the "magic" 150-mile-an-hour barrier with a new record of 150.370 to win the pole. The brush-cut, impetuous Jones was called the hottest driver to whirl around the Indy track since the heyday of the Mad Russian, Bill Vukovich. But Vukovich had wrestled cars through the turns, while Jones smoothed them through with a silky touch. "Parnelli drives romantically," said racing car owner John Zink.

Much of the prerace publicity had focused on Mickey Thompson's rear-engine Buick, but it was lost in the smoke of the dinosaurs and dropped out with rear-end ailments halfway through the race. Parnelli Jones leaped from the pole to head the pack for the first 150 miles. Two previous winners, Rodger Ward and A. J. Foyt, grimly tried to keep from being lapped as Jones circled the course at better than 146 miles an hour. At the 320-mile mark Jones had won all the $150 lap prizes but three. But when Jones pitted for the second time to take on fuel, Ward's Leader Card swept into the lead. Jones smoked out of the pits in pursuit, but his car seemed to lag; its brakes were gone, and Jones faded into the pack.

1962's TOP TEN

Race open to nonstock supercharged engines with a piston displacement of 170.856 cubic inches or less; nonstock nonsupercharged engines with a piston displacement of 256.284 cubic inches or less; diesel engines with a piston displacement of 335.61 cubic inches or less; and turbine engines, no size limitation.

NO.	DRIVER	CAR	ENGINE	CYL.	BORE	STROKE	PISTON DISPL.	TIME	MPH	WINNINGS*
3	Rodger Ward	Leader Card "500" Roadster	Offenhauser	4	4.281	4.375	251.9	3:33:50.33	140.293†	$124,515
7	Len Sutton	Leader Card "500" Roadster	Offenhauser	4	4.281	4.375	251.9	3:34:01.85	140.167	44,566
2	Eddie Sachs	Dean-Autolite Special	Offenhauser	4	4.281	4.375	252.0	3:34:10.26	140.075	26,591
27	Don Davis	J. H. Rose Truck Line Special	Offenhauser	4	4.281	4.375	251.9	3:34:38.46	139.768	16,716
54	Bobby Marshman	Bryant Heating and Cooling Special	Offenhauser	4	4.281	4.375	251.9	3:36:09.27	138.790	14,316
15	Jim McElreath	Schulz Fueling Equipment Special	Offenhauser	4	4.281	4.375	251.9	3:36:22.02	138.653	9,866
98	Parnelli Jones	Agajanian's Willard Battery Special	Offenhauser	4	4.281	4.375	251.9	3:36:33.18	138.534	33,516
12	Lloyd Ruby	Thompson Industries Special	Offenhauser	4	4.291	4.375	253.4	3:37:06.33	138.182	8,541
44	Jim Rathmann	Simoniz Vista Special	Offenhauser	4	4.281	4.375	251.9	3:39:07.05	136.913	8,041
38	Johnny Boyd	Metal-Cal Special	Offenhauser	4	4.281	4.375	251.9	3:39:37.19	136.600	8,841

* Total prizes for winning entries. Total awards in race, $426,152: Speedway prizes, $320,428; accessory prizes, $75,724; lap prizes, $30,000. † New record.

Opposite page: The field goes through the pace lap on the resurfaced front stretch. At top is the exit from the pits. Left: Rodger Ward holds a paper that spells the reason for his grin. With him are his mother and (far l.) one of his sons. Below: Ward in the winning A. J. Watson roadster. The first two finishers were owned by Bob Wilke, a Milwaukee manufacturer. Watson cars finished one-two-three and won three other places in the top ten. Watson's pit crew worked so smoothly that Ward's three pit stops used only 60 seconds, Sutton's 61. "Sutton," commented *Sports Illustrated*, "was content to finish 11 seconds behind Ward without ever risking Wilke's ire by attempting to dice with him."

The curly-haired, amiable, 41-year-old Ward, his sights on a second "500" triumph, led with only 100 miles to go. He swiveled the Leader Card into the pits where A. J. Watson, the builder and crew chief, helped to refuel it. Out on the track another Leader Card roadster, also built by Watson, swept into first. Ward whipped out of the pits and went by his teammate, Len Sutton, when Sutton—with 75 miles to go—brought his car in for fuel. The two Leader Cards blew one-two the rest of the way, Ward taking the checker 11 seconds ahead of his teammate with a new record average speed of better than 140 miles an hour, a full mile an hour faster than Foyt's record of a year earlier.

Watson roadsters had finished one-two-three and had won the "500" a fourth straight year. And for the second time in two years, front-engine roadsters had outperformed the solitary rear-engine entry. But the roadsters' long line of "500" victories was rapidly coming to an end. Another rear-engine challenger was on the way from England. The new challenger's name: Lotus Powered by Ford.

Rodger Ward: The way it was

How does one grow up wanting to drive at Indianapolis? Rodger Ward, in the winner's circle,

told the way it was for him: *When I was very young I thought that race drivers were the roughest, the toughest, and the greatest people alive. I wanted to be like them. I shouldn't admit this now, but at 14 I put my first car together out of junk parts and raced another kid down back streets at night. It wasn't going so fast that grabbed me. It was getting into a car and beating someone.*

1963

Oil on the Track, a Punch in the Mouth

"Racing drivers," Dan Gurney once said, "are the kind of people who reach out and touch when they see a wet-paint sign."

That kind of curiosity had impelled Gurney to challenge the "dinosaurs," the heavy roadsters that had won every "500" since 1953. The tall, spare, 32-year-old Gurney was rated by many as America's best sports car driver after his 1962 victory in the French Grand Prix. At his own expense he had brought British car designer Colin Chapman, of Lotus, Limited, to Indianapolis to watch the 1962 race (in which Gurney drove a rear-engine Buick that broke down). Then Gurney took Chapman to Dearborn, Michigan, to confer with Benson Ford. Gurney talked Ford into a return to racing by the Ford Motor Company, almost 30 years having washed away the memory in Dearborn of the disappointing Miller-Fords. Chapman went back home to his Lotus factory and designed a car that was independently sprung and rear-engined, its frameless, "monocoque," chassis superlight. Ford engineers modified an aluminum Fairlane V-8 for the Lotus Powered by Ford. In 1963's trials two of the Lotus-Fords, one driven by Gurney, the other by Scotland's Jim Clark, qualified at over 149 miles an hour. Parnelli Jones won the pole for the second straight year in the Offy roadster that he called Ol' Calhoun, the Agajanian's Willard Battery Special. It qualified at a record 151.153 miles an hour.

The streamlined Lotuses "looked like go-carts next to the burly Offys," said one reporter. Since there was no drive shaft running from a front engine to the rear wheels, the Lotus drivers appeared to be sitting on the pavement as they scooted around the track. The Ford engine consumed gasoline instead of the quick-firing, lower-miles-per-gallon alcohol injected into the Offys. At a feisty 1,300 pounds and with their springy independent suspension, the Lotus-Fords rode easier on their tires than the heavier (1,600- to 1,800-pound), torsion-bar suspended roadsters. Colin Chapman predicted the Lotus-Fords would need only one pit stop, while roadsters normally needed at least three for tires and refueling. But the roadsters burst more rapidly off the turns and outdragged the Lotuses down the straights.

Back for the "500" after a four-year absence were the Novis, the howling, supercharged lions that had a history of setting records in trials and coming apart in races. Now they were owned by Andy Granatelli, a former driver on his way to fame as a TV pitchman for STP Oil Treatment. Granatelli's "500" luck was nearly as bad as the Novis' (he'd broken bones in one of his first tries as a driver; as an owner his best finish was a second in 1952). This year three of Granatelli's Novis qualified, and Bobby Unser and Jim Hurtubise put two of them in the front rows with clockings of around 150 miles an hour. The rotund Granatelli, enthralled like most fans by the screaming Novis, talked confidently of a one-two finish.

On a sunny Memorial Day a crowd estimated at 250,000—many seated in six new grandstands built since 1959—watched the cars swirl through the pace lap. On the backstretch of the first lap a Novi whined by Parnelli Jones to win the first lap prize of $150, but by midrace all three Novis, predictably, had chugged into the pits. Ahead after 150 miles was the hot-footed Jones in his pearl-grey roadster. Right behind him and pecking at his tail were Dan Gurney and Jim Clark in their yellow-striped Lotus-Fords. The vast throng was witnessing the most dramatic—and saddest—of duels: the old trying to stave off the new.

Above: Two challengers to the traditional Offy roadster showed up for this "500." On the left is a low, wide Mickey Thompson job that carried a Chevrolet V-8. In the center is the old-fashioned roadster, Rodger Ward at the wheel. At the right is a Colin Chapman Lotus-Ford, Dan Gurney the pilot. Right: A side view of the Lotus-Ford, Jim Clark at the wheel. Note how much lower the driver sits in the Lotus compared to the roadster.

From the pits Fengler bent to watch Jones go by, then told the starter to put down the black flag. "There is no question that there was a certain amount of oil on the track," Fengler said later, "but in my opinion the oil had stopped spewing."

Reprieved, Jones edged ahead of the slowed-up Clark to win by 34 seconds. After the race Eddie Sachs growled that Jones had "jeopardized the life of every driver," and the next day, at a post-race luncheon, Sachs called Jones a liar and caught a punch in the mouth. But Clark, the one who would have gained most, said, "I would have been sorry to see Parnelli Jones black-flagged."

The orthodox Offy roadster had won again. But the Lotus-Ford's second-place finish had shaken the faith of roadster owners. "The old cars," mourned Lindsey Hopkins, "have got to go." And go they soon would.

Near the halfway point Gurney had to slip into the pits for a premature stop because of wheel problems ("They took the heart out of me," he said later). Two other pit stops pushed him back into the pack and he finished seventh.

With 100 miles to go Jones swerved in for a third pit stop to take on fuel. He came out still ahead, but Clark's Lotus-Ford was only 11 seconds behind. The two cars clung together, bang-bang thunderclaps as they shot by an electrified crowd, Clark now only four seconds behind.

Suddenly, with 50 miles left in the race, Clark saw smoke puff from Jones's roadster. Jones's car was trailing oil that slicked the track. In fourth place Eddie Sachs spun. Clark's Lotus skidded, and he slowed. "I would much rather be second," he said later, "than dead."

Chief steward Harlan Fengler told the starter to get out the black flag to call Jones in for consultation. Clark's Lotus-Ford would have swept to victory. The owner of Jones's car, J. C. Agajanian, begged Fengler to take a closer look.

Parnelli Jones: Not the only one

Of the great oil-leak controversy, Parnelli Jones said later: *There's no doubt I put oil on the track. But most of the oil that leaked did not go onto the track. It hit the exhaust and burned, and that's where the puffs of smoke came from. Anyway, I don't think the oil my car laid on the track was any more than anyone else's. Everyone leaks. I had about half a tank of oil left so there wasn't that much I could have put on the track.*

(Continued on page 217)

Top: Eddie Sachs's car throws a wheel on the 181st lap. On the previous lap he'd spun while running fourth. Right: While five pit men tend to the car, a sixth pokes drinks over the wall to driver Bob Christie.

Goodyear

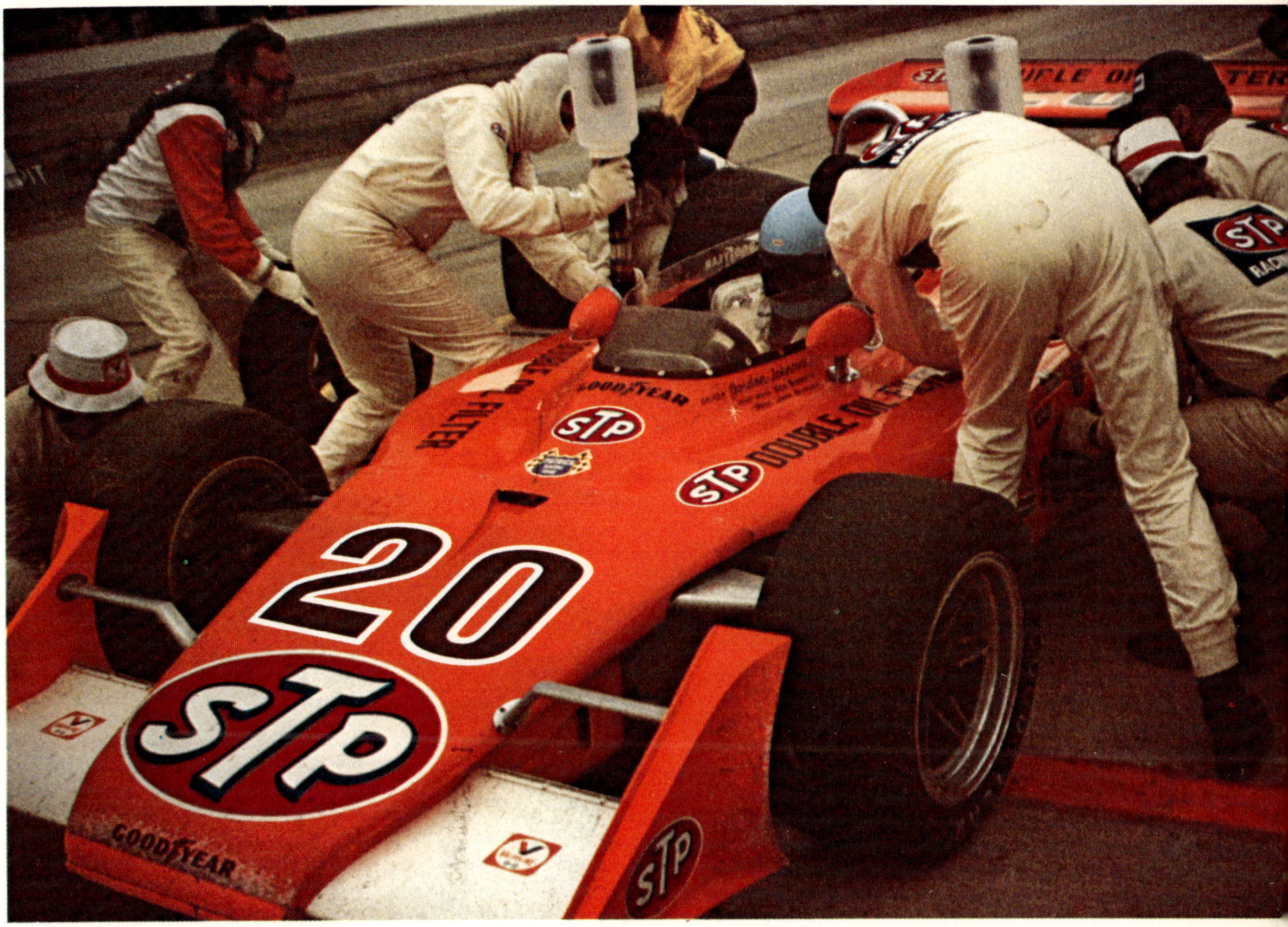

Gordon Johncock's STP pit crew tends to his Eagle-Offy during the 1973 race. The right tires are being changed. The left tires get the least wear on Indy's left-handed turns and often go the full 500 miles without a change. Johncock went on to win the race, which was stopped after 332.5 miles due to rain.

Bobby Unser skims his Jorgensen Eagle around the track in 1975's "500." Unser chalked up his second Indy victory in the rain-shortened race, which was halted by a sudden downpour after 435 miles.

Goodyear

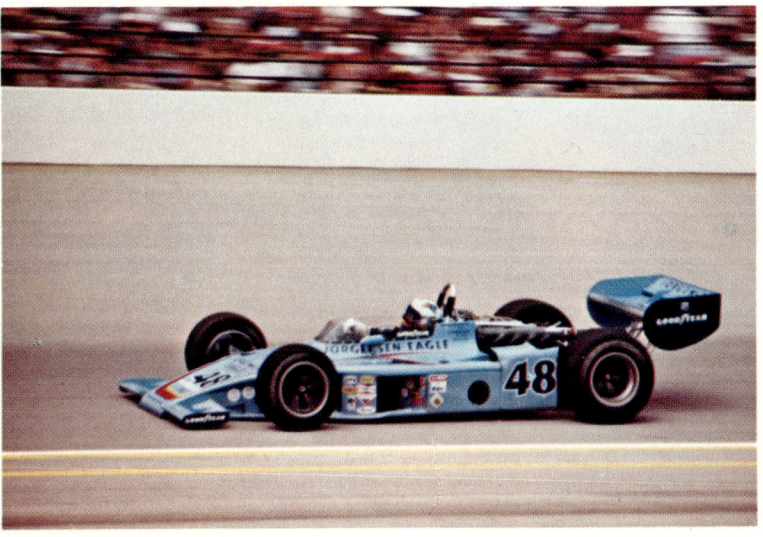

Below: Johnny Rutherford on his way to victory in 1974 in his turbocharged McLaren. This was Rutherford's first win in 11 years at Indianapolis. Opposite page: Camera-clicking fans and a cautious press gather around A. J. Foyt, the muscled one in the short-sleeved red shirt, during a practice session before the 1976 "500." The independent, gruff Foyt was fined by track steward Tom Binford when he went out for a practice run without wearing the required fire-retardant underwear. To a track announcer who complimented him on a run that had left A. J. unhappy, the burly Texan growled: "The darn thing wasn't handling. If you had your eyes open, you could have seen that." Left: A member of the McLaren team makes adjustments on Johnny Rutherford's Hy-Gain McLaren/Goodyear car before the 1976 race. The proliferation of sponsors has become necessary to foot bills that run as high as $200,000 a year to prepare, run, and maintain a car for Indianapolis. Most cars, with their spare $25,000 engines, cost around $100,000. As a result, no sponsor makes money even if his car wins the "500."

Pete Koeber

Steve Sutton

216d

Don Eldredge, Jr.

Opposite page, top: An Offy engine in the rear of a racer before the 1976 race. The engine, made of an aluminum and magnesium alloy, weighs about 600 pounds. At 9,000 rpm it produces from 900 to 1,000 horsepower. The most successful engine ever to race in the "500," the Offy has powered 24 of the last 30 winners to the checker. Bottom: On race day, 1976, fans mingle outside Gasoline Alley. There are three rows of garages, about 25 in a row. Right: Wally Dallenbach's Sinmast-Goodyear Wildcat is towed out of its garage for the start of the 1976 race. The typical Indianapolis car is 16 feet long and about 6 feet wide. Below: Front-row cars line up for the 1976 race. Johnny Rutherford's McLaren-Offy (No. 2) is on the pole. In the middle is Gordon Johncock's Wildcat, with a Drake-Goosen-Sparks engine, an offshoot of the Offy. Tom Sneva's McLaren-Offy is on the outside. Rutherford won this shortest of all the "500s," stopped by rain after 255 miles. Johncock finished third, and Sneva was sixth.

Johnny Rutherford's McLaren pit crew refuels his car during the 1976 race. Each pit storage tank is limited to 275 gallons of methanol. In addition each car can carry up to 75 gallons in its tanks at the start of the race. The total of 350 gallons weighs about a ton and a quarter. A compact passenger car could drive from New York to Los Angeles and back again on an equivalent amount of gasoline. The race cars use methanol instead of gasoline because it burns cooler and thus is less likely to burn out pistons. At top racing speed most cars in the "500" consume a gallon of fuel every mile and a half.

216f

Goodyear

Don Eldredge, Jr.

Above: The third-row cars are surrounded by crewmen as they line up for the start of the 1976 race. No. 40, on the inside, is Wally Dallenbach's Wildcat-Drake; in the middle is Gary Bettenhausen's Eagle-Offy; on the outside is Billy Vukovich's Eagle-Offy. Dallenbach finished fourth, Bettenhausen 28th, Vukovich 31st. Left: Signs that can be waved at the driver if the two-way radio fails sit in A. J. Foyt's pit during the 1976 race. Pit crews commonly have various printed messages such as the command to pit shown here. Special messages can be scrawled on the blackboard, a practice that dates back to the first race, in 1911.

Steve Sutton

Top: Parnelli Jones sports the hairstyle of the time and a sombrero in Victory Lane. Also in a cowboy hat is J. C. Agajanian, who saved the day for his car. Bottom: Ol' Parnelli in the car he called Ol' Calhoun. They snatched the lion's share of a purse that had swollen to almost half a million dollars, double the purse of ten years earlier. With four tunnels feeding cars under the track, 40,000 to 50,000 autos were estimated to be parked on the infield on race day.

1963's TOP TEN

Race open to nonstock supercharged engines with a piston displacement of 170.856 cubic inches or less; nonstock nonsupercharged engines with a piston displacement of 256.284 cubic inches or less; diesel engines with a piston displacement of 335.61 cubic inches or less; and turbine engines, no size limitation.

NO.	DRIVER	CAR	ENGINE	CYL.	BORE	STROKE	PISTON DISPL.	TIME	MPH	WINNINGS*
98	Parnelli Jones	Agajanian's Willard Battery Special	Offenhauser	4	4.281	4.375	251.9	3:29:35.40	143.137†	$148,513
92	Jim Clark	Lotus Powered by Ford	Ford‡	8	3.760	2.870	255.6	3:30:09.24	142.752	55,238
2	A. J. Foyt	Sheraton Thompson Special	Offenhauser	4	4.281	4.375	251.9	3:30:57.34	142.210	32,413
1	Rodger Ward	Kaiser Aluminum Special	Offenhauser	4	4.281	4.375	251.9	3:32:37.80	141.090	21,288
4	Don Branson	Leader Card "500" Roadster	Offenhauser	4	4.281	4.375	251.9	3:32:58.11	140.866	18,588
8	Jim McElreath	Bill Forbes Racing Team Special	Offenhauser	4	4.281	4.375	251.9	3:32:58.43	140.862	14,388
93	Dan Gurney	Lotus Powered by Ford	Ford‡	8	3.760	2.870	255.6	3:34:10.61	140.071	13,063
10	Chuck Hulse	Dean Van Lines Special	Offenhauser	4	4.281	4.375	251.9	3:34:11.26	140.064	12,063
84	Al Miller	Thompson Harvey Aluminum Special	Chevrolet‡	8	3.750	2.880	255.0	3:35:00.98	139.524	12,513
22	Dick Rathmann	Chapman Special	Offenhauser	4	4.281	4.375	251.9	3:36:04.09	138.845	10,463

* Total prizes for winning entries. Total awards in race, $494,030: Speedway prizes, $382,300; accessory prizes, $81,730; lap prizes, $30,000. † New record.
‡ Rear-engine.

1964

"You Are Sitting on Gasoline"

A. J. Foyt had thought hard about it. Now he had made his decision. He had been invited to drive one of the new rear-engine Fords that American designers were building for the 1964 race. "I don't think the Fords can make it," Foyt told friends. "I'm sticking with the so-called antique front-engine roadster."

Foyt, on his way to becoming the United States Auto Club's driving champion for the fourth time in five years, had been described this way by one of his mechanics: "Foyt has an unshakable faith that he is right and everybody else is wrong."

But even Foyt may have questioned the rightness of his decision after Jim Clark whisked a rear-engine Lotus Powered by Ford around the track at a record 158.828 miles an hour to win the pole before a first-day qualifying crowd of 235,000. And next to him on the front row were two other rear-engine Fords—a British-made Lotus driven by Bobby Marshman and an A. J. Watson-built car driven by Rodger Ward, his eyes fixed on a third "500" win.

A. J. Watson, whose roadsters had won the last five races, had accepted the British challenge and built this rear-engine racer—the Kaiser Aluminum Special. All told, there were seven rear-engine Fords in the race. Consuming gasoline, they got twice the mileage of the Offy roadsters that used alcohol blends. The Fords would have to stop only once to refuel, the Offys at least twice.

Before a race-day crowd estimated at 250,000 —another new grandstand had been added along the No. 3 turn—Clark led the pack out of the No. 4 turn and into the straightaway to begin the second lap.

Behind him rookie Dave MacDonald's car suddenly swung out of control and ricocheted off the inside wall like a crazed billiard ball. His full tank of gasoline exploded into a balloon of orange flame and black smoke. A path of fire leaped across the track, snaring two other cars. Veteran Eddie Sachs slammed into MacDonald's flaming wreckage and his rear-engine Ford exploded with a shattering whoosh. Sachs was killed instantly, and MacDonald, his lungs burned, died a few hours later.

The red flag stopped the race—the first time a "500" had been halted because of a crash (rain interrupted the 1926 race). Almost two hours later the solemn-faced drivers filed out in the positions they held at the red flag. In their Lotus-Fords Clark and Marshman diced for the lead for the first 100 miles. Then both dropped out with mechanical troubles and those two hot-tempered chargers, A. J. Foyt and Parnelli Jones, locked the noses of their Offy roadsters together in a fierce duel that ended when Jones's car caught fire during a pit stop.

Now it was A. J. Foyt all alone to carry the Offy roadster banner as Rodger Ward, in his Watson-built rear-engine Ford, swept up from the pack to challenge him for the lead. The veteran Ward, perhaps rattled by the race's disastrous start, set his fuel mixture too rich, ran out of fuel, and had to make a fifth pit stop—"two more than we needed," he said later with a rueful smile. "The car was capable of winning—

Spectators scatter (l.) as the cars of Dave MacDonald and Eddie Sachs explode. Seven cars were involved in the crash, which took the lives of MacDonald and Sachs and left Ronnie Duman badly burned. Before the next "500" new regulations regarding the construction and location of fuel tanks were enacted.

Opposite page: A. J. Foyt (No. 1) noses into view as he closes on lapped cars, his roadster hugging the inside of the curve. Above: Parnelli Jones leaves his car and the race on the 55th lap, diving from the cockpit when his tank suddenly caught fire after a pit stop. He was placed 23d. Left: One of Jones's crew slips and falls during an earlier pit stop as Ol' Calhoun, Jones's No. 98, is shoved on its way. The race was telecast on closed circuit to theaters across the nation. One viewer was Eddie Sachs's son. Said Sachs's aunt: "His wife had begged Eddie to get out of the game, but he insisted he could win the big race and refused to quit until he did."

Majorettes strike a pose before the race. Behind them is the starting line, the strip of bricks that is the only remnant of the 3 million that originally paved the track.

1964's TOP TEN

Race open to nonstock supercharged engines with a piston displacement of 170.856 cubic inches or less; nonstock nonsupercharged engines with a piston displacement of 256.284 cubic inches or less; diesel engines with a piston displacement of 335.61 cubic inches or less; and turbine engines, no size limitation.

NO.	DRIVER	CAR	ENGINE	CYL.	BORE	STROKE	PISTON DISPL.	TIME	MPH	WINNINGS*
1	A. J. Foyt	Sheraton Thompson Special	Offenhauser	4	4.281	4.375	251.9	3:23:35.83	147.350†	$153,650
2	Rodger Ward	Kaiser Aluminum Special	Ford‡	8	3.760	2.874	255.2	3:25:00.18	146.339	56,925
18	Lloyd Ruby	Bill Forbes Racing Team Special	Offenhauser	4	4.281	4.375	251.9	3:27:52.31	144.320	35,650
99	Johnny White	Demler Special	Offenhauser	4	4.281	4.375	251.9	3:29:29.30	143.206	20,700
88	Johnny Boyd	Vita Fresh Orange Juice Special	Offenhauser	4	4.281	4.375	251.9	3:30:45.31	142.345	17,625
15	Bud Tingelstad	Federal Engineering, Detroit Special	Offenhauser	4	4.281	4.375	251.9	Flagged	198 laps	15,375
23	Dick Rathmann	Chapman Special	Offenhauser	4	4.281	4.375	251.9	Flagged	197 laps	13,500
4	Bob Harkey	Wally Weir Mobilgas Special	Offenhauser	4	4.281	4.375	251.9	Flagged	197 laps	12,200
68	Bob Wente	Morcroft-Taylor Special	Offenhauser	4	4.281	4.375	251.9	Flagged	197 laps	11,350
16	Bobby Grim	Konstant Hot Special	Offenhauser	4	4.281	4.375	251.9	Flagged	196 laps	10,000

* Total prizes for winning entries. Total awards in race, $506,575: Speedway prizes, $397,150; accessory prizes, $79,425; lap prizes, $30,000.   † New record.
‡ Rear-engine.

the car should have won—but the driver didn't do a good job."

Ahead by almost a lap, Foyt sighted Ward down the barrel of his hood and kept him there. He scooted to his second "500" triumph with an average speed of 147.350 miles an hour, shattering Parnelli Jones's 143.137 mark, set a year earlier. Foyt earned the richest purse yet—$153,650—but talked bitingly of the new rear-engine cars and their tanks of gasoline: "I am afraid of those rear-engine cars. I am scared of having all that gasoline around me in that type of chassis. You are sitting on gasoline, you have gasoline on each side of you. I can carry just as much fuel in my front-engine car—my so-called antique car—with a much greater safety margin." Now he was openly scornful: "People thought this antique front-engine roadster couldn't hack it against the high-powered Fords, against the rear-engine cars. We just didn't think the Fords could make it. We were right."

But A. J. Foyt would not be right for long.

A. J. Foyt
"You got to race alone"

Late that night, after the race, A. J. Foyt talked of being a winner on a day two other drivers died. *I am sorry those guys died. We are all sorry they died. That is racing. You can't let this get you down. . . . You got to carry on in racing. . . . Maybe you haven't noticed it about me, but I haven't any close friends in racing. You can't let anyone get too close to you in this game. If they get killed, it breaks your heart, and if you are going to race, you got to race alone.*

A. J. Foyt wears a Goodyear cap after the race, even though he'd driven on Firestones (below). Early in the year the temperamental A. J. used Goodyears, switched to Firestones for the race, but said he would not accept the $7,500 prize from the company for using Firestones. Goodyear had returned to racing to challenge Firestone's "500" domination, which dated back to 1920.

1965

Trouble Came in Second

Like helmeted kings on thrones, they sat in the cockpits of the three gaudy shells in the front row as the cars rolled around the course for the parade lap. Any one of the three aristocrats of racing was favored to win this year's "500." On the pole was grim Texas perfectionist A. J. Foyt, who had rocketed his Sheraton Thompson Special through the 10-mile trials to a new record of 161.233 miles an hour. Reluctantly, the patriotic Foyt had switched from his beloved American front-engine roadster to a British rear-engine Lotus-Ford. Next to Foyt was Scotland's Jim Clark, the former world Grand Prix champion, and next to him Dan Gurney, a sports car champion on both sides of the Atlantic. Both Clark and Gurney rode in Lotus-Fords, and behind them hung California charger Parnelli Jones, also at the wheel of a Lotus-Ford.

Of the 33 qualifying cars, only four were front-engine Offy roadsters, the car that had won every race here since 1953. Most owners and drivers had seen the handwriting on the wall ever since Clark's Lotus-Ford whisked in second in 1963. They had garaged their front-mounted roadsters and bought rear-engine Fords like the Lotus-Ford, its dual overhead-camshaft V-8 snapped into a 1,300-pound chassis that was a 500-horsepower bullet.

This year all the Fords gulped alcohol instead of gasoline. One reason was the explosion that had killed Eddie Sachs and Dave MacDonald the year before. And another was the decision to go for alcohol's higher horsepower despite its low mileage. Miles-per-gallon was not a critical factor this year; a new rule required each car to make at least two pit stops. No one could try to stretch his fuel supply and stop only once.

Here again was Andy Granatelli, his two wailing Novis plastered with STP stickers. But on the first lap, as many in the huge crowd—estimated at close to 300,000—groaned, one of the Novis dropped out with a grumbling transmission. "All day that was the way it was," reported Bob Ottum in *Sports Illustrated*. "Records and cars fell with almost every lap."

A bolt of blue and red that streaked from sunshine to shadow, Clark's Lotus Powered by Ford barreled through the first lap at a record 151 miles an hour. On the 2d lap A. J. Foyt rolled high on the No. 1 turn, surprising Clark, and blasted by him on the backstretch. Behind them, locked in another wheel-to-wheel dice, bellowed Dan Gurney and Parnelli Jones, as rookie Mario Andretti snipped at their rears. On the 3d lap Clark zoomed by Foyt and began to pocket $150 lap prizes. By the 100-mile mark Clark led Foyt by a minute and zoomed in for a pit stop.

In previous "500s" the British Lotus-Ford crew had been slow on pit stops. This year Colin Chapman had signed Glen and Leonard Wood, two good old country boys from the stock car racing circuit, to boss the pit, and they shoved Clark on his way in only 21 seconds (a second stop delayed Clark only 25 seconds).

Halfway through the race, Clark still led Foyt by a lap and was averaging better than 151 miles an hour. Then, as the crowd let out a surprised "Oooooh," Foyt jerked his car into the pits, shut off the engine, yanked off his gloves, and snapped, "Transmission's gone."

The new breed at Indy hums to the fore as three Lotus-Fords dice for the early lead. Jim Clark rides in No. 82, A. J. Foyt in No. 1, Parnelli Jones in No. 98. As a new safety measure, the race was now flagged to a stop five minutes after the winner finished.

Only 14 cars were still running. Clark was far ahead. Drivers feathered back to stay in the race and win the big prizes. ("Use your head!" one pit signaled its driver.) In his Lotus-Ford, Parnelli Jones hung in second place, almost three laps behind Clark, but his fuel tank was nearly dry and Mario Andretti was in hot pursuit. With his engine hammering, Jones ran for home and got by the finish two minutes behind Clark—and only six seconds ahead of Andretti. Clark, a Scotsman, became the first foreign driver to win here since Dario Resta, in 1916. In only their third year of trying, Colin Chapman and Ford had won the "500." Clark's 150.686 average speed was 3 miles an hour faster than Foyt's record of a year earlier. For the first time since 1947, an Offy-powered car was not crowned the winner.

Parnelli Jones, despite his second-place finish, muttered unhappily about his "funny car." "There are more moving parts in these new babies, more things that can break," he said. He called his car "trouble." For Parnelli and the other American drivers, more trouble was on the way from England. This trouble's name was Graham Hill.

Jim Clark: Death wish

In his shy way, Jim Clark talked of the emotions of a "500" driver and crowd: *A driver must control his emotions. If you let your emotions go and you get angry or excited, you'd be a menace to yourself. But today there were no real tense moments for me out there. The crowd, of course, is always tense. I think this crowd is disappointed if the driver recovers and there is no accident. They look forward to crashes and, yes, maybe even seeing people killed.*

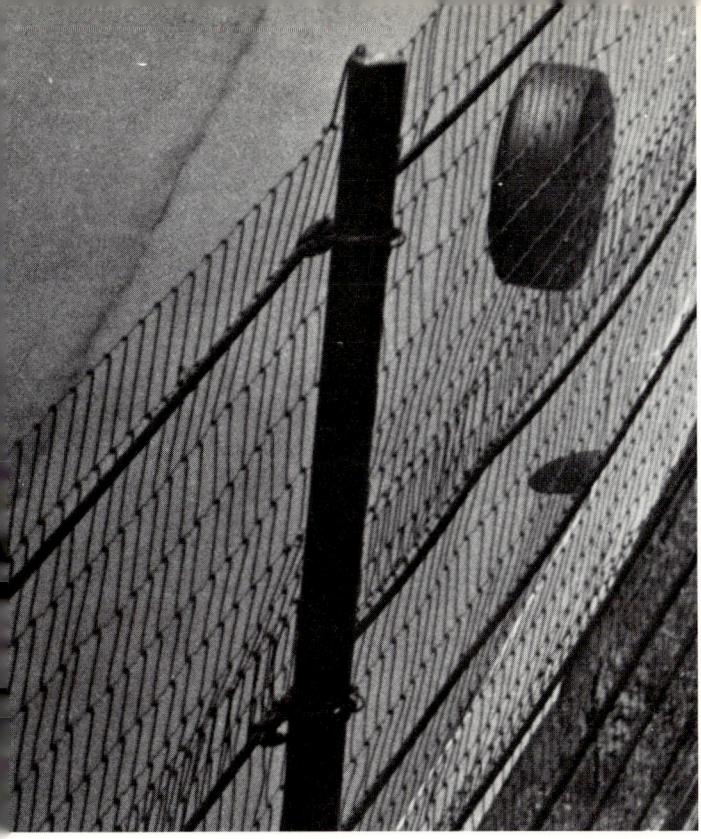

Left: A wheel flies into the new safety screen that protected spectators as Bud Tingelstad's car skids out of control on the No. 3 turn. He was not hurt. Bottom: Jim Clark in his winning Lotus-Ford. "Mmmmm, no," he said calmly after the race, "there were no tense moments out there." A. J. Foyt called the Lotus-Fords "funny cars" and mourned for the vanishing roadsters, but rookie of the year Mario Andretti raved about his 1,300-pound Brawner-Ford. "It is ready to take out on a road course right now," he said. "She can turn right, too... not just turn left, like most Indy cars." On a sunny day—"Tony Hulman weather," they said in Indianapolis— the crowd was estimated at a record 305,000. The purse had now grown past $600,000.

1965's TOP TEN

Race open to nonstock supercharged engines with a piston displacement of 170.856 cubic inches or less; nonstock nonsupercharged engines with a piston displacement of 256.284 cubic inches or less; diesel engines with a piston displacement of 335.61 cubic inches or less; and turbine engines, no size limitation.

NO.	DRIVER	CAR	ENGINE	CYL.	BORE	STROKE	PISTON DISPL.	TIME	MPH	WINNINGS*
82	Jim Clark	Lotus Powered by Ford	Ford†	8	3.760	2.870	255.1	3:19:05.34	150.686‡	$166,621
98	Parnelli Jones	Agajanian's Hurst Special	Ford†	8	3.760	2.870	255.1	3:21:04.32	149.200	64,661
12	Mario Andretti	Dean Van Lines Special	Ford†	8	3.760	2.870	255.1	3:21:10.70	149.121	42,551
74	Al Miller	Jerry Alderman Ford Lotus	Ford†	8	3.760	2.870	255.1	3:24:39.89	146.581	26,641
76	Gordon Johncock	Weinberger Homes Special	Offenhauser	4	4.295	4.375	253.5	3:24:53.62	146.417	21,981
81	Mickey Rupp	G. C. Murphy Stores Special	Offenhauser†	4	4.310	4.375	255.3	Flagged	198 laps	13,971
83	Bobby Johns	Lotus Powered by Ford	Ford†	8	3.760	2.870	255.1	Flagged	197 laps	16,886
4	Don Branson	Wynn's Special	Ford†	8	3.760	2.870	255.1	Flagged	197 laps	16,376
45	Al Unser	Sheraton Thompson Special	Ford†	8	3.760	2.870	255.1	Flagged	196 laps	14,416
23	Eddie Johnson	Chapman Special	Offenhauser	4	4.305	4.375	254.7	Flagged	195 laps	14,606

* Total prizes for winning entries. Total awards in race, $628,399: Speedway prizes, $500,493; accessory prizes, $97,906; lap prizes, $30,000.   † Rear-engine.
‡ New record.

1966

A Junkyard Blooms on the Straightaway

The Golden Girl strutted, baton whirling, sequined costume glittering in the cool morning sunlight as she led the Purdue University band down the straightaway. Minutes later 50 massed bands rended the air with "On the Banks of the Wabash." Ed Ames crooned "Back Home in Indiana," the song that had preceded "500s" for as long as most anyone here could remember. Colored balloons swarmed high, bombs burst. At 10:58 A.M. Tony Hulman's voice sounded over the loudspeakers: "Gentlemen, start your engines!" The 50th running of the Indianapolis 500 was about to begin.

With a coughing roar, almost $2 million worth of shiny machinery burst into vibrating life. Each chassis cost from $15,000 to $25,000, the engines about $30,000 apiece. With other costs, including one or two spare engines, on each entry was staked an investment of at least $100,000.

In the pole position, as the cars rolled around for the parade and pace laps, was 26-year-old Mario Andretti, who had driven his rear-engine Ford, the Dean Van Lines Special, to a new qualifying record of better than 165 miles an hour. On his right was the previous year's winner, Scottish gentleman farmer Jim Clark. This year Clark was driving for Andy Granatelli, who had junked the luckless Novi, ending its 25 years at Indy without a "500" victory. Granatelli had switched to Colin Chapman's Lotus-Fords. Back in the middle of the formation, driving a British-made Lola-Ford for Texas millionaire John Mecom, Jr., was 37-year-old Graham Hill, a rookie at the "500" but a former world driving champion on the Grand Prix circuit.

On the green flag Andretti shot from the pole to lead the flashing cars down the straightaway in what has been called "the most heart-stopping and breathless moment in all of sports." As the cars hurtled by the stands, two drivers in the middle of the pack saw an opening and both lunged for it. One of the drivers, Billy Foster, sensed the other car pinching in on his left and swung right. His car slammed into the wall, losing two wheels. The nose cone sliced off and bounded across the track in front of the thundering herd. Cars spun, slid, and slowed, and in an eye's blink the waist of the track was choked with colliding metal. Wheels, springs, and jagged metal fragments showered out of the sky amid the screeches, squeals, and wham-wham-wham of ramming steel. His car crushed against a wall, A. J. Foyt leaped out and scaled the wall as cars banged round him. A wheel hit Arnie Knepper's helmet, and he thought for a moment that a car had pancaked on him. Debris struck five spectators in the stands.

No one, amazingly, was badly hurt. But as the yellow lights flashed, 11 cars were stretched smoking on the track, bellies and backs ripped. Five other cars wobbled to the pits, where frantic repairs would begin as soon as the race resumed.

After more than an hour's delay, the race was restarted, the 17 unscathed survivors going off in cautious single file. Mario Andretti again led, but his rear-engine Ford faltered and Jim Clark shot by in Granatelli's STP Ford. He, in turn, lost the lead to Lloyd Ruby in his new Eagle-Ford, built by Dan Gurney; but Ruby, his car leaking oil, was black-flagged. With 100 miles to go, Granatelli and Colin Chapman thought that their STP Ford was ahead. But the leader, as the illuminated scoreboard on the straightaway indicated, was Jackie Stewart, in a Lola-Ford. Granatelli

Wheels sail wildly as 16 cars screech into each other on the straightaway of the first lap. Coming safely through the maelstrom are Graham Hill (24) and Roger McCluskey (8).

signaled to Clark that he was in the lead and Clark slowed—a mistake that would cost them some $79,000, the difference between first- and second-place prize money.

Stewart still led with just 25 miles to go. Behind him only eight cars were left, one of them Graham Hill's Lola-Ford. As Stewart rounded the No. 4 turn, his Bowes Seal Fast Special shuddered to a stop, a victim of low oil pressure. As Stewart was shoved into the pits, Graham Hill swept by to take the checker. Behind him, on a "victory" lap, roared Jim Clark, still thinking he had won.

Minutes later there were howls from Clark, Granatelli, and Chapman, but a look next day at the timing tapes showed that Hill had run 41 seconds faster than Clark. Hill, averaging a slow 144 miles an hour, had become the first rookie to win the "500" since George Souders in 1927. Hill had led for only 10 laps, the fewest for a winner since Joe Dawson won only 2 laps in 1912.

There were also cries for a safer start and less jockeying into the No. 1 turn after the second early-lap disaster in three years. Needed, said some observers, were better trained drivers to handle cars that had become much faster and trickier. But coming up was something even faster and trickier.

Gurney and Foyt: "Those clowns..."

Two angry veterans lashed out at the jockeying on the first lap:

Dan Gurney: *Those clowns... I was hit four times in there. Wouldn't you think that a bunch of grown men, all supposedly experienced race drivers, could drive together down a simple stretch of straight road?*

A. J. Foyt: *I ain't ever going to run in one of those races again unless I can start from up front. You got to be free to drive clean away from those crazy sons of bitches. This is supposed to be a 500-mile race. This first lap ain't no old drag strip, you know.*

During time trials Bob Veith skids to a stop, his car's tail aflame, and watches firemen put out the blaze amid a curtain of smoke.

At the wheel of the Stoddard-Dayton that paced the first "500" in 1911 is Ray Harroun. He died in 1968. Next to him is Cliff Bergere, who, until 1975, held the record for the most miles driven in "500s" —6,142.5. Bottom: Graham Hill and the winning Lola-Ford. He died in a plane crash in 1975. At the finish only seven cars were running —the fewest in any "500" so far.

1966's TOP TEN

Race open to supercharged four-cycle overhead camshaft engines with a piston displacement of 170.856 cubic inches or less; nonsupercharged four-cycle overhead camshaft engines with a piston displacement of 256.284 cubic inches or less; American stock production block design, single nonoverhead camshaft, removable head, supercharged engines with a piston displacement of 203.4 cubic inches or less; American stock production block design, single nonoverhead camshaft, removable head, nonsupercharged engines with a piston displacement of 305.1 cubic inches or less; two-cycle engines, supercharged or not, with a piston displacement of 170.856 cubic inches or less; diesel engines, two- or four-cycle, supercharged or not, with a piston displacement of 335.61 cubic inches or less; rotating combustion engines, nonsupercharged, with a displacement of 256.284 cubic inches or less; and turbine engines, energy or fuel cells, hydraulic accumulators, and steam engines complying with USAC specifications.

NO.	DRIVER	CAR	ENGINE*	CYL.	BORE	STROKE	PISTON DISPL.	TIME	MPH	WINNINGS†
24	Graham Hill	American Red Ball Special	Ford	8	3.760	2.872	255.1	3:27:52.53	144.317	$156,297
19	Jim Clark	STP Gasoline Treatment Special	Ford	8	3.760	2.872	255.1	3:28:33.66	143.843	76,992
3	Jimmy McElreath	Zink-Urschel-Slick Trackburner Special	Ford	8	3.760	2.872	255.1	3:28:42.42	143.742	42,586
72	Gordon Johncock	Weinberger Homes Special	Ford	8	3.760	2.872	255.1	3:29:40.00	143.084	26,381
94	Mel Kenyon	Gerhardt Special	Offenhauser	4	4.281	4.375	251.9	Flagged	198 laps	21,987
43	Jackie Stewart	Bowes Seal Fast Special	Ford	8	3.760	2.872	255.1	Out	190 laps	25,767
54	Eddie Johnson	Valvoline Special II	Offenhauser	4	4.281	4.375	251.9	Out	175 laps	17,615
11	Bobby Unser	Vita Fresh Orange Juice Special	Offenhauser‡	4	4.125	3.125	168.0	Flagged	171 laps	6,562
6	Joe Leonard	Yamaha Eagle	Ford	8	3.760	2.872	255.1	Out	170 laps	15,822
88	Jerry Grant	Bardahl-Pacesetter Homes Special	Ford	8	3.760	2.870	255.1	Flagged	167 laps	15,055

* All cars rear-engine.   † Total prizes for winning entries. Total awards in race, $691,808: Speedway prizes, $545,293; accessory prizes, $116,515; lap prizes, $30,000.   ‡ Turbocharged.

1967

Granatelli Brings a Turbine

"That's no racing car," muttered A. J. Foyt, "it's a damn *air*plane."

He was speaking of Andy Granatelli's newest entry, a broad-hipped, two-foot-high, 12-foot-long, Day-Glo red torpedo. Dotted with STP decals, the new car was powered by an industrial Pratt-Whitney turbine engine. The same kind of turbine zipped yachts through water and whooshed planes through the stratosphere. Foyt estimated its horsepower at double what most piston engines could deliver. Leaving a thin whine in its wake, the turbine-powered car had shot through the qualifying laps at better than 166 miles an hour. "If it stays legal," growled Foyt, "every driver is going to demand one and this race is going to become a proving ground for jet aircraft."

The only car picked to beat Granatelli's 1,750-pound, four-wheel-drive turbine was a rear-engine Brawner-Ford, Mario Andretti at the wheel, that had qualified at a record 168.982 miles an hour to win the pole. On the inside in the second row was A. J. Foyt, twice a "500" winner. He was driving a rear-engine Coyote-Ford that he had built himself as his red-white-and-blue answer to the invasion of the Lotus-Fords from England.

On a cold, cloudy morning, with rain squalls drilling the rim of the city, most of the estimated 300,000 spectators had eyes and binoculars on the red turbine, driven by Parnelli Jones, as the field swept toward the No. 1 turn, at the bottom of the stretch. From the pole Andretti jumped into the lead. He looked up and saw a red streak high up on the turn where racers weren't supposed to tread. The turbine's four-wheel drive gripped the incline securely as it whipped by Andretti to sweep through the first lap at a record 154 miles an hour. For the next 17 laps it broke a string of lap records. But then rain sheeted down and the race was stopped. After a wait of almost five hours, the race was put off until the next day, May 31. This would be the first "500" to be run over two days.

That night, at dinner, most drivers told each other that the turbine would run away from the field. But others recalled that the car had been plagued during the trials by a rash of gearbox ailments. "I feel certain it won't go the 500 miles without breaking down," Foyt said. And he told Speedway owner Tony Hulman: "I'm so certain I'm going to win that I ought to charge you for keeping my money overnight."

The next morning the cars started off in single file, Parnelli Jones's turbine at the head, in the positions they had held when the race was halted. Jones again wailed the turbine away from the pack. Trying to keep up, Andretti's Brawner-Ford threw a wheel. Only two drivers—Gurney and Foyt—could keep the red blur at their backs and weren't lapped. Then Gurney chugged to the pit with a burned piston and Foyt alone tried to catch the turbine.

In the pit Andy Granatelli told himself his years of bad "500" luck had finally ended. His car had only 8 miles to go as it roared by the applauding grandstands. Suddenly the car bucked, shivered, and shook itself out of gear. A $6 ball bearing had failed in the gearbox. A frustrated Jones coasted the car toward the pit and the anguished Granatelli.

An exuberant Foyt came by, saw the turbocar in the pit, and rammed his Coyote-Ford toward the finish line. As he blasted his way out of the No. 4 turn on the final lap, something instinctual made him slow down. His instinct had served him

Top: On the pace lap Mario Andretti tucks in behind the Camaro pacer. Bottom: An angry Andretti kicks the tire that flew off his Brawner-Ford and left him and the car in the infield as spectators.

233

1967's TOP TEN

Race open to supercharged four-cycle overhead camshaft engines with a piston displacement of 170.856 cubic inches or less; nonsupercharged four-cycle overhead camshaft engines with a piston displacement of 256.284 cubic inches or less; American stock production block design, single nonoverhead camshaft, removable head, supercharged engines with a piston displacement of 203.4 cubic inches or less; American stock production block design, single nonoverhead camshaft, removable head, nonsupercharged engines with a piston displacement of 305.1 cubic inches or less; two-cycle engines, supercharged or not, with a piston displacement of 170.856 cubic inches or less; diesel engines, two- or four-cycle, supercharged, with a piston displacement of 203.4 cubic inches or less; diesel engines, two- or four-cycle, nonsupercharged, with a piston displacement of 305.1 cubic inches or less; gas turbine engines, axial flow design compressors, with a total inlet annulus area of 23 square inches or less; gas turbine engines, centrifugal design compressors, with a total inlet annulus area of 28.5 square inches or less; rotating combustion engines, nonsupercharged, with a displacement of 256.284 cubic inches or less; and energy or fuel cells, hydraulic accumulators, and steam engines complying with USAC specifications.

NO.	DRIVER	CAR	ENGINE	CYL.	BORE	STROKE	PISTON DISPL.	TIME	MPH	WINNINGS*
14	A. J. Foyt	Sheraton Thompson Special	Ford†	8	3.760	2.872	255.1	3:18:24.22	151.207‡	$171,527
5	Al Unser	Retzloff Chemical Special	Ford†	8	3.760	2.872	255.1	Flagged	198 laps	67,127
4	Joe Leonard	Sheraton Thompson Special	Ford†	8	3.760	2.872	255.1	Flagged	197 laps	43,177
69	Denis Hulme	City of Daytona Beach Special	Ford†	8	3.760	2.872	255.1	Flagged	197 laps	28,177
2	Jim McElreath	John Zink Trackburner	Ford†	8	3.760	2.872	255.1	Flagged	197 laps	22,957
40	Parnelli Jones	STP Oil Treatment Special	Pratt-Whitney§#	0	—	—	—	Out	196 laps	55,767
8	Chuck Hulse	Hopkins Special	Offenhauser†¶	8	3.760	2.872	255.1	Out	195 laps	18,397
16	Art Pollard	Thermo King Auto Air Conditioning Special	Offenhauser†¶	4	4.125	3.125	168.0	Flagged	195 laps	16,928
6	Bobby Unser	Rislone Special	Ford†	8	3.760	2.872	255.1	Flagged	193 laps	15,773
41	Carl Williams	George R. Bryant Special	Ford†	8	3.760	2.872	255.1	Out	189 laps	16,173

* Total prizes for winning entries. Total awards in race, $734,834: Speedway prizes, $566,016; accessory prizes, $128,818; lap prizes, $40,000. † Rear-engine. ‡ New record. § Turbine-powered. # Four-wheel drive. ¶ Turbocharged.

Right: A. J. Foyt, winner of three "500s." He drove in as many as 50 races a year. "They all add up," he said. An all-night card player with his crew, he confessed to homesickness. "But I love racing. I don't fear death. I don't think about it." Below: Foyt and the winning Coyote-Ford, which needed only two pit stops. Opposite page, top: Andy Granatelli (l.) and Colin Chapman stand with the turbocar (No. 40), Parnelli Jones at the wheel, and a Lotus-Ford, Jim Clark at the wheel. Less than a year later Clark was killed in Europe. Far right: Top view of the turbocar, turbine on the right.

well: Five cars were spinning and smoking in the middle of the stretch after a collision.

Foyt weaved through the tangle to win with a record speed of better than 151 miles an hour. Immediately the red flag waved the other cars off the track to avoid the wreck. For the first time, only one driver had completed the 200 laps. Foyt joined Wilbur Shaw, Mauri Rose, and Louis Meyer as the only three-time "500" winners.

Foyt's tires were made by Goodyear, which had come here in the early sixties to challenge Firestone. This was the first year since 1919, when a Goodrich Silvertown cord tire had won, that Firestone newspaper ads could not proclaim the day after Memorial Day that Firestone once more had won the "500."

A disappointed Granatelli promised he would try again with his turbine. "It should be outlawed," groused Foyt. But the turbine would be back—with a funny-looking snout.

A. J. Foyt:
A peek at disaster

In the winner's circle, Foyt told how he had finished amid smoking wrecks: *Something made me slow as I came around that No. 4 turn of the final lap. I peeked around the turn and saw all that smoke. I dropped her into low and pulled down to the inside of the track. And as soon as I could see where everybody was spinning to, I stood on it again and drove her on through to the finish line.*

1968

Showdown at the Old Corral

The shrimp-red blur streaked down the straightaway toward the No. 1 turn. This STP turbocar left no sound except a faraway whine of power. It hit the turn going fast enough to traverse a football field in one second. It swerved high onto the bank, too high, and Mike Spence felt the tail skid. He tried to lock the front wheels. The car slammed into the wall, there was a flash of fire, a wheel hurtled into the air, and Spence's helmet rolled down the track, its chin strap still fastened. A few hours later Spence was dead, killed in a practice run of one of Colin Chapman's newest creations.

Chapman, designer of the Lotus-Ford, had joined Andy Granatelli's STP team. Chapman sculpted a new chassis for Granatelli's airplane-type turbine engine. The car had a wedge-shaped nose—the "doorstop," they called it on Gasoline Alley. In one of these Lotus-turbines Spence had whistled through one lap at 169 miles an hour, only a smidgen shy of the qualifying record, and on another run he had died.

Spence's death shook Colin Chapman. A month earlier Chapman's Lotus team had lost Jim Clark, the 1965 Indianapolis winner, killed in a race in Germany. For Granatelli, Spence's crash was another setback in his bitter battle with the United States Auto Club (USAC) to qualify turbines for the "500." The club, its membership overwhelmingly made up of piston men, had imposed a new rule that limited the turbine's air flow, cutting its power by about 25 percent. Dan Gurney, the builder of Eagle-Fords, summed up the opposition: "It's just as if you introduced a baseball that had some new ingredient in it that everyone who hit it would sock it over the fence for a home run. ... Suddenly everyone would be hitting home runs. Nobody would come to see baseball."

Retorted Granatelli: "USAC stands in the way of progress."

With some 250,000 fans watching on a Saturday two weeks before Memorial Day, two of the STP Lotus-turbines—one driven by Joe Leonard, the other by Graham Hill—hummed to new qualifying records of better than 171 miles an hour. Leonard won the pole, Hill the No. 2 position. Carrying the flag on the front row for the piston engines would be 34-year-old, 6-foot Bobby Unser. In the No. 3 slot, he was at the wheel of a car built by Dan Gurney. Its Eagle chassis was powered by a rear-mounted Offy; it was the first Offy-driven car since 1963 to earn a starting spot in the front row ("Hurrah," cried an oldtimer, "the Offys are back home in Indiana"). This new-generation Offy had a turbocharger, a device that retunneled exhaust gases to give the car an extra boost. At 4,500 rpm the turbocharger shot the Offy's horsepower toward 600—close to what the restricted turbines could muster.

Popping by Joe Leonard's turbine at the 20-mile mark, Bobby Unser led for most of the first half of the race. Behind him cars spun, crashed, or just came apart. Bobby Unser saw his younger brother, Al, smack into a wall; but a little later, going by the pits, he saw Al wave that he was all right. "I felt a thousand percent better," Bobby said later.

With 90 miles to go three cars led the shattered field. Unser was first, Lloyd Ruby was grabbing at his tailpipe in another turbocharged Offy, and then came Leonard in an STP turbocar—two pistons against what Granatelli called his "car of tomorrow."

Unser had to swerve into the pits for fuel. He lumbered out, unable to shift to low because of

A giant balloon, one of many lofted before the race, seems to be swelling out of the cockpit of a racer in the foreground. In this race Lloyd Ruby's Offy whirled through the fastest lap run up to that time in "500" traffic: 168.666 miles an hour.

gear complications, and he lost time while he picked up enough speed for the turbocharger to kick on. Ruby's Offy and Leonard's turbocar were ahead of him. But then Ruby's car began to sputter, and it dropped back. Leonard rammed into first place, Unser clinging to his rear.

Now it was *mano a mano,* Leonard against Unser, turbine against piston. There were some 50 miles to go.

Both saw the yellow lights flash on. A car had crashed and was aflame. While crews dodged onto the track to haul away the wreck, the field slowed to 120 miles an hour and cars could not pass each other. Unser had to dawdle behind Leonard. If the lights stayed on for a few more minutes, Leonard's turbocar would coast to victory.

For the second straight year Andy Granatelli watched from the pit as one of his cars ran toward Victory Lane . . . only 11 laps, then 10 laps, then 9 laps away.

On flashed the green lights. Leonard stamped on the floor. The car leaped ahead, then suddenly folded. "It was like a jet airplane taking off," Leonard said later, "and then plunk. It was like you're driving on a road and you turn off the key."

Later it was found that not enough fuel was being fed the flame in the turbine's combustion chamber while the car noodled along at 120. When Leonard jabbed the throttle, the fuel pump's drive shaft couldn't take the sudden strain and snapped. But Andy Granatelli had another explanation: "Maybe somebody up there doesn't want me to win."

Bobby Unser zoomed by the checker to win with a new record speed—152.882 miles an hour—the ninth time in the last ten years a new record had been posted. All three of Colin Chapman's Lotus-turbines had failed to finish. Piston owners talked of banning the turbines from future races. "The great showdown came and they won," growled Granatelli. "They have beaten us and now they want to ban us."

Bobby Unser: "That was stupid"

In recalling his first "500" victory, Bobby Unser remembered a faulty gearshift: *One of my secret tricks was that I had four gears and nobody knew it. I had two for the pits and two for racing. The third gear was especially for running with a full fuel load. It would pick up rpm real fast to get the car lifting quick. The fourth was for running near empty. But I had to hold the car in third gear with my right hand. Then I decided that was stupid because I ended up driving with my left hand. And pretty soon I got a blister on my palm and then another blister on top of that one. So finally I just left the shift there jiggling around and drove the rest of the race with both hands on the wheel.*

Opposite page: Joe Leonard whizzes the STP Lotus-turbocar out of the pit. Below: Bobby Unser. Right: Unser in his winning Eagle-Offy, built by Dan Gurney. "Hell," said Bobby, "I've never run a full 500 miles before and I wasn't even sure I could last all that time under that abuse. But I did." He won $175,000 plus the Torino pace car and other products. The rookie of the year was Billy Vukovich, who finished seventh.

1968's TOP TEN

Race open to supercharged four-cycle overhead camshaft engines with a piston displacement of 170.856 cubic inches or less; nonsupercharged four-cycle overhead camshaft engines with a piston displacement of 256.284 cubic inches or less; American stock production block design, single nonoverhead camshaft, removable head, supercharged engines with a piston displacement of 203.4 cubic inches or less; American stock production block design, single non-overhead camshaft, removable head, nonsupercharged engines with a piston displacement of 305.1 cubic inches or less; two-cycle engines other than diesel engines, supercharged or not, with a piston displacement of 170.856 cubic inches or less; diesel engines, two- or four-cycle, supercharged, with a piston displacement of 203.4 cubic inches or less; diesel engines, two- or four-cycle, nonsupercharged, with a piston displacement of 305.1 cubic inches or less; gas turbine engines with a total inlet annulus area of 15.999 square inches or less; and rotating combustion engines, nonsupercharged, with a displacement of 256.284 cubic inches or less.

NO.	DRIVER	CAR	ENGINE*	CYL.	BORE	STROKE	PISTON DISPL.	TIME	MPH	WINNINGS†
3	Bobby Unser	Rislone Special	Offenhauser‡	4	4.125	3.125	168.0	3:16:13.76	152.882§	$175,139
48	Dan Gurney	Olsonite Eagle	Gurney Weslake Ford	8	4.007	3.000	305.0	3:17:07.57	152.187	65,094
15	Mel Kenyon	City of Lebanon, Indiana, Special	Offenhauser‡	4	4.125	3.125	168.0	3:21:02.43	149.224	44,959
42	Denis Hulme	Olsonite Eagle	Ford	8	3.760	2.872	255.1	3:21:08.71	149.146	26,624
25	Lloyd Ruby	Gene White Company Special	Offenhauser‡	4	4.125	3.125	168.0	3:21:58.83	148.529	30,364
59	Ronnie Duman	Cleaver-Brooks Special	Offenhauser‡	4	4.125	3.125	168.0	Flagged	199 laps	19,204
98	Billy Vukovich	Wagner-Lockheed Brake Fluid Special	Offenhauser‡	4	4.125	3.125	168.0	Flagged	198 laps	18,519
90	Mike Mosley	Zecol-Lubaid Special	Offenhauser‡	8	3.760	2.872	255.1	Flagged	197 laps	17,489
94	Sam Sessions	Valvoline Special	Offenhauser‡	4	4.125	3.125	168.0	Flagged	197 laps	15,729
6	Bobby Grim	Gene White Company Special	Offenhauser‡	4	4.125	3.125	168.0	Flagged	196 laps	15,169

* All cars rear-engine. † Total prizes for winning entries. Total awards in race, $712,269: Speedway prizes, $562,059; accessory prizes, $110,210; lap prizes, $40,000. ‡ Turbocharged. § New record.

1969

A Shriek, a Kiss, and a Hoist

The sun came up pale white on what they call "a hot one" in Indiana. Andy Granatelli sniffed the morning heat and winced. For his 17th try at winning a "500," he'd entered 11 cars, the most ever by one owner, and qualified three. "If he had to enter 33," said a friend, "he'd do it to win." Twice in the past two years he'd watched in anguish as a Granatelli car collapsed while it was ahead and within sniffing distance of the finish. Now Granatelli could visualize the nightmare: His car comes down the homestretch far ahead and runs out of fuel.

This year Andy's turbocars were gone, banished by a United States Auto Club edict that reduced turbine engines to a size that couldn't win at Indianapolis. But the wedge-shaped front that Britain's Colin Chapman had carved onto Granatelli's luckless Lotus-turbines of 1968 was copied by other designers. Even A. J. Foyt, "who fiercely resents changes by anyone not waving the American flag," in the words of one reporter, had given the "doorstop" nose to his Coyote-Fords.

Nearly all the 33 qualifiers were powered by rear-mounted turbocharged Fords or Offys. The turbochargers were ravenous on fuel; it was the rare car that got 2 miles a gallon. So the three pit stops mandatory since 1968 were also necessary, to refuel. But with a limit of 325 gallons of fuel per car, most everyone was concerned whether the turbocharged cars would finish—especially on a hot day when they'd burn fuel faster.

After having failed to win over the years with the temperamental Novis and then with the radical turbocars, Granatelli had joined the crowd: His STP Oil Treatment Special was much like everybody else's car, its turbocharged Ford engine mounted in the rear of a chassis designed by his mechanic Clint Brawner. With the 5-foot-2-inch Mario Andretti—on his way to a third national driving championship—at the wheel, the car won a front-row spot next to Foyt's Coyote, which was on the pole. Bobby Unser, 1968's winner, sat on the outside in a new Bardahl Special.

At the start, Andretti beat Foyt and Unser to the first turn and stayed in front for the first 5 laps. Then he glanced at a temperature gauge, saw the engine was heated, and slowed. Foyt popped into the lead. For the next 200 miles four cars clustered together like colored beads: Foyt's, Roger McCluskey's (a Foyt Coyote-Ford), Andretti's, and veteran Lloyd Ruby's.

Bad luck rode next to Ruby. Leading, he went into his pit to refuel. A mechanic accidentally tapped him on the helmet, and Ruby thought it was the signal to go. But the fuel hose was still gripped to his tank. He blasted out of the pit, ripped away a hunk of the side of his car, and was through for the day.

Minutes later Foyt ruptured a manifold, and a 22-minute stay in the pits put him back in the ruck. His teammate, McCluskey, tried to stay on the track one lap too many, ran out of fuel, and had to free-wheel to the pits, ending his bid for first.

Suddenly there was Andretti all alone at the head of the pack in the STP Special. There were 250 miles to go and all he had to do was nurse his fuel supply and pray the car held together. He feathered back to 155 miles an hour and threaded his way carefully through a dwindling field (only 12 cars were running at the finish).

From the pit the squat Granatelli watched his car whirl closer and closer to the prize that had eluded him so long. Remembering how his cars

Top: Jim McElreath leaps onto the wall of the first turn after his Hawk-Offy caught fire. Cars' tanks could hold up to 75 gallons of fuel, a mixture of alcohol and nitromethane. Bottom: As Jim watches, the fire is extinguished.

had led in the last laps of the previous two races —and lost—he refused to accept congratulations, sweltering silently in a red blazer. Then, as Andretti swept by the finish line to win the record $200,000 first prize, a shrieking Granatelli ran puffing to Victory Lane, kissed Andretti, and shouted congratulations in Italian and English. He hoisted the diminutive Mario onto his broad back. Despite the slowed-down pace of the last 250 miles, Andretti had set a "500" record, his 156.876-mile-an-hour average almost 4 miles an hour faster than Unser's record of a year earlier.

Forever the huckster, Granatelli shouted into microphones to millions listening on radio or watching on closed-circuit theater TV: "I guess we had more STP in our Ford."

One listener was Al Unser, at home in New Mexico with a broken leg. Ahead for him was the "500's" only brother act.

Andy Granatelli: Happy—but...

After coming heartbreakingly close twice in a row, Andy Granatelli told how it felt to be a winner at last: *I didn't believe it until I saw Mario a hundred feet from the flag. Look at our luck. The Novi set so many records, and a couple of times they were close to winning and fell apart. Then those last two years with the turbines... I'm happy, but it's not the same as it would have been with the Novis or the turbines.*

1969's TOP TEN

Race open to supercharged four-cycle overhead camshaft engines with a piston displacement of 161.703 cubic inches or less; nonsupercharged four-cycle overhead camshaft engines with a piston displacement of 256.284 cubic inches or less; American stock production block design, single nonoverhead camshaft, removable head, supercharged engines with a piston displacement of 203.4 cubic inches or less; American stock production block design, single nonoverhead camshaft, removable head, nonsupercharged engines with a piston displacement of 320.355 cubic inches or less; special rocker arm, single nonoverhead camshaft, removable head, nonsupercharged engines with a piston displacement of 305.1 cubic inches or less; two-cycle engines other than diesel engines, supercharged or not, with a piston displacement of 170.856 cubic inches or less; diesel engines, two- or four-cycle, supercharged, with a piston displacement of 203.4 cubic inches or less; diesel engines, two- or four-cycle, nonsupercharged, with a piston displacement of 305.1 cubic inches or less; gas turbine engines with a total inlet annulus area of 11.999 square inches or less; and rotating combustion engines, nonsupercharged, with a displacement of 256.284 cubic inches or less.

NO.	DRIVER	CAR	ENGINE*	CYL.	BORE	STROKE	PISTON DISPL.	TIME	MPH	WINNINGS†
2	Mario Andretti	STP Oil Treatment Special	Ford‡	8	3.650	1.902	159.0	3:11:14.71	156.867§	$206,727
48	Dan Gurney	Olsonite Eagle	Gurney	8	4.113	3.000	319.0	3:13:07.74	155.337	67,732
1	Bobby Unser	Bardahl Special	Offenhauser‡#	4	4.030	3.125	159.0	3:14:41.45	154.090	45,647
9	Mel Kenyon	Krohne Grain Transport Special	Offenhauser‡	4	4.030	3.125	159.0	3:17:08.32	152.177	30,612
92	Peter Revson	Repco-Brabham Special	Repco Brabham	8	3.655	3.030	254.3	Flagged	197 laps	25,722
44	Joe Leonard	City of Daytona Beach Special	Ford‡	8	3.650	1.902	159.0	Flagged	193 laps	21,602
66	Mark Donohue	Sunoco-Simoniz Special	Offenhauser‡#	4	4.030	3.125	159.0	Flagged	190 laps	21,512
6	A. J. Foyt	Sheraton Thompson Special	Ford‡	8	3.650	1.902	159.0	Flagged	181 laps	50,251
21	Larry Dickson	Bryant Heating and Cooling Special	Ford‡	8	3.650	1.902	159.0	Flagged	180 laps	17,426
97	Bobby Johns	Wagner-Lockheed Brake Fluid Special	Offenhauser‡	4	4.030	3.125	159.0	Flagged	171 laps	19,841

* All cars rear-engine. † Total prizes for winning entries. Total awards in race, $805,127: Speedway prizes, $614,147; accessory prizes, $150,980; lap prizes, $40,000. ‡ Turbocharged. § New record. # Four-wheel drive.

Opposite page, top: During practice Jochen Rindt skids but stops safely. A year later he was not as lucky, dying at Monza. Bottom: Lloyd Ruby (No. 4) holds the inside, ahead of Joe Leonard (No. 44) and Wally Dallenbach (No. 22). Left and below: Mario Andretti and his winner, whose front Andretti called "swoopy." He was supposed to drive a Lotus-Ford but wrecked it in practice. He could have driven another Lotus, instead chose a backup car, this Hawk-Ford, and won.

1970

"I Don't Think Indy Likes Me"

Through the short north chute and into the No. 4 turn buzzed the star-spangled, red, white, and blue Mongoose-Offy, nicknamed the Silent Majority Special by one of its politically minded owners. Stretched in the cockpit was the 42-year-old Lloyd Ruby, who, like the silent majority's president, had known what it was like to be a loser. Ruby, wrote an observer, was driving "like a man possessed." From 25th at the start of the race, he'd weaved through traffic during the first 50 miles to nudge into seventh place, and he was beating his way toward the leaders.

Three times since 1966 Lloyd Ruby had led in a "500." Each time his car had broken under him. On the eve of this race he'd spun during a practice run and almost kissed a wall. "I believe," drawled the Texan, "that I've plumb run out of bad luck."

The Silent Majority Special (real name: Daniels Cablevision Special) had been one of some 60 racers that had bleeped and blatted around the Speedway since May 1. The weeks of practice and qualifying runs had drawn more than a half-million spectators to the Speedway. Day in and day out, the humid air was split by the drone of the engines, nearly all of them turbocharged Ford V-8s or Offy four-bangers mounted in the rear of Eagles, Mongooses, Coyotes, Lolas, Colts, and other chassis, most with identical wedge fronts.

This was the dapper, 69-year-old Tony Hulman's 25th anniversary as the owner of the Speedway. Since 1945 he had given the 61-year-old *grande dame* of car racing a new figure and face: track resurfaced with asphalt; a museum near the main gate that housed cars and other mementos of "500s" past; a motel that bordered the nine-hole golf course on the infield; a long row of stately new grandstands that seated more than 225,000. And this year Hulman and the Speedway would be offering auto racing's first million-dollar purse.

Favored to win the biggest first prize in auto racing history was Al Unser, the 31-year-old younger brother of the 1968 Indy winner. He gripped the wheel of a blue and gold P. J. Colt-Ford named the Johnny Lightning "500" Special by its sponsor, a toy company. Unser had hurried the Johnny Lightning through the 4 qualifying laps at 170 miles an hour to win the pole. Next to Unser, in a Gurney-Ford, sat Johnny Rutherford. On the outside was A. J. Foyt, grimly seeking his fourth "500" crown. So far he had won $375,000 at the Speedway, more than anyone else (the closest was Bobby Unser, with $198,000). "He's a millionaire," said Foyt's chief mechanic, Jud Phillips, "but he has a desire to win this thing four times—and even if he does, I don't think he'll retire." Far back in the ninth row, Lloyd Ruby hung over the wheel of his Silent Majority Special, convinced his bad luck was behind him.

With grey rain clouds hanging over the track—the race was delayed an hour by showers—Al Unser outsprinted Rutherford and Foyt to the first corner and led for 120 miles. Ruby, meanwhile, had been wiggling his way through the pack, and he picked off Bobby Unser, Johnny Rutherford, and Al Unser to growl into first place. But no sooner was he in the lead than Ruby learned his luck was still bad: Studs snapped and oil spurted onto the exhaust pipe. His car a smoking torch, Ruby skidded onto the grassy infield and leaped out. "It just ain't meant for me to win at this place," he said later. "I don't think Indy likes me. Every year I try to change her opinion, but every year she wins."

Al Unser retook the lead and hurtled through

In the track-sniffing chassis that reminded some people of four-wheeled anteaters, Al Unser (No. 2) creeps by Mark Donohue (No. 66) late in the race—proving to Donohue what Al's Johnny Lightning could do.

the first 200 miles averaging a record 161 miles an hour. He edged away from Foyt, his closest pursuer, until he sighted the Texan's white Sheraton Thompson Special up ahead of him. Then Unser heeded owner Parnelli Jones's advice: "Take it easy and don't try to break the car." Unser swung in behind Foyt's Coyote-Ford and conserved his car's strength and fuel by "drafting." He let Foyt's draft suck him along, while Foyt—in front—had to wring the utmost out of his car.

With 100 miles to go and Unser ahead by almost a lap, the "500" cognoscenti reminded each other that no pole winner had won the race since 1963. Anything could happen—and did. A car crashed, spilling oil, and other cars spun on the slicked pavement. Foyt twisted by but broke his gearbox and limped the rest of the way to finish tenth. The yellow lights glowed for 17 minutes. Unser coasted under the yellow at 120 miles an hour while Mark Donohue, Dan Gurney, and rookie Donnie Allison had to lockstep in place behind him. When the green finally came on, Unser still had his lap lead and there were only 19 laps to go. He won by almost a lap with a 155-mile-an-hour average, below the record set the previous year. It was only the second "500" since 1958 to end with no new record in the book.

In 1939, the year Al Unser was born, Wilbur Shaw had won about $35,000 with an average speed of 115 miles an hour. In 1970 Al Unser had won almost ten times that much in prize money and endorsements. But to win money at Indianapolis in the 1970s, drivers were about to discover, you'd need wings.

1970's TOP TEN

Race open to supercharged four-cycle overhead camshaft engines with a piston displacement of 161.703 cubic inches or less; nonsupercharged four-cycle overhead camshaft engines with a piston displacement of 256.284 cubic inches or less; American stock production block design, single nonoverhead camshaft, removable head, supercharged engines with a piston displacement of 203.4 cubic inches or less; American stock production block design, single nonoverhead camshaft, removable head, nonsupercharged engines with a piston displacement of 320.355 cubic inches or less; special rocker arm, single nonoverhead camshaft, removable head, nonsupercharged engines with a piston displacement of 305.1 cubic inches or less; two-cycle engines other than diesel engines, supercharged or not, with a piston displacement of 170.856 cubic inches or less; diesel engines, two- or four-cycle, supercharged, with a piston displacement of 203.4 cubic inches or less; diesel engines, two- or four-cycle, nonsupercharged, with a piston displacement of 305.1 cubic inches or less; gas turbine engines with a total inlet annulus area of 11.999 square inches or less; and rotating combustion engines, nonsupercharged, with a displacement of 256.284 cubic inches or less.

NO.	DRIVER	CAR	ENGINE*	CYL.	BORE	STROKE	PISTON DISPL.	TIME	MPH	WINNINGS†
2	Al Unser	Johnny Lightning "500" Special	Ford	8	3.650	1.902	159	3:12:37.04	155.749	$271,697
66	Mark Donohue	Sunoco Special	Ford	8	3.650	1.902	159	3:13:09.23	155.317	86,427
48	Dan Gurney	Olsonite Special	Offenhauser	4	4.030	3.125	159	3:15:49.25	153.201	58,977
83	Donnie Allison	Greer-Foyt Special	Ford	8	3.650	1.902	159	3:16:21.86	152.777	36,002
14	Jim McElreath	Greer-Foyt Special	Ford	8	3.650	1.902	159	3:17:07.95	152.182	32,577
1	Mario Andretti	STP Oil Treatment Special	Ford	8	3.650	1.902	159	Flagged	199 laps	28,202
89	Jerry Grant	Nelson Iron Works Special	Offenhauser	4	4.030	3.125	159	Flagged	198 laps	26,977
38	Rick Muther	The Tony Express	Offenhauser	4	4.030	3.125	159	Flagged	197 laps	25,302
75	Carl Williams	McLaren	Offenhauser	4	4.030	3.125	159	Flagged	197 laps	22,352
7	A. J. Foyt	Sheraton Thompson Special	Ford	8	3.650	1.902	159	Out	195 laps	24,902

* All cars rear-engine and turbocharged. † Total prizes for winning entries. Total awards in race, $1,000,002: Speedway prizes, $754,407; accessory prizes, $205,595; lap prizes, $40,000.

Opposite page: Art Pollard steps away from his blazing Pollard's Car Wash Special, a Kingfish-Offy, after it blew a piston on the 28th lap and caught fire. Left: Al Unser. Below: Unser in his winning P. J. Colt-Ford; the P. J. stood for Parnelli Jones, the car's co-owner, who organized the team. The chief mechanic was George Bignotti.

Al Unser:
A show of force

Characterizing it as a "comfortable" ride, Al Unser recalled his first "500" win: *I was careful to keep the car between the walls. The only trouble was on that 172d lap, when the yellow came on. I got off the throttle right away. As I entered the third turn, I saw a big mess on the track. There was fuel oil spilled, and I hit the brakes and slid a little sideways.... The second lap after the green light came on, I passed Foyt and Donohue. I had to prove I could pass 'em whenever I wanted to. Once I showed that, I let 'em get back around.*

Mike Mosley's helmet can be seen in his No. 4 as flames sheet around him after his car crashed. In the rear is Bobby Unser in his burning car. Unser hit the wall after dodging Mosley. Unser was not hurt, but Mosley had a broken leg and severe burns.

1971

A Lurch of the Heart—and Four Near Miracles

Steve Krisiloff's McNamara-Ford elbowed out of the No. 3 turn and sped down the short north chute, a glimmer of blue and yellow in the sunlight. Its drone was suddenly punctuated by the bursts of a machine gun gone wild. The Ford engine had blown. Oil cascaded onto the track. Into the goo slid Mel Kenyon in his Kuzma-Kenyon-Ford. His car spun and crashed into the wall. Kenyon began to wiggle his way out of the harness that held him in the cockpit. "Out of the corner of my eye," he said later, "I saw the other car coming. I dived right back into the cockpit."

That other car, driven by Gordon Johncock, slid across the oil and slammed into Kenyon's wreck. Then it vaulted over Kenyon. "Johncock's car went right over my head," Kenyon said later. "And I have the wheel marks on my helmet to prove it."

Johncock's car came down and bellied into Mario Andretti's. Fragments of four cars were scattered over the track, but the four drivers walked away. It was the second of four near miracles on this 60th anniversary of the first "500."

Now in the lead as the cars swirled into the 13th lap growled Mark Donohue's McLaren-Offy. This car was one of three McLaren M-16s that had set Indianapolis agog the past 29 days. Donohue had flashed through one practice lap at 181 miles an hour, faster than any previous lap ever run in the old brickyard. He won the No. 2 slot in the first row. In another McLaren, Peter Revson won the pole with a record run over the 4 laps of 178 miles an hour, 7 miles an hour faster than the old record, set by Joe Leonard in Andy Granatelli's turbocar in 1968. In the third McLaren, Australia's Denis Hulme took the No. 4 spot, the inside in the second row.

These McLaren M-16s—designed by Britain's Bruce McLaren, who had died a few months earlier in a crash—sprouted two small spoiler wings in front and a large wing in the rear. In effect, they were upside-down airplane wings: Instead of lifting a car up, they pushed it down. "If you can keep all four wheels on the road all the time," said Donohue, "particularly when you are going through banked corners, you obviously go much faster than a car that has a wheel up in the air part of the time."

In the midst of the new McLaren M-16s was Al Unser, in the No. 3 spot on the first row, driving a brand-new Johnny Lightning "500" Special, a twin of last year's winning Colt-Ford. "Our only hope of winning," he said, "is to put pressure on those new M-16s and hope they won't hold up."

On a sunny, cloudless day the crowd, estimated at 260,000, saw the pace car swerve out of control as it pulled off the track at the start of the race and wallop into a photographers' stand. Twenty people were carted to hospitals, some with broken limbs, but no one was killed—No. 1 of the day's four near miracles.

Minutes later came near miracle No. 2, when Kenyon ducked under Johncock's wheel as four cars skidded and crashed in a pond of oil, again without a fatality. Over the next 50 laps Donohue's McLaren M-16 pulled away from Al Unser's Johnny Lightning to lead by 30 seconds. On the 66th lap Donohue went around at 174.961 miles an hour, 6 miles an hour faster than any previous lap run in traffic at the Speedway. On the 67th—as Unser had hoped—the McLaren broke down. Donohue parked it on the infield grass. "When I saw Donohue was out," said Unser, the new leader, "my heart did an extra lurch because I

249

knew everyone else had a chance now."

Near miracle No. 3 happened on the 113th lap, when two cars smashed into each other on the main straightaway. Both drivers walked away, and two dozen cars somehow weaved through the smoking debris scattered over 300 feet of track.

With only 33 laps to go, Al Unser still led, pressed by his brother Bobby and Peter Revson in the only surviving McLaren M-16. Early in the race Revson's McLaren had lagged. "The steering felt heavy," he explained. "I wasn't about to go all out until I knew it would stay together." Now, feeling more confident, Revson closed down on the Unsers. Then came near miracle No. 4. Mike Mosley's car lost a wheel, spun, and slammed down the banked northwest turn into Mark Donohue's parked McLaren. The two cars exploded. Gary Bettenhausen, whose father, Tony, had died here in 1961, stopped his car and helped pull out Mosley, badly burned but alive.

That crash kept the yellow lights on for 20 laps and froze Revson behind Al Unser's Johnny Lightning. At the green Revson took off after Unser, but he ran out of track. Unser (on his 32d birthday) won by 23 seconds to become the fourth driver—Wilbur Shaw, Mauri Rose, and Bill Vukovich were the others—to win back-to-back "500s." And his time was a new record.

A Colt-Ford now had won the last two "500s." "We were lucky," said Al Unser. "We have got to make changes to at least keep up with the McLarens." But next year there would be no keeping up with at least one McLaren.

Al Unser:
"I would have been history"

A winner for the second straight year, Al Unser talked about the race: *We were lucky to win and lucky that no one was killed. I wanted to put the pressure on the McLarens from the beginning. We hoped our reliability factor would hold up and theirs wouldn't—and that's what happened. As for me, the only time I came close to trouble was when David Hobbs and Rick Muther tangled on the backstretch [of the 113th lap]. I came out of the fourth turn and saw them banging around and debris flying. I started to lock up my brakes. Trouble was, I couldn't see any place to go, so I decided to try the low route. I pushed on the throttle and took off for the inside. If one of those cars had come sliding back down across the track, I would have been history.*

1971's TOP TEN

Race open to supercharged four-cycle overhead camshaft engines with a piston displacement of 161.703 cubic inches or less; nonsupercharged four-cycle overhead camshaft engines with a piston displacement of 256.284 cubic inches or less; American stock production block design, single nonoverhead camshaft, removable head, supercharged engines with a piston displacement of 203.4 cubic inches or less; American stock production block design, single nonoverhead camshaft, removable head, nonsupercharged engines with a piston displacement of 320.355 cubic inches or less; special rocker arm, single nonoverhead camshaft, removable head, nonsupercharged engines with a piston displacement of 305.1 cubic inches or less; two-cycle engines other than diesel engines, supercharged or not, with a piston displacement of 170.856 cubic inches or less; diesel engines, two- or four-cycle, supercharged, with a piston displacement of 203.4 cubic inches or less; diesel engines, two- or four-cycle, nonsupercharged, with a piston displacement of 305.1 cubic inches or less; gas turbine engines with a total inlet annulus area of 11.999 square inches or less; and rotating combustion engines, nonsupercharged, with a displacement of 256.284 cubic inches or less.

NO.	DRIVER	CAR	ENGINE*	CYL.	BORE	STROKE	PISTON DISPL.	TIME	MPH	WINNINGS†
1	Al Unser	Johnny Lightning "500" Special	Ford	8	3.760	1.800	158	3:10:11.56	157.735‡	$238,454
86	Peter Revson	McLaren	Offenhauser	4	4.030	3.125	159	3:10:34.44	157.419	103,198
9	A. J. Foyt	ITT-Thompson Special	Ford	8	3.650	1.902	159	3:12:13.37	156.069	64,759
42	Jim Malloy	Olsonite Eagle	Offenhauser	4	4.281	2.750	158	3:14:04.65	154.577	38,669
32	Billy Vukovich	Sugaripe Prune Special	Offenhauser	4	4.281	2.750	158	3:14:05.77	154.563	32,447
84	Donnie Allison	Purolator Special	Ford	8	3.650	1.902	159	Flagged	199 laps	30,093
58	Bud Tingelstad	Sugaripe Prune Special	Offenhauser	4	4.030	3.125	159	Flagged	198 laps	28,206
43	Denny Zimmerman	Fiore Racing Enterprises Special	Offenhauser	4	4.030	3.125	159	Flagged	189 laps	27,658
6	Roger McCluskey	Sprite Special	Offenhauser	8	3.650	1.902	159	Flagged	188 laps	22,980
16	Gary Bettenhausen	Thermo King Special	Offenhauser	4	4.030	3.125	159	Flagged	178 laps	24,419

* All cars rear-engine and turbocharged. † Total prizes for winning entries. Total awards in race, $1,001,604: Speedway prizes, $787,700; accessory prizes, $173,904; lap prizes, $40,000. ‡ New record.

Opposite page: Al Unser and the winning P. J. Colt-Ford. Its owner, Parnelli Jones, said of the new McLarens: "We got caught. It's like when the Lotus-Fords put the roadsters out of business. Now we have to catch up again." Unser's time was three and a half hours faster than Ray Harroun's time of 60 years earlier. Unser made four pit stops, second-place finisher Peter Revson only the mandatory three, but Unser was in the pits 18 fewer seconds, almost his margin of victory. Right: Driver George Follmer encased in helmet and wrapped in flame-resistant mask. Some drivers' helmets held two-way radios for talking to the pit crew during the race. Also new this year: women in Gasoline Alley. After a court order, two female reporters were allowed into the pits and garages.

Top: Mike Mosley, badly burned a year earlier, falls in flames from his car, which lost a wheel and hit a wall. Bottom: While spectators gape, Mike bats out the fire on his legs. He had second-degree burns. Mosley was in the lead when the crash occurred.

1972

A Stall on the Yellow, a Blunder in the Pit

"A couple of years ago, you went flat out down the straightaways and backed off when you hit the corners. But now you can stay on the throttle through some of the corners—two or three. If I were brave enough, I think I could drive flat out all the way."

Speaking was Bobby Unser. A few hours earlier he had toed his Eagle-Offy Olsonite Eagle around the old brickyard at an average of 195.940 miles an hour to win the pole with a speed that shattered Peter Revson's year-old record by a quantum jump of 17 miles an hour. Two other cars also ripped by the 190-mile-an-hour barrier. Revson took the No. 2 spot in his orange Gulf McLaren-Offy with a 192, and Mark Donohue, with a 191, won the outside in a Sunoco McLaren-Offy. All 33 qualifiers screamed by Revson's old record of 178. Cale Yarborough barely got into the race with an average speed of 178.864 that would have won the pole a year earlier.

What had put a hotfoot to this year's cars were wings, grippier tires, and high-boost engines. Every car now flaunted spoiler wings in front and inverted airfoils in the rear, the "low-level aviation" look introduced by the McLaren M-16s a year earlier. The wings' downthrust glued cars to the track through the corners, as did new Goodyear and Firestone "slick" tires, nearly treadless, that bit hard into the turns. And mechanics set bigger turbochargers at high boosts to whip their straining Offys and Fords to as high as 900 horsepower.

A price had been paid for all this speed—in dollars and blood. Drivers had blown more than 40 engines during practice and the trials, each engine costing a minimum of $25,000. In a practice run Jim Malloy's Eagle-Offy snapped out of control and rocketed into the wall on the No. 3 turn. Malloy was lifted out with all four limbs broken. He died a few days later—the first to be killed at the Speedway since 1968 and the 50th to die in the running of 56 "500s."

In the midst of all the frenzy for speed, Mark Donohue made a daring decision. He "detuned" his Offy to trim away 200 horsepower. In 1971 he'd set a race record, running a lap at over 174 miles an hour, but in the next lap his McLaren-Offy had collapsed. He decided to gamble on a "weakened" Offy. "It will be harder to pass anyone on the straights," he said, "but the car won't be working as hard as it was in last year's race."

On a still, hot May 27—the race was held the Saturday before Memorial Day—Bobby Unser whirled off the pole in his Eagle-Offy to jump ahead of three McLaren-Offys, driven by Donohue, Revson, and Gary Bettenhausen. Revson dropped out early with a cracked gearbox, and Unser peeled out of the race after 75 miles with a broken distributor rotor.

In his dark blue Sunoco McLaren, Gary Bettenhausen rammed to the head of the pack. The grandstand crowd let out an explosive roar: Bettenhausen, whose father had died here in 1961, was a sentimental favorite to win. For most of the race he stayed ahead, winning more than $20,000 in lap money. Tugging at his rear were Jerry Grant in an Eagle-Offy and Donohue in the other Sunoco McLaren. Donohue's gamble had paid off: His "weakened" Offy purred smoothly, while faster cars curled out of the race with smoking engines. With only 60 miles to go Bettenhausen led Grant by a straightaway, Donohue by almost a lap. Then the yellow lights flashed on—a hunk of metal had been spotted on the back straight.

Above: The downthrust of their wings gluing their treadless tires to the track, Sam Sessions's Lola-Ford (No. 52) and Joe Leonard's Parnelli-Offy boom by the pits. Right: Leonard walks to his racer, the wires for a two-way radio trailing from his helmet. Opposite page: Mark Donohue and the winning McLaren-Offy. Donohue ran the fastest lap of the race, 187.539 miles an hour, to break by almost 13 miles an hour his 1971 record for the fastest lap run in a "500." Donohue, a Brown University graduate, and owner Roger Penske were called "Indy's slide-rule boys" because of their precision. Donohue was killed in 1975 at the Austrian Grand Prix.

1972's TOP TEN

Race open to supercharged four-cycle overhead camshaft engines with a piston displacement of 161.703 cubic inches or less; nonsupercharged four-cycle overhead camshaft engines with a piston displacement of 274.590 cubic inches or less; stock production block design, single nonoverhead camshaft, removable head, supercharged engines with a piston displacement of 209.3 cubic inches or less; stock production block design, single nonoverhead camshaft, removable head, nonsupercharged engines with a piston displacement of 355.136 cubic inches or less; special rocker arm, single nonoverhead camshaft, removable head, supercharged engines with a piston displacement of 180 cubic inches or less; special rocker arm, single nonoverhead camshaft, removable head, nonsupercharged engines with a piston displacement of 320.355 cubic inches or less; two-cycle engines other than diesel engines, supercharged or not, with a piston displacement of 170.856 cubic inches or less; diesel engines, two- or four-cycle, supercharged, with a piston displacement of 203.4 cubic inches or less; diesel engines, two- or four-cycle, nonsupercharged, with a piston displacement of 305.1 cubic inches or less; gas turbine engines with a total inlet annulus area of 11.999 square inches or less; and rotating combustion engines, nonsupercharged, with a displacement of 256.284 cubic inches or less.

NO.	DRIVER	CAR	ENGINE*	CYL.	BORE	STROKE	PISTON DISPL.	TIME	MPH	WINNINGS†
66	Mark Donohue	Sunoco McLaren	Offenhauser	4	4.281	2.750	159	3:04:05.54	162.962‡	$218,767
4	Al Unser	Viceroy Special	Offenhauser	4	4.281	2.750	159	3:07:16.49	160.192	95,257
1	Joe Leonard	Samsonite Special	Offenhauser	4	4.281	2.750	159	3:08:17.51	159.327	58,797
52	Sam Sessions	Gene White Firestone Special	Ford	8	3.760	1.800	159	3:09:22.88	158.411	39,582
34	Sam Posey	Norris Eagle	Offenhauser	4	4.281	2.750	159	Flagged	198 laps	37,410
5	Lloyd Ruby	Wynn's Special	Ford	8	3.760	1.800	159	Flagged	196 laps	29,506
60	Mike Hiss	STP-Pylon Window Wiper Blade Special	Offenhauser	4	4.281	2.750	159	Flagged	196 laps	30,869
9	Mario Andretti	Viceroy Special	Offenhauser	4	4.281	2.750	159	Out	194 laps	24,821
11	Jimmy Caruthers	Steed U.S. Armed Forces Special	Ford	8	3.760	1.800	159	Flagged	194 laps	23,093
21	Cale Yarborough	Bill Daniels GOP Special	Ford	8	3.760	1.800	159	Flagged	193 laps	22,132

*All cars rear-engine and turbocharged. †Total prizes for winning entries. Total awards in race, $1,011,845: Speedway prizes, $831,000; accessory prizes, $140,845; lap prizes, $40,000. ‡New record.

The cars had to slow—this year to 80 miles an hour. Some drivers, including Bettenhausen, had predicted that engines would stall at that slow a pace. When Bettenhausen saw the green, he stood on the throttle and, sure enough, his engine coughed, bucked, and stalled.

Grant popped into the lead, pursued by Donohue in the surviving Sunoco McLaren. There were only 35 miles to go as Donohue inched closer to Grant, whose Eagle seemed to be straining. Suddenly, the pudgy Grant veered into the pit and gestured frantically at his left front wheel, which was vibrating. The crew hastily changed the wheel as Donohue blew by to lead for the first time in the race. As Grant's wheel was changed, a fuel hose was coupled to his Eagle. The hose ran to a teammate's tank—a blunder that would be costly.

When Grant veered out of the pit he was almost a lap behind Donohue, who had only 13 laps to go. Donohue held on to finish 47 seconds—almost a lap—ahead of Grant. Donohue had led for only 13 laps, but he had run the fastest "500" ever—just a few minutes over three hours. And he had topped Al Unser's record average of 157 miles an hour by almost 6 miles an hour. Unser, winner of the previous two "500s," rolled in third, behind Grant, in his new Parnelli-Offy; but there was a plum to sweeten Al's disappointment at having come so close to being the first driver to win three straight "500s." He was moved up to second in the official standings when Grant was dropped to 12th for having taken on someone else's fuel—a penalty that cost him some $72,000. "It was the fastest race in Indy history and also one of the most confusing," someone wrote. The next year's race would not be as fast, but it would be even more confusing.

Gary Bettenhausen: "I felt like crying"

In his garage a disappointed Gary Bettenhausen talked of the collapse of his McLaren when it had only 30-odd miles to go to win: *My car was just perfect until the yellow flag went out. Then the temperature went up to 200 ... 230 ... 240 ... The motor began popping and banging, and when we got the green flag I lost the motor. I put the car on the grass near the No. 3 turn. I got out and sat awhile. Somebody gave me a beer. I felt like crying. In fact, I did. I guess it's not meant for a Bettenhausen to win here. Yeah, I thought of my father quite a few times during the race when I was going good and then when the motor went. I know how much he wanted to win here.*

WINNER MARK DONOHUE

1973

Fire and Water and Death

At 190 miles an hour the sky-blue Cobre Special hurtled toward the No. 1 turn—"Old Indy's favorite ambush site," in the words of one reporter—where more drivers had been killed than anyplace else on this grey ribbon of track. At the wheel was Art Pollard, a 46-year-old grandfather. As the car swept into the turn, it veered toward the wall as though nudged by an invisible finger. The Cobre hit and exploded into an orange ball of flame. One horrified witness saw Pollard looking back as though searching for what had shoved him. He was pulled from the flaming wreckage, his lungs scorched, and hours later he died.

His death was the second in the new winged cars that had thrust drivers within grasping distance of a new "magic" barrier—200 miles an hour. A year earlier Jim Malloy had died just as mysteriously in a winged Eagle-Offy. Both Pollard's and Malloy's cars had veered sharply out of the groove and nosed for the wall.. The wings, thought some drivers, stirred up turbulence that blew cars out of the groove to their destruction.

But Pollard's death did not slow the racers. Before the more than 200,000 fans watching the first weekend of trials, 35-year-old Johnny Rutherford, Pollard's closest friend in racing, slammed a McLaren-Offy around the oval to come within a few heartbeats of that magic 200—a record 199.071-mile-an-hour run for one lap. He won the pole with a record-breaking 198.413. Next to him was Bobby Unser, the 1968 winner, in an Eagle-Offy; and on the outside sat last year's winner, Mark Donohue, in another Eagle-Offy. Both had qualified at better than 197 miles an hour. The average time for the field was 192—14 miles an hour faster than the record of only two years earlier. "Now everyone," said British driver David Hobbs dryly, "is engaged in the art of low-level aviation."

New stands built since 1971 had added more seats to the Speedway, and a crowd estimated at 325,000 waited as high winds and drenching rains lashed the track on Monday, May 28. The rains ceased, the track dried, and the race started four hours late. As the cars took the green flag and swept by the grandstand, David (Salt) Walther's car jumped to the right, perhaps taking flight in the turbulence created by the traffic. His car hit another, then pinwheeled down the track, spitting flames and pieces of metal into the faces of spectators massed behind the protecting screen. Some drivers managed to swerve around Walther's flaming McLaren—A. J. Foyt shot right under it—but several others crashed. Walther was pulled badly burned from the wreck, and more than a dozen spectators were burned or bashed by debris; there were, however, no deaths.

The red flag stopped the race, and more rain put it off until the next day. But rain streamed down on Tuesday, aborting the start. At 2:10 P.M. on Wednesday, before a crowd of no more than 150,000, Tony Hulman said "Gentlemen, start your engines" for the third time in three days. This time the cars sped off safely. Driving for Andy Granatelli's STP team in an Eagle-Offy, David (Swede) Savage zoomed into the lead, lost it during a pit stop, and came out streaking after new leader Al Unser. As Savage slid into the No.

The race begins in good order (top). But moments later (bottom) flames and debris swirl through the air as Salt Walther's car explodes. Escaping (l. to r.): Jerry Grant (No. 48), Wally Dallenbach (No. 62), and Mel Kenyon (No. 19).

4 turn, a rear wing tore off. The car whirled out of control and crashed nose first into the wall. Tires arched through the flames and smoke, and the car skidded along the white concrete wall. "Holy Christ, what a mess!" Savage shouted over his helmet radio to his pit crew. Other drivers stopped and yanked him out of a flaming, upside-down cockpit. "He was conscious and almost cocky in the ambulance," reported *Sports Illustrated*'s Robert F. Jones, "but both of his legs were badly broken and bent up almost into his groin. His eyes appeared to be glued shut and his hair was singed." Thirty-two days later he was dead.

An STP mechanic, running to Savage's wreck, was hit by a truck and killed instantly. The race was stopped for almost an hour and a half. When it resumed Al Unser still led in his Viceroy Special, but he was being pressed by another of Granatelli's Day-Glo-red STP Eagle-Offys. The driver was 150-pound Gordon (Wee Gordie) Johncock, who had started in the fourth row. He went by Unser at the 180-mile point. "The groove was becoming slicker," a grinning Gordie said later. "Other guys were going high on the turns, but by cutting my car down low I could get by people. Sometimes I had two of my wheels on the grass."

As Unser faded and then dropped out of the race, the 36-year-old Johncock was pressed by Billy Vukovich, son of the Mad Russian, in another Eagle-Offy. They ran together as though wired, but Wee Gordie kept half a lap between them until rain began to patter onto the asphalt. The red flag ended the race at 332.5 miles. It was the shortest race run at the Speedway since 1916 (when a 300-mile race was scheduled) and the first "500" to be abbreviated since 1950. Johncock and Granatelli won $236,000 of another million-dollar purse. This was Granatelli's second "500" win and the sixth for his chief mechanic, George Bignotti. But with a mechanic dead and a driver dying, there were no smiles on the STP team's faces. "I'm happy for Gordie," said Granatelli, "but this has been an ugly day."

The rains pelted the emptying Speedway as drivers, owners, and United States Auto Club officials pondered a question as old as this race: How do we slow down these cars?

Right: Models of racers, built by the Indianapolis 500 Shrine Club, tool around the track before the race. Bottom: The crowd watches Joe Leonard's Parnelli-Offy smoke out of the pits. Smoke also rose in the infield—from barbecues. "It's the world's biggest fried chicken picnic," wrote a reporter. Before the race the crowd applauded two dozen ex-POWs, recently returned from North Vietnam, as they rode around the track in white Cadillacs.

Billy Vukovich: "Something has to be done"

Despite his mother's wish that he never become a race driver, Billy Vukovich had come to the Speedway seeking the prizes won by his father. After finishing second he shouted, *I'm rich! I'm rich, rich, rich!* But later he said: *Something has to be done to make the race safer. We're the drivers and we know we're putting our lives on the line. That's OK. No one's forcing us to drive. But what about the spectators? They should never be in danger. One answer is to reduce the fuel we can carry in our cars so all that alcohol doesn't go up in flames in the faces of people. And if we could use only 200 gallons in a race instead of 350, we'd have to get about two and a half miles a gallon, which would slow us up.*

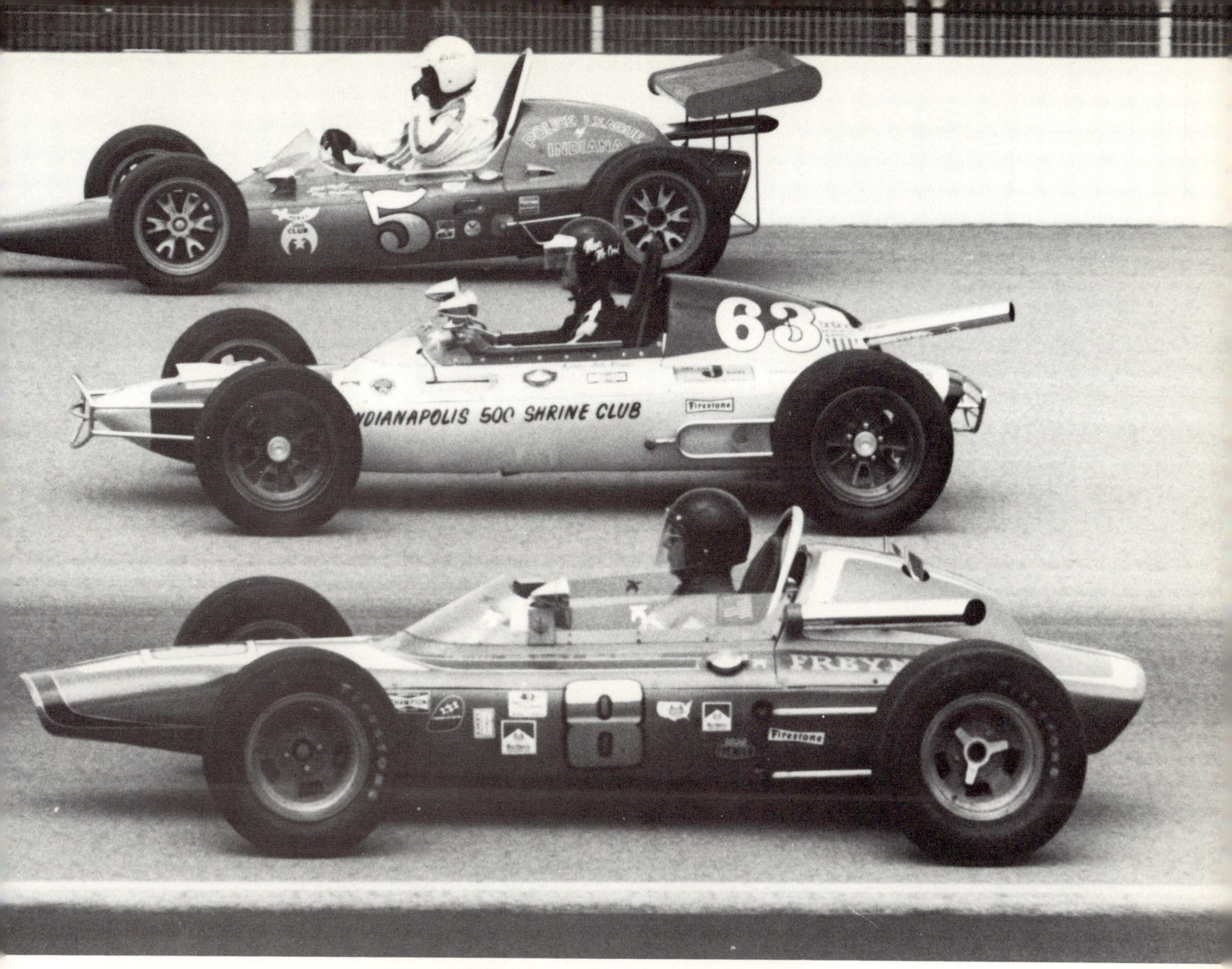
POLICE LEAGUE of INDIANA
5
63
INDIANAPOLIS 500 SHRINE CLUB
Firestone

STP

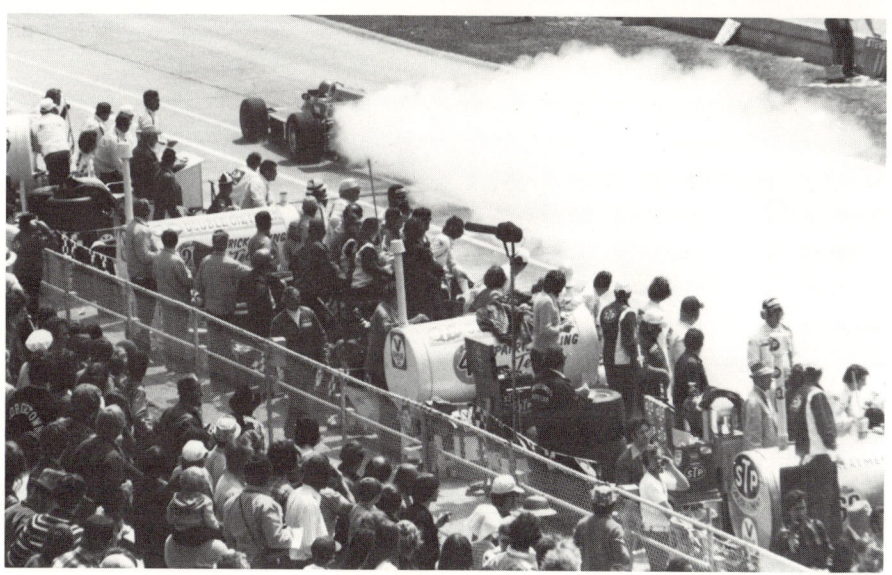

Below: His Eagle-Offy in flames and crumpling around him, Swede Savage hits the track with his hands down, helmeted head bent. He is wearing a uniform that automatically drenched itself with foam at high temperatures; it probably prevented an instant death by fire. Opposite page: Wee Gordie Johncock and the winning Eagle-Offy, its front bearing the unmistakable Granatelli stamp. This was the third "500" postponed by rain, the others in 1915 and 1967. Knowing at the start that the race would be official after 101 laps if rain stopped the race, drivers sprinted for the lead, making more likely a fiery smashup.

1973's TOP TEN

Race open to supercharged four-cycle overhead camshaft engines with a piston displacement of 161.703 cubic inches or less; nonsupercharged four-cycle overhead camshaft engines with a piston displacement of 274.590 cubic inches or less; stock production block design, single nonoverhead camshaft, removable head, supercharged engines with a piston displacement of 209.3 cubic inches or less; stock production block design, single nonoverhead camshaft, removable head, nonsupercharged engines with a piston displacement of 355.136 cubic inches or less; special rocker arm, single nonoverhead camshaft, removable head, supercharged engines with a piston displacement of 180 cubic inches or less; special rocker arm, single nonoverhead camshaft, removable head, non-supercharged engines with a piston displacement of 320.355 cubic inches or less; two-cycle engines other than diesel engines, supercharged or not, with a piston displacement of 170.856 cubic inches or less; diesel engines, two- or four-cycle, supercharged, with a piston displacement of 203.4 cubic inches or less; diesel engines, two- or four-cycle, nonsupercharged, with a piston displacement of 305.1 cubic inches or less; gas turbine engines with a total inlet annulus area of 11.999 square inches or less; and rotating combustion engines, nonsupercharged, with a displacement of 256.284 cubic inches or less.

NO.	DRIVER	CAR	ENGINE*	CYL.	BORE	STROKE	PISTON DISPL.	TIME†	MPH	WINNINGS‡
20	Gordon Johncock	STP Double Oil Filters	Offenhauser	4	4.375	2.600	157	2:05:26.59 (133)	159.036	$236,022
2	Billy Vukovich	Sugaripe Prune Special	Offenhauser	4	4.281	2.750	159	2:06:51.50 (133)	157.262	97,512
3	Roger McCluskey	Lindsey Hopkins Buick Co. Special	Offenhauser	4	4.281	2.750	159	2:05:58.28 (131)	155.988	60,752
19	Mel Kenyon	Atlanta Falcons Special	Ford	8	3.760	1.800	159	2:07:01.13 (131)	154.701	34,487
5	Gary Bettenhausen	Sunoco-DX McLaren	Offenhauser	4	4.281	2,750	159	2:05:51.65 (130)	154.933	37,965
24	Steve Krisiloff	Elliot's Norton Special	Offenhauser	4	4.281	2.750	159	2:06:52.39 (129)	152.515	30,861
16	Lee Kunzman	Ayr-Way/Lloyd's Special	Offenhauser	4	4.281	2.750	159	2:05:40.88 (127)	151.574	26,349
89	John Martin	Unsponsored Special	Offenhauser	4	4.281	2.750	159	2:07:04.21 (124)	146.376	25,376
7	Johnny Rutherford	Gulf McLaren	Offenhauser	4	4.281	2.750	159	2:07:23.49 (124)	146.007	29,903
98	Mike Mosley	Lodestar Special	Offenhauser	4	4.281	2.750	159	1:51:37.74 (120§)	161.248	23,675

*All cars rear-engine and turbocharged. † Race stopped at 332.5 miles due to rain; figures in parentheses show number of laps run. ‡ Total prizes for winning entries. Total awards in race, $1,006,105: Speedway prizes, $829,200; accessory prizes, $136,905; lap prizes, $40,000. § Not running at finish.

A group of fans let it be known who is their favorite. The fastest lap of the race was spun off by Wally Dallenbach on the 2d lap—191.408 miles an hour, the fastest ever in a "500," some 23 miles an hour above the fastest lap of only six years earlier.

1974

Classic and "Sanitary"

Stretched inside the orange McLaren-Offy as the 33 cars swept around the pace lap, 36-year-old Johnny Rutherford reminded himself of what he had repeated perhaps a dozen times this morning: "Take it easy on the start and don't try to pass 24 cars on the first lap." He was stuck way back in 25th place, in the ninth row. Only three drivers had started farther back in previous "500s" and won. But Gentleman Johnny, as the other drivers called him, thought he had the fastest car in the race. He'd qualified at 190.446 miles an hour; only A. J. Foyt's Coyote-Foyt had been faster. But Johnny hadn't qualified on the first day. So here he was back in the ruck, and there was Supertex, as the drivers called the crusty Foyt, riding the pole in the first row and taking dead aim at the fourth "500" victory he hungered for so badly.

Speedway officials fervently hoped this race would be free of the burning, bloody carnage of last year. New rules had been drawn up by the United States Auto Club to make the race safer. Cars could consume only 280 gallons of alcohol, down from 350. To get more miles per gallon, mechanics had to drop boost pressures in their turbochargers, which meant slower speeds. Cars could carry only 40-gallon tanks, down from 75, which made them less incendiary. Rear wing-spreads had been clipped from 64 to 43 inches; the cars didn't "glue" as tightly to the track and thus had to slow on the turns. The average for the 33 qualifiers dropped from 1973's record 192 miles an hour to 182.

For the 39-year-old, taciturn Foyt, this was his 17th "500"—a record. His orange Coyote was powered by a Ford V-8 he had modified. (Ford had decided to leave racing in the early seventies for economic reasons.) Nearly all the other cars in the race carried the same 159-cubic-inch Offy. After Foyt won the pole, he became the heavy favorite to win the race. In the 57 previous "500s," 38 of the winners had come from the first three rows—23 from the first row, ten from the second, and five from the third. But only eight drivers had come off the pole to win, the most recent Al Unser in 1970.

On a cool, partly cloudy morning, promptly at 11 o'clock, starter Pat Vidan waved the green flag from a new control stand. The crowd let out a relieved roar as the field swept safely through the No. 1 turn. Another heavy roar—this one of surprise—rose from the southwest stands. Spectators saw Johnny Rutherford's McLaren streak by nine cars in the first three-fifths of a mile, as he forgot his promise to go easy at the start. He swept from 16th to third in the first 30 miles while, up ahead, Foyt had bolted by Wally Dallenbach to jump into first. At 50 miles Rutherford swooped inside Bobby Unser to grab second. He pushed toward Foyt and soon was only a split second behind and drafting in Supertex's wake. Both cars pitted at the 120-mile point. Quick pit work would be critical in this race with so many stops needed to refuel the smaller tanks; at least six would be necessary compared to a mandatory four in recent years. Both Rutherford and Foyt got out quickly, and Rutherford still churned at Foyt's tail when both went in again at 185 miles. Rutherford stormed out in 14 seconds, but Foyt's crew got their signals mixed and he came out 54 seconds later a straightaway behind Rutherford. Gentleman Johnny pulled away to lead by almost half a lap.

As Rutherford began the last 150 miles, a car

hit a wall—the only crack-up so far—and the yellow lights went on. The field went 5 laps at a cautionary 80 miles an hour. When the green flashed A. J. pulled even with Rutherford on the straightaway and blasted off the second turn into the lead. With only 130 miles to go, the crowd roared for Supertex to win that fourth "500."

The roaring died as the crowd saw smoke billow from the Texan's Coyote. A scavenger pump had failed and clots of oil spurted out of Foyt's turbocharger. He was black-flagged, came in briefly, tried one more lap, then veered off the track and drove straight into Gasoline Alley without a word to anyone. "The disappointment," wrote a reporter, "he kept to himself."

With his fastest pursuer gone, Rutherford cut his boost from 78 inches of mercury to 72. Bobby Unser moved his Eagle-Offy to within half a lap of Rutherford. Rutherford raised his boost and moved away to finish 22 seconds ahead of Unser. Running fourth, hard-luck Lloyd Ruby ran out of fuel only 13 laps from home and was placed ninth. Only Rutherford and Unser went the full 200 laps. In recent "500s" cars had fought for the runner-up spots for five minutes after the winner took the checker; then all were flagged and placed according to their time and number of laps run. But there was a disturbance by fans at one corner of the track—there had been some nude "streaking" earlier—and the cars were flagged after Unser took second.

Despite that ragged finish, the race had been a classic one—Rutherford coming through the field to win. Not since 1936, when Louis Meyer fought his way up from the 28th spot, had a winner come from so far back. Although new rules had been imposed to slow the race, Rutherford's average speed was second only to Mark Donohue's record, set in 1972. And it had been what was called a "sanitary" race, the worst injury a cut ankle. "I hope," Rutherford said, "this race eases some people's minds, that we're not a bunch of idiots trying to rub out a lot of people." "We needed a race like this," a relieved Speedway official told newspaperman Ray Marquette. "My God, how we needed one like this."

Opposite page: In the pace car, an Olds, beauty queens wave to the crowd. In the race Dick Simon (No. 44) in an Eagle-Foyt, Gary Bettenhausen (No. 8) in a McLaren-Offy, and Jimmy Caruthers (No. 21) in an Eagle-Offy run wing-tip to wing-tip through the first lap. By the 2d lap Simon and Bettenhausen had dropped out with engine trouble. Right: From a new control stand, about where the old suspension bridge once stood, an official gives the checker to the winner. The Speedway's new chief steward, Tom Binford, was credited with enforcing a safe race.

1974's TOP TEN

Race open to supercharged four-cycle overhead camshaft engines with a piston displacement of 161.703 cubic inches or less; nonsupercharged four-cycle overhead camshaft engines with a piston displacement of 274.590 cubic inches or less; stock production block design, single nonoverhead camshaft, removable head, supercharged engines with a piston displacement of 209.3 cubic inches or less; stock production block design, single nonoverhead camshaft, removable head, nonsupercharged engines with a piston displacement of 355.136 cubic inches or less; special rocker arm, single nonoverhead camshaft, removable head, supercharged engines with a piston displacement of 180 cubic inches or less; special rocker arm, single nonoverhead camshaft, removable head, nonsupercharged engines with a piston displacement of 320.355 cubic inches or less; two-cycle engines other than diesel engines, supercharged or not, with a piston displacement of 170.856 cubic inches or less; diesel engines, two- or four-cycle, supercharged, with a piston displacement of 203.4 cubic inches or less; diesel engines, two- or four-cycle, nonsupercharged, with a piston displacement of 305.1 cubic inches or less; gas turbine engines with a total inlet annulus area of 11.999 square inches or less; and rotating combustion engines, nonsupercharged, with a displacement of 256.284 cubic inches or less.

NO.	DRIVER	CAR	ENGINE*	CYL.	BORE	STROKE	PISTON DISPL.	TIME	MPH	WINNINGS†
3	Johnny Rutherford	McLaren	Offenhauser	4	4.281	2.750	159	3:09:10.06	158.589	$245,031
48	Bobby Unser	Olsonite Eagle	Offenhauser	4	4.375	2.600	159	3:09:32.38	158.278	99,503
4	Billy Vukovich	Sugaripe Prune Special	Offenhauser	4	4.281	2.750	159	Flagged	199 laps	63,811
20	Gordon Johncock	STP Double Oil Filter	Offenhauser	4	4.375	2.600	159	Flagged	198 laps	37,078
73	David Hobbs	Carling Black Label McLaren	Offenhauser	4	4.281	2.750	159	Flagged	196 laps	32,074
45	Jim McElreath	Thermo King Special	Offenhauser	4	4.281	2.750	159	Flagged	194 laps	27,970
11	Duane Carter, Jr.	Cobre Firestone	Offenhauser	4	4.281	2.750	159	Flagged	191 laps	27,758
79	Bob Harkey	Peru Circus Special	Ford	8	3.761	1.800	160	Flagged	189 laps	23,985
9	Lloyd Ruby	Unlimited Racing	Offenhauser	4	4.281	2.750	159	Out	187 laps	23,182
55	Jerry Grant	Cobre Firestone	Offenhauser	4	4.281	2.750	159	Flagged	175 laps	22,016

*All cars rear-engine and turbocharged. † Total prizes for winning entries. Total awards in race, $1,015,686: Speedway prizes, $817,500; accessory prizes, $158,186; lap prizes, $40,000.

Johnny Rutherford: "A little more incentive"

A winner at last, after 11 runs in the "500," Rutherford spoke of his battle with A. J. Foyt: *Any time A. J. is around, you've got a race on your hands. I could catch A. J. at will, but I couldn't pass. I was faster in the corners, but A. J. was faster on the straights, and unfortunately you have to pass on the straights. Had he stayed in, I don't know if I could have beaten him. It would have been a tooth-and-nail thing. . . . I always said if I ever finished this race, I'd win or be in the top three. And today I finished and won. I think being so far in the back was a little more incentive for me. I need to work under adversity sometimes.*

Johnny Rutherford enjoys the perks of a winner. Opposite page: He is kissed by his wife, Betty, in Victory Circle. Then he drinks from the traditional quart of milk. At left he poses with the Borg-Warner Trophy at the victory dinner the following night. With him are Betty and their children, Angela and John IV. Below: He waves from the winning McLaren-Offy. His arms had been broken and badly burned in racing accidents. "When you're hurt so badly and you see so many killed," he said with his Texan's drawl after the race, "there is some thought of quitting... But I said to myself, 'What the hell else would I do?'"

1975

At the Finish, a Regatta

Two out of every three drivers said the same thing in an informal poll before the race: If A. J. Foyt went the distance, he would win.

For the second year in a row, Foyt, or Supertex, as the other drivers called him with awe in their voices, had won the pole. He thrilled more than 200,000 fans at the first day of qualifying when he blew his Coyote-Foyt around one lap at over 195 miles an hour, a bright red blur that whirled out of the turns and shot sickeningly close to the walls. "I thrilled the hell out of myself a couple of times out there," he said. Murmured Bobby Unser: "There is no way anyone can beat him."

For the first time in "500" history, three former winners started in the front row: Foyt, Gordon Johncock in the middle, Bobby Unser on the outside. The year-old safety rules—smaller wings, less fuel—had kept a lid on speeds. Foyt qualified at 193, well below the record of 198.

Sixteen of the 33 cars were Dan Gurney-produced Eagles and seven were McLarens from Britain; of the rest, the most notable were Foyt's Coyote and two Wildcats built by George Bignotti, the master-mechanic winner of six "500s." Twenty-seven of the cars carried the same $25,000, four-cylinder, turbocharged Offy that generated about 1,000 horsepower. The four-banging Offy's main challenger was A. J. Foyt's modified Ford V-8.

So far Supertex had won $743,698 at the Speedway, only $6,000 behind all-time winner Al Unser (Bobby Unser was third with $481,-019). Foyt was only 71 laps away from passing Cliff Bergere's all-time record of 6,142 miles of Speedway driving. And he needed to run first for only 68 more laps to go over Parnelli Jones's record of $75,050 in total lap prizes.

On a steamy, cloudy May 25, a Sunday, some 300,000 spectators watched the pace lap with high hopes of seeing Supertex become the first driver to win four "500s." For the second year in a row, the grandstand crowd let out a roar as the field swung safely through the first turn. Gordon Johncock swooped high over Foyt to take the lead, with Bobby Unser beating at their heels. At 25 miles Supertex drew another happy roar from the packed stands as his red dart blasted by Johncock on the main straight. But weaving through the pack came Wally Dallenbach in a Wildcat-Drake that swallowed up Supertex's lead. At 150 miles Dallenbach arrowed by Foyt, and over the next 240 miles Dallenbach pulled away to lead by as much as a mile.

Back in fifth place hung young Tom Sneva, a former junior high principal, in a McLaren-Offy, and he was about to infect the cockpits of the two leaders with his bad luck. A little after the race's midway point, Sneva's car drifted into the wheel of a car behind him. Like a cheerleader, Sneva's Norton Spirit cartwheeled down the track. It crunched, burning, against a wall. Sneva was pulled out, alive but badly burned. Other cars swerved around the smoking debris. Foyt's tires picked up a hunk of metal and he had to pit. He came out well behind Dallenbach, Johnny Rutherford, and Bobby Unser. But Dallenbach's bright red Wildcat had gulped debris in dodging onto the grass to go around Sneva's wreck. With about 100 miles to go and ahead by 20 seconds, Dallenbach's Wildcat let out an anguished screech on the main straight and hiccuped to a stop on the first turn; a piston was burned, the car was done.

Rutherford sped by, then pitted for fuel. Bobby Unser, tank freshly topped, zoomed by to lead. During the last hour the sky above the Speedway

In their cockpits, roll bars behind them and rearviews on both sides, four drivers prepare to attempt to qualify for the 59th "500." Top: Al Unser (l.) and Mike Hiss. Bottom: A. J. Foyt (l.) and Dick Simon.

Left: Coming out of turn No. 2, Mike Hiss (No. 94) spins and ends up against the wall. The car did not explode into flames and Hiss climbs out unhurt. New gas tanks held the fuel in "cells," making the cars less incendiary. Right: Flames roar from the rear of Tom Sneva's Norton Spirit McLaren, a Roger Penske car, after its rear wheel "tripped" at 170 miles an hour over another car's front wheel. Sneva's car somersaulted down the track, a fiery whirl as it came apart on the asphalt and against the wall, rear wheels (r.), engine, and wings (l.) flying away. "I thought," Sneva said later, badly burned, "that I was upside down in a racing car. I thought it was a dream—but it really was happening." A short while later he won the Michigan 150.

had darkened from a dusty grey to a menacing black. Umbrellas flowered on the infield. Out on the track Gary Bettenhausen's car lost a wheel on the main straight and bounced along the wall in front of the crowd on three wheels. Parts of his Eagle-Offy scattered across the track. The yellow lights came on, locking Rutherford into second place at 80 miles an hour, behind Bobby Unser's blue Jorgensen Eagle.

The yellow lights still flared in the darkness as rain suddenly deluged the track. Within seconds the main straight was sloshy with water. Starter

Pat Vidan pulled in his yellow flag and waved the red flag and the checker, ending the race at 435 miles. In one of the weirdest finishes in "500" history, cars skimmed wildly on the water-carpeted track like out-of-control boats, bumping each other, but at speeds so slow no one was hurt.

Through the darkness and downpour, squinting for the finish line, Bobby Unser slid his Jorgensen Eagle by the checker ("Is that it?" his voice crackled incredulously over his two-way radio to Dan Gurney in the pits as he cruised down the darkened backstretch on a precautionary lap).

Behind him floated Johnny Rutherford and Foyt. Supertex had led for 53 laps but once more had failed to win that cherished fourth "500." In winning his second "500"—and the fourth for the Unser brothers—Bobby Unser had run at an average of 149 miles an hour, well below the record of 162. In this second "500" in three years to be shortened by rain, he had won a quarter of a million dollars from a purse that topped the million-dollar mark for the sixth straight year. Ahead was a seventh straight million-dollar race —and a driver named Janet.

This drawing, courtesy of the Goodyear Motor Sports Club, shows what happens during a pit stop at the "500." Pit man No. 1 is rushing with an air wrench to pull off the right front wheel and put on the wheel at his left. No. 2 is jacking up the right side for the wheel changes. No. 3 grips an air wrench to pull off the right rear wheel. No. 4 is inserting a quick-release fuel hose from a gravity-fed refueling rig to fill the cells in the fuel tank. The No. 5 man is plugging in another hose to catch the overflow when the cells are filled. No. 6, not allowed in the pit, pushes a drink to the driver at the end of a pole. No. 7 is a United States Auto Club fire marshal poised with a fire extinguisher. The pit crew can change those two outside tires and top off the tank with fuel in the time it takes you to read this caption.

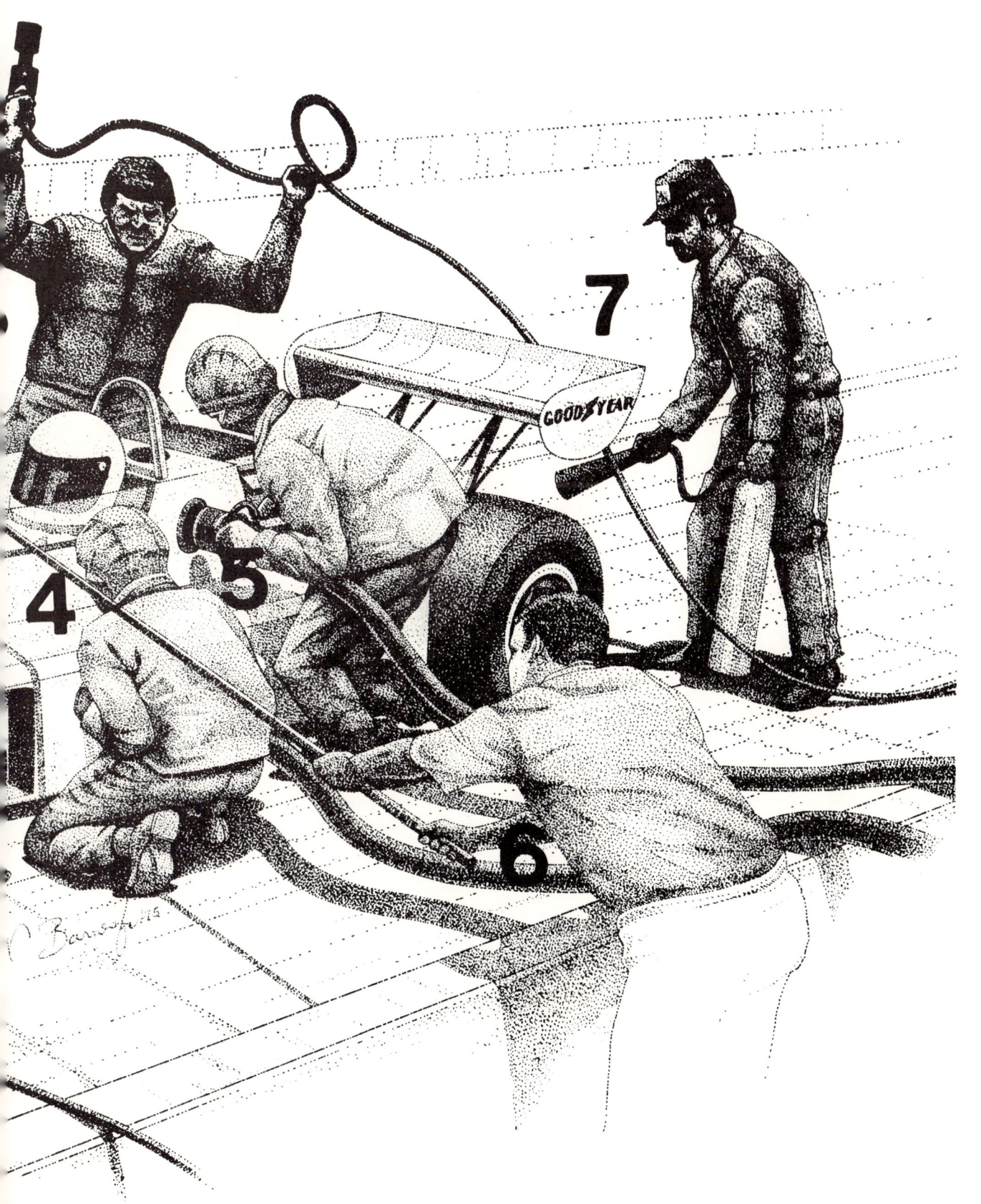

Bobby Unser:
Wrong ones and a right one

Of the crash of Tom Sneva's car, Bobby Unser recalled: *It was a bad wreck—the worst one that I've ever seen at Indianapolis. As I went by I couldn't tell the engine from the chassis. There was stuff lying all over the track and it could have finished the race right there for me. I made the decision—real quick—to go down low to avoid the debris, and it happened to be the right decision. This time. God knows, in my time I've made wrong ones.*

Left: The Almost Made It award is held by Al Loquasto, with a "500" princess at the awards ceremony. Al was next in line to attempt qualification when 6:00 P.M. rolled around, closing the trials. Above: Bobby Unser waves to the crowd, the "500" queen and Borg-Warner Trophy behind him. Opposite page: Bobby and the winning Eagle-Offy. Of second-place Johnny Rutherford, Bobby said: "I outran Johnny earlier in the race when I was running with less boost and less power. My car was faster, and there was just no doubt about it." The date of the race, May 25, the Sunday before Memorial Day, was the earliest ever for a "500."

THE WINNER
BOBBY UNSER

1975's TOP TEN

Race open to supercharged four-cycle overhead camshaft engines with a piston displacement of 161.703 cubic inches or less; nonsupercharged four-cycle overhead camshaft engines with a piston displacement of 274.590 cubic inches or less; stock production block design, single nonoverhead camshaft, removable head, supercharged engines with a piston displacement of 209.3 cubic inches or less; stock production block design, single nonoverhead camshaft, removable head, nonsupercharged engines with a piston displacement of 355.136 cubic inches or less; special rocker arm, single nonoverhead camshaft, removable head, supercharged engines with a piston displacement of 180 cubic inches or less; special rocker arm, single nonoverhead camshaft, removable head, nonsupercharged engines with a piston displacement of 320.355 cubic inches or less; two-cycle engines other than diesel engines, supercharged or not, with a piston displacement of 170.856 cubic inches or less; diesel engines, two- or four-cycle, supercharged, with a piston displacement of 203.4 cubic inches or less; diesel engines, two- or four-cycle, nonsupercharged, with a piston displacement of 305.1 cubic inches or less; gas turbine engines with a total inlet annulus area of 11.999 square inches or less; and rotating combustion engines, nonsupercharged, with a displacement of 256.284 cubic inches or less.

NO.	DRIVER	CAR	ENGINE*	CYL.	BORE	STROKE	PISTON DISPL.	TIME†	MPH	WINNINGS‡
48	Bobby Unser	Jorgensen Eagle	Offenhauser	4	4.375	2.650	159	2:54:55.08 (174)	149.213	$214,031
2	Johnny Rutherford	Gatorade McLaren	Offenhauser	4	4.281	2.750	159	2:55:59.08 (174)	148.308	97,886
14	A. J. Foyt	Gilmore Racing Team	Ford	8	3.760	1.800	161	2:56:43.70 (174)	147.684	74,676
11	Duane Carter, Jr.	Cobre Tire	Offenhauser	4	4.281	2.750	159	2:56:08.55 (169)	143.918	33,424
15	Roger McCluskey	Silver Floss Sauerkraut Special	Offenhauser	4	4.281	2.750	159	2:55:01.75 (167)	143.119	31,002
6	Billy Vukovich	Cobre Tire	Offenhauser	4	4.281	2.750	159	2:55:00.75 (166)	142.276	28,473
83	Bill Puterbaugh	McNamara D.I.A. Special	Offenhauser	4	4.375	2.600	159	2:55:58.29 (165)	140.648	28,786
97	George Snider	Leader Card Lodestar	Offenhauser	4	4.281	2.750	159	2:56:00.94 (165)	140.612	24,688
40	Wally Dallenbach	Sinmast Wildcat	Drake	4	4.281	2.750	159	2:42:04.54 (162§)	149.930	42,711
33	Bob Harkey	Dayton-Walther Special	Offenhauser	4	4.281	2.750	159	2:56:09.47 (162)	137.944	22,899

* All cars rear-engine and turbocharged. † Race stopped at 435 miles due to rain; figures in parentheses show number of laps run. ‡ Total prizes for winning entries. Total awards in race, $1,001,321: Speedway prizes, $839,500; accessory prizes, $121,821; lap prizes, $40,000. § Not running at finish.

1976

Of Lady Janet and Gentleman Johnny

Exactly at 5:00 A.M. the bomb exploded with the same dull boom that had echoed over these flat Indiana plains back in 1911—the signal to open the Speedway gates. Camped at the walls of the Speedway was a snoozing, beery army. The night before, it had flowed over the suburban greenness, propelled on wheels, dressed mostly in blue denim, and trailing beer cans. For most of the night booted young men and barefoot young women had strummed, sung, smoked, danced, drunk—most of all they drank—while occasionally brawling (the police made more than 100 arrests). Now, as the sun peered like a bloodshot eye over the horizon, they crept out of vans, tents, and sleeping bags and swayed unsteadily toward the double-decked grandstands that were etched against the sun's slanting rays. By 11:00 A.M., the starting time for this 60th running of the "500," a crowd said by one Speedway official to be "more than 350,000," the largest up to now, had settled into the 234,000 seats (paying $10 to $50 a ticket) or had sprawled out over the infield to witness what would turn out to be the shortest of all the "500s."

This "500" had danced through May dangling a provocative question: Would a woman grip the wheel of one of the racers for another "first" for women entering traditional domains of men? This year two women were in United States Auto Club (USAC) cockpits. One was black-flagged at a Phoenix race for being too slow, but the other—Janet Guthrie, a 38-year-old New York City physicist and sports-car driver—finished 15th in the Trenton 200, then came to Indianapolis to take the driving test for "500" rookies. She passed, "scaring the hell" out of the car's owner by buzzing close to the walls with a daring reminiscent of A. J. Foyt himself. But her car was balky during the trials and did not reach qualifying speeds. Then A. J. loaned her a Coyote-Foyt, and she sent it humming around a practice lap at nearly 181 miles an hour. Few observers doubted that Guthrie would have been able to qualify the car for the "500." But Foyt said his team had never planned to run two cars in the race and pointed out the lack of a fully prepared pit crew to service the second car. Guthrie, though disappointed, thanked Foyt, who said, "All I intended to do was to prove, in my own mind, what she can do. And she did prove that ladies can drive race cars."

For this year's race USAC had mandated "popoff valves" that kept boost pressures of turbochargers at 75 inches, down from 80. Most drivers agreed with Johnny Rutherford, the 1974 winner, who said, "The new rules will make for closer, more exciting dicing. Passing is going to be more of a problem because of all the cars being so equal. No one can dial in some extra boost to get around another guy."

Speeds of the qualifying field were markedly slower because of the drop in boost pressure. Rutherford—Gentleman Johnny and Mr. Nice Guy to the other drivers—won the pole in his McLaren-Offy with a 188.957 clocking. Next to him was Gordon Johncock, the 1973 winner, in one of George Bignotti's new cars, a Wildcat-Drake. On the outside was Tom Sneva, the fortunate survivor of that spectacular crash a year earlier, in a McLaren-Offy. In the second row, in his Coyote-Foyt, sat Supertex, A. J. Foyt, poised for his 19th "500," more than any other driver ever, and the leader now in "500" miles with 6,402.5. But what he didn't have was that

Janet Guthrie (right) looks like any other race driver (below) inside the cockpit as she confers with owner Rolla Vollstedt. "Like 99 out of 100 rookies," said driver Dick Simon, "she was shying away from the walls during her rookie tests. Janet was furious with herself. She borrowed a rented car and stuck a four-inch welding rod out the right-hand door and went around the track until she wore down that rod and scraped the door besides."

fourth "500" checker he'd sought since 1968.

At 11:00 A.M. the 75-year-old Tony Hulman told the gentlemen to start their engines. Fluffy, dirty clouds had obscured the sun, and the weather bureau switched its forecast from a 30 percent chance of rain to a 60 percent chance.

Rutherford, on the pole, was a 4–1 Las Vegas favorite, even though only eight previous winners had come from the pole, the last in 1970. Rutherford beat the pack to the first corner in his Hy-Gain McLaren and he led for the first 3 laps. Then, as the grandstand crowd roared, there was Supertex booming by Sneva and Johncock to close on Gentleman Johnny. On the backstretch Foyt bellowed by Rutherford and took the lead as he whipped into turn No. 3. But the Coyote hit a water slick and slid toward the wall. "I just knew A. J. was going to hit it," Rutherford said later. "But he got it straightened out. I repassed him and gave him a wave as I went by."

Foyt, without a wave, went by Rutherford to recapture the lead and he led until lap 13, when he pitted. Near the 50-mile point the leaders—Rutherford, Foyt, Johncock, Sneva, Wally Dallenbach, and Duane (Pancho) Carter, Jr.—thundered in a compact herd down the main straightaway. They rushed by slower cars as the grandstand crowd stood and screamed. On the infield beer-soaked sleepers awoke and squinted groggily to see what the shouting was all about.

"We had some great racing out there," Rutherford said later. "With everyone so equal in horsepower, it was a chore to pass anyone. I know when a whole gaggle of us would come out of the turns and head down the stretch side by side, it was wild. It made my heart beat pretty hard."

On his second pit stop Rutherford's right tires were changed. "The car came to life after that," he said. "I was surprised at some of the people I could pass."

Empty seats (l.) are filled (below) as the crowd jams a grandstand facing the pits and starting line. Seats cost $10 to $50. Other fans paid $5 to sit on the infield (opposite page, far r.). Many picnic, buy souvenirs, or watch prerace parades and see little or none of the race. "The '500,'" a reporter wrote in 1934, "really is a picnic on a national scale.... People sleep through it and start home without knowing which cars finished one, two, three.... Yet all these people had got what they came for—a thrill or two at some stage of the race and the feeling they were part of a great national event." And he added: "It is the feature event of the wheat and corn and motor-car belt's first summer Holiday."

Clinging behind Rutherford, Foyt's Coyote bucked and pitched through the turns. Foyt radioed to his crew, "I'm really loose. I'm going into the turns hooking it to the right [because the car was pushing left]. My heart won't stand this much longer."

There had been only one crash. But yellow lights flicked on frequently as debris was removed and cars towed off. With the green on again, Rutherford, Foyt, and Johncock were running in that order as they whirled into the 101st lap, the race now official. Moments later rain spattered the track. Red lights—new this year—winked on, signaling the drivers to pit their cars.

Foyt wheeled in and ordered the Coyote's nose removed. He peered in at the suspension and saw a broken swaybar. "No wonder the damned thing wouldn't handle," he said, seeing how close he'd come to splintering against a wall.

While his crew fixed the swaybar, Foyt argued that Rutherford had gained on him during the yellow. "I had that big lead of 23 seconds [by Foyt's count] and Johnny cut it to four under the yellow," he said, "and now I end up . . . behind him." An electropacer system, installed in 1972, was supposed to stop any sneaking up during the yellow, but Foyt claimed the officials weren't cracking down on poachers. Foyt had, however, made five pit stops, Rutherford only four.

The rain ceased, but there was a delay of more than two hours while the track dried. Then, as the cars prepared to file back onto the track, rain again pelted down, and steward Tom Binford ended the race. The winner of this 255-mile "500" was Johnny Rutherford, 15.4 seconds ahead of an anguished Foyt.

This was the second straight "500" stopped by rain and the third in four years that hadn't gone all the way. Rutherford had been second a year earlier when rain blocked his pursuit of Bobby

Unser. As Foyt stomped off to his garage, slamming the door behind him, Rutherford—a fellow Texan—said, "I know how A. J. feels. A year ago we lost because of the rain. This year we won." And then he summed up what all the winners from Ray Harroun to himself had found about this ribbon of track that runs nowhere except into itself. "You hang around this place long enough," said Johnny Rutherford, "you learn a few things."

Bobby Unser: What makes a "500" winner?

The winner in 1968 and 1975, Bobby Unser talked of what makes a "500" winner. *Most drivers never learn how to win here. Each year you can pick maybe a half-dozen drivers, plus one dark horse, and be pretty sure one of them is going to be the winner. Most drivers just drive the car; they go fast, but they never know how to win. They get the lead, they freeze and someone else goes by them. I want to win a third '500,' not because I'd be one of the few to win three times. I want to win three because this is the biggest race in the world. Hell, this is the biggest sporting event in the world.*

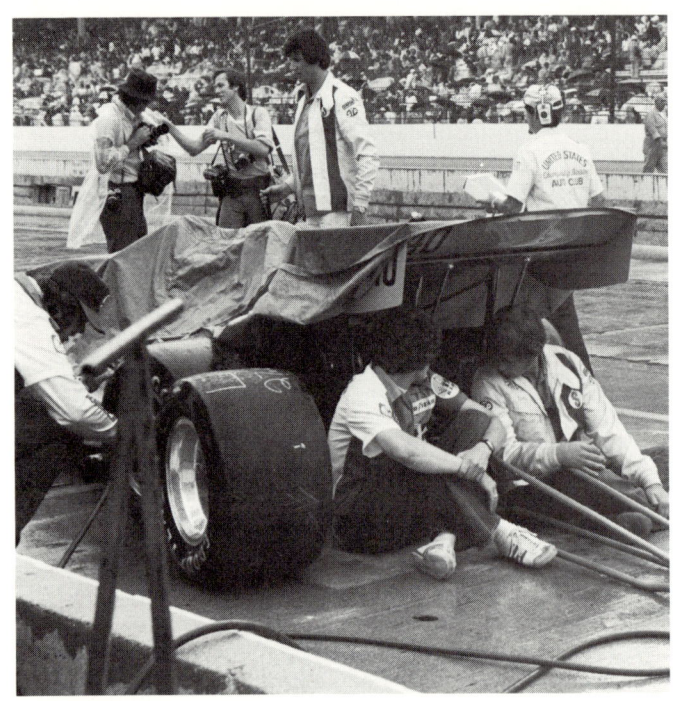

1976's TOP TEN

Race open to supercharged four-cycle overhead camshaft engines with a piston displacement of 161.703 cubic inches or less; nonsupercharged four-cycle overhead camshaft engines with a piston displacement of 274.590 cubic inches or less; stock production block design, single nonoverhead camshaft, removable head, supercharged engines with a piston displacement of 209.3 cubic inches or less; stock production block design, single nonoverhead camshaft, removable head, nonsupercharged engines with a piston displacement of 355.136 cubic inches or less; and special rocker arm, single nonoverhead camshaft, removable head, nonsupercharged engines with a piston displacement of 320.355 cubic inches or less.

NO.	DRIVER	CAR	ENGINE*	CYL.	BORE	STROKE	PISTON DISPL.	TIME†	MPH	WINNINGS‡
2	Johnny Rutherford	Hy-Gain McLaren/Goodyear	Offenhauser	4	4.281	2.750	159	1:42:52.48 (102)	148.725	$256,121
14	A. J. Foyt	Gilmore Racing Team	Foyt	8	3.760	1.800	161	1:43:07.84 (102)	148.354	103,296
20	Gordon Johncock	Sinmast-Goodyear Wildcat	Drake-Goosen-Sparks	4	4.281	2.750	159	1:44:37.43 (102)	146.238	67,675
40	Wally Dallenbach	Sinmast-Goodyear Wildcat	Drake-Goosen-Sparks	4	4.281	2.750	159	1:42:57.13 (101)	147.156	38,049
48	Duane Carter, Jr.	Jorgensen Eagle	Offenhauser	4	4.370	2.650	159	1:42:58.06 (101)	147.134	33,777
68	Tom Sneva	Norton Spirit	Offenhauser	4	4.281	2.750	159	1:43:10.84 (101)	146.830	30,960
21	Al Unser	American Racing Wheels Special	Cosworth	8	3.375	2.250	161	1:44:04.08 (101)	145.578	27,441
6	Mario Andretti	CAM2 Motor Oil Special	Offenhauser	4	4.281	2.750	159	1:44:44.04 (101)	144.652	28,331
77	Salt Walther	Dayton-Walther Special	Drake-Goosen-Sparks	4	4.281	2.750	159	1:43:48.73 (101)	144.492	23,728
3	Bobby Unser	Cobre Tire	Offenhauser	4	4.281	2.750	159	1:43:59.80 (100)	144.235	23,992

* All cars rear-engine and turbocharged.   † Race stopped at 255 miles due to rain; figures in parentheses show number of laps run.   ‡ Total prizes for winning entries. Total awards in race, $1,037,775: Speedway prizes, $850,000; accessory prizes, $147,275; lap prizes, $40,500.

Above: Johnny Martin (No. 98) in his Dragon-Offy is passed by Rutherford (No. 2). Opposite page and left: The rain drives a car and crew under shelter, Betty and Johnny Rutherford under an umbrella. Even Rutherford's team manager conceded that Foyt, his car healthy again, would probably have caught Johnny if rain hadn't ended the race. Below: The two-time winner in his McLaren-Offy. He was the ninth driver to win from the pole and the tenth to win the race twice.

Since 1911 these Speedway bricks have marked the beginning and end of each "500."

INDEX

Agabashian, Fred, 104a, 144, 162, 164, 172, 177, 201: quoted, 162
Agajanian, J. C., 161, 166, 169, 216, 217
Aitken, Johnny, 12, 14, 23, 35, 37
Allen, Leslie, 87
Alley, Tom, 32, 41, 52
Allison, Donnie, 246, 247, 251
Allison, Jim, 8
Ames, Ed, 228
Amick, George, 194, 195
Anderson, Eddie (Rochester), 157
Anderson, Gil, 21, 32
Andres, Emil, 120, 130, 140, 152: quoted, 130, 140
Andretti, Mario, 104b, 104g, 225, 226, 227, 228, 233, 241, 242, 243, 247, 249, 254, 280
Andrews, Keith, 181, 187
Ansterberg, Ernie, 61
Ardinger, Herb, 105, 122, 144
Arnold, Billy, 78, 82, 84, 86, 87, 89, 91, 92, 97, 105

Ball, Bobby, 163
Ballinger, Clay, 95: quoted, 95
Banks, Henry, 139, 163
Barringer, George, 115, 127
Batten, Norman, 65, 71, 73, 78
Baugh, Sammy, 145
Belcher, Fred, 17
Benny, Jack, 157
Bergere, Cliff, 75, 78, 82, 90, 96, 98, 105, 118, 127, 133, 134, 135, 142, 146, 164, 231, 268: quoted, 78, 134
Bettenhausen, Gary, 216h, 250, 251, 253, 255, 261, 265, 270: quoted, 255
Bettenhausen, Tony, 141, 163, 172, 182, 184, 194, 195, 199, 206, 250
Bignotti, George, 247, 258, 268, 276
Billman, Mark, 98
Binford, Tom, 216c, 265, 279
Blanchard, Harold F., 100
Bloemker, Al, 128, 155, 166
Boillot, Georges, 27, 29
Bordino, Pietro, 67
Bourke-White, Margaret, 106
Boyd, Johnny, 179, 190, 195, 199, 212, 222
Boyer, Joe, 58, 60, 61, 65, 76, 134: quoted, 61
Boyle, Mike, 124

Brabham, Jack, 104b, 204, 206, 207, 208: quoted, 208
Branson, Don, 202, 217, 227
Brawner, Clint, 241
Brisko, Frank, 105, 131
Brown, Walt, 144, 161
Bruce-Brown, David, 12, 14, 17
Bryan, Jimmy, 167, 169, 175, 177, 179, 181, 187, 190, 194, 195
Burman, Bob, 8, 32

Cantlon, William (Shorty), 84, 86, 87, 108, 142
Cantrell, Bill, 153
Carey, Bob, 96
Carlson, Billy, 29, 32
Carter, Duane, Jr. (Pancho), 265, 275, 278, 280
Carter, Duane, Sr., 146, 163, 169, 199
Caruthers, Jimmy, 254, 265
Chandler, William, 37
Chapman, Colin, 214, 215, 225, 226, 228, 230, 234, 236, 241
Chassagne, Jean, 45
Cheesbourg, Bill, 195
Chevrolet, Arthur, 35, 38, 42
Chevrolet, Gaston, 41, 42, 44, 45, 46, 76
Chevrolet, Louis, 35, 38, 41, 42, 44, 46, 48, 53
Chiron, Louis, 82
Chitwood, Joie, 140, 152, 158
Christiaens, Josef, 29, 37
Christie, Bob, 202, 216
Clark, George, 25
Clark, Jim, 104b, 214, 215, 216, 217, 218, 225, 226, 227, 228, 230, 231, 234, 236: quoted, 226
Cobe, Harry, 17
Cole, Hal, 149
Comer, Fred, 61, 71, 78
Connor, George, 115, 118, 152, 158, 169
Cooper, Earl, 32, 58, 61, 63, 68
Cooper, John, 204
Cortner, Bob, 197
Corum, L. L., 56, 58, 60, 61, 87, 101, 134
Crockett, Larry, 177
Cross, Art, 169, 172, 175
Cummings, Bill (Wild Bill), 87, 91, 98, 103, 104, 105, 108, 118

Dahl, Arlene, 169
D'Alene, Wilbur, 37
Dallenbach, Wally, 216e, 216h, 243, 256, 262, 263, 268, 275, 278, 280
Davies, Jimmy, 162, 172, 182
Davis, Don, 204, 212
Davis, Floyd, 133, 134, 135, 144
Dawson, Joe (Smiling Joe), 17, 18, 20, 21, 24, 27, 37, 230: quoted, 20
Daywalt, Jimmy, 172, 182
de Cystria, Prince, 56
DelRoy, Frank, 86, 108: quoted, 86, 108
DePalma, Ralph, 11, 12, 14, 16, 17, 18, 20, 31, 32, 33, 35, 38, 40, 41, 42, 44, 45, 46, 48, 50, 52, 53, 54, 67, 104, 175: quoted, 20
DePaolo, Peter, 32, 42, 44, 50, 61, 63, 65, 67, 68, 71, 72, 76, 81, 83, 86, 92: quoted, 32, 44, 65
DeVore, Billy, 118, 122, 127, 140
Devore, Earl, 75
Dickson, Larry, 243
DiMaggio, Joe, 145
Dinsmore, Duke, 144
Disbrow, Louis, 25
Donohue, Mark, 104e, 243, 245, 246, 247, 249, 250, 253, 254, 255, 256, 264
Drake, Dale, 155
Duesenberg, August, 27, 35, 38, 40, 42, 53, 54, 58, 61, 65, 68, 72, 75, 81, 84, 95, 104
Duesenberg, Fred, 27, 35, 38, 40, 42, 50, 53, 54, 58, 60, 61, 63, 65, 68, 70, 72, 75, 81, 84, 95, 104
Duff, John, 71
Duman, Ronnie, 219, 239
Duncan, Len, 176
Dunham, Jimmy, 109
Durant, Cliff, 46, 50, 54, 56, 96
Durant, Louis, 140
Duray, Arthur, 27, 29
Duray, Leon, 67, 76, 80, 81, 106, 116

Earhart, Amelia, 106
Edenburn, W. D. (Eddie), 89, 100
Elisian, Ed, 192, 194: quoted, 194
Elliott, Frank, 56, 71, 75
Endicott, Bill, 20
Evans, Dave, 75, 87, 91, 101

283

Index

Faulkner, Walt, 155, 158, 161, 175, 182
Fengler, Harlan, 216
Fetterman, I. P., 52
Firestone, Harvey, Jr., 94
Firestone, Harvey, Sr., 94
Firestone, Raymond, 194
Fisher, Carl, 6, 8, 11, 12, 18, 21, 31, 35, 37, 38, 40, 42, 56, 58, 76
Flaherty, Pat, 158, 182, 185, 186, 187: quoted, 187
Fohr, Myron, 152
Follmer, George, 251
Fontaine, Louis, 33, 46
Forberg, Carl, 163
Ford, Benson, 94, 214
Ford, Edsel, 92, 94
Ford, Henry, 58, 92, 94, 95, 106, 109
Ford, Henry, II, 94
Ford, Percy, 49
Foster, Billy, 228
Fox, Frank, 15
Fox, Malcolm, 98, 100: quoted, 100
Foyt, A. J. (Supertex), 9, 78, 104h, 192, 194, 199, 206, 207, 208, 211, 213, 216c, 216h, 217, 218, 221, 222, 223, 225, 226, 227, 228, 233, 234, 235, 241, 243, 244, 246, 247, 251, 256, 263, 264, 266, 268, 271, 275, 276, 278, 279, 280, 281: quoted, 223, 230, 235
Frame, Fred, 78, 82, 89, 90, 92, 96, 97, 100
Free, Roland, 142
Freeland, Don, 177, 187, 195

Gable, Clark, 157
Gardner, Chet, 101, 108, 122
Gardner, W. H., 82
Garroway, Dave, 194
Gleason, Jimmy, 76, 78, 82, 90
Goldsmith, Paul, 199, 202
Goux, Jules, 23, 24, 25, 27, 29, 41, 70: quoted, 24
Granatelli, Andy, 104e, 104g, 214, 225, 228, 230, 233, 234, 235, 236, 238, 241, 242, 249, 256, 258, 260: quoted, 242
Grant, Harry, 29, 231, 247, 253, 255, 256, 265
Green, Cecil, 158
Greer, Jane, 172
Griffith, Cliff, 169, 187
Grim, Bobby, 222, 239
Gulotta, Tony, 75, 76, 78, 89, 101, 118
Gurney, Dan, 211, 214, 215, 216, 217, 225, 228, 233, 236, 239, 243, 246, 247, 268, 271: quoted, 230
Guthrie, Janet, 6, 227, 276
Guyot, Albert, 25, 27, 29, 41, 49

Haibe, Ora, 37, 49, 52
Hall, Ira, 96
Hall, Norm, 207
Hanks, Sam (Steady Sam), 169, 172, 186, 187, 188, 190, 191, 194, 202: quoted, 191
Hannagan, Steve, 81, 100
Hansen, Mel, 131
Harkey, Bob, 222, 265, 275
Harris, Lawson, 100, 114
Harroun, Ray (the Bedouin), 11, 12, 14, 16, 17, 20, 35, 37, 65, 70, 118, 166, 231, 251, 280: quoted, 166
Hartley, Gene, 190
Hartz, Harry, 50, 52, 53, 54, 56, 61, 67, 68, 70, 71, 72, 84, 86, 89, 91, 92, 96, 123
Haupt, Willie, 25
Hearne, Eddie, 41, 45, 52, 56, 75
Hellings, Mac, 149
Henderson, Pete, 34, 37, 45
Henry, Ernest, 23
Hepburn, Ralph (Hep), 71, 80, 90, 108, 116, 118, 126, 135, 136, 139, 146, 151
Herman, Al, 182
Hickey, Denny, 41
Hill, Bennett, 49, 61, 63, 65, 164
Hill, Graham, 104g, 226, 228, 230, 231, 236
Hill, Jim, 74
Hinnershitz, Tommy, 135, 149
Hiss, Mike, 254, 268, 270
Hobbs, David, 250, 256, 265
Hodge, Loren, 29: quoted, 29
Holland, Bill, 142, 144, 146, 148, 149, 151, 152, 153, 155, 157, 158, 161: quoted, 144
Hopkins, Lindsey, 179, 197, 204, 216
Horan, Joe, 20
Horn, Ted, 108, 112, 115, 118, 122, 127, 128, 131, 135, 139, 140, 144, 146, 149, 164
Houck, Jerry, 96
Householder, Ronney, 118
Houser, Norman, 152
Huff, Joe, 96
Hughes, Hughie, 20
Hulman, Anton (Tony), 8, 139, 145, 153, 157, 161, 179, 182, 183, 185, 192, 194, 202, 227, 228, 233, 244, 256, 278: quoted, 153
Hulme, Denis, 234, 239, 249
Hulse, Chuck, 217, 234
Hurtubise, Jim, 104a, 104b, 201, 203, 214

Jackson, Jimmy, 140, 144, 149, 152
Jeffkins, Rupert, 18
Jenkins, Johnny, 20
Johncock, Gordon (Wee Gordie), 104g, 216a, 216e, 227, 231, 249, 258, 260, 261, 265, 268, 276, 278, 279, 280
Johns, Bobby, 227, 243
Johnson, Art, 37
Johnson, Eddie, 195, 199, 202, 227, 231
Johnson, Jigger, 91
Johnson, Luther, 101
Jones, Milton, 90
Jones, Parnelli, 104g, 211, 212, 214, 216, 217, 218, 221, 223, 225, 226, 233, 234, 246, 247, 251, 268: quoted, 216
Jones, Robert F., 258

Keck, Howard, 164, 175, 179
Keech, Ray, 78, 81, 82, 83
Keene, Charles, 29
Keller, Al, 190, 207
Kenyon, Mel, 231, 239, 243, 249, 256, 261
Kimberly, Jim, 204
Klein, Seth, 68, 151, 155, 170
Knepper, Arnie, 228
Kreis, Peter, 67, 68, 103
Krisiloff, Steve, 249, 261
Kunzman, Lee, 261
Kurtis, Frank, 153, 155, 157, 161, 164, 185, 197, 204, 211

Landis, Carole, 144
Larson, Jud, 195
LeBegue, Rene, 131
Leonard, Joe, 231, 234, 236, 238, 239, 243, 249, 254, 258
Lewis, Dave, 63, 65, 67, 68
Lindbergh, Charles, 73
Linden, Andy, 161, 163, 182, 190
Litz, Deacon, 81, 84, 91, 98, 105, 108
Lockhart, Frank, 53, 68, 70, 71, 72, 75, 76, 81
Loquasto, Al, 274

McCluskey, Roger, 229, 241, 251, 261, 275
McCoy, Ernie, 172
MacDonald, Dave, 218, 219, 225
McDonogh, Bob, 61, 72, 75
McElreath, Jim, 212, 217, 231, 234, 241, 247, 265
McGrath, Jack, 161, 163, 172, 175, 177, 179
MacKenzie, George (Doc), 108, 109, 115
McLaren, Bruce, 249
McQuinn, Harry, 122, 123, 135, 148: quoted, 123, 148
Magill, Mike, 197
Malloy, Jim, 251, 253, 256
Mansfield, Jayne, 208
Mantz, Johnny, 152
Marchese, Carl, 82
Marmon, Howard, 12, 14
Marquette, Ray, 264
Marshall, Cy, 84, 144
Marshman, Bobby, 207, 212, 218
Martin, John, 261, 281

284

Index

Matlock, Spider, 92
Mauro, John, 149
Mays, Rex, 106, 111, 128, 130, 131, 133, 135, 144, 151
Mecom, John, Jr., 228
Merz, Charlie, 17, 20, 23, 24, 25
Meyer, June (Mrs. Louis), 110
Meyer, Louis, 76, 78, 79, 81, 82, 83, 84, 87, 95, 97, 98, 100, 101, 103, 104, 110, 111, 112, 114, 115, 118, 124, 126, 128, 146, 148, 155, 235, 264, 281: quoted, 83, 112, 118
Meyer, Zeke, 96, 101, 115
Miller, Al (1934, 1936 races), 105, 114
Miller, Al (1963, 1965 races), 217, 227
Miller, Chet, 78, 86, 90, 108, 115, 122, 124, 135, 146, 164, 167, 170
Miller, Eddie, 49
Miller, Harry, 40, 41, 46, 50, 53, 54, 58, 61, 63, 65, 68, 70, 72, 75, 81, 84, 92, 95, 106, 109, 126, 136, 204
Milton, Tommy, 40, 44, 45, 46, 48, 49, 50, 53, 54, 56, 57, 58, 63, 67, 72, 75, 96, 111, 153, 157: quoted, 56
Moore, Lou, 78, 92, 97, 101, 105, 120, 123, 133, 134, 142, 144, 151, 155
Mosley, Mike, 239, 248, 250, 252, 261
Mourre, Antoine, 61
Mulford, Ralph, 12, 16, 17, 20, 25, 37, 45, 49
Murphy, Jimmy, 40, 45, 50, 52, 53, 54, 56, 57, 58, 61, 63, 76, 84, 86, 151
Muther, Rick, 247, 250
Myers, T. E. (Pop), 35, 76, 113, 116, 139

Nalon, Duke, 123, 146, 148, 149, 151, 161, 163
Nazaruk, Mike, 161, 163, 177
Newby, Arthur, 8
Niday, Cal, 177

O'Brien, Erin, 197, 198
O'Connor, Pat, 176, 182, 186, 187, 190, 192, 194
O'Donnell, Eddie, 32
Offenhauser, Fred, 46, 50, 95, 104, 106, 155
Oldfield, Barney, 11, 27, 28, 29, 35, 37, 46, 48, 51, 89
Olson, Ernie, 53: quoted, 53
Ottum, Bob, 225

Parsons, Johnnie, 152, 155, 157, 158, 159, 161, 169, 187: quoted, 157, 182

Patschke, Cy, 14
Penske, Roger, 254, 270
Petillo, Kelly, 103, 106, 108, 109, 112, 128
Phillips, Jud, 244
Pilette, Theodore, 25
Pirrung, Gil, 109
Pixley, Ray, 115
Pollard, Art, 234, 247, 256
Portor, Odis, 69
Posey, Sam, 254
Puterbaugh, Bill, 275

Rathmann, Dick, 187, 192, 194, 217, 222
Rathmann, Jim, 169, 172, 181, 188, 190, 191, 195, 197, 199, 201, 202, 203, 206, 212: quoted, 203
Rathmann, Kay (Mrs. Jim), 202
Reece, Jimmy, 169, 187, 192, 195
Resta, Dario, 31, 32, 35, 36, 37, 54, 76, 226
Revson, Peter, 243, 249, 250, 251, 253
Rickenbacker, Eddie, 27, 29, 32, 34, 35, 48, 76, 81, 83, 84, 89, 92, 94, 98, 100, 101, 103, 113, 117, 120, 124, 139
Ricker, Chester S., 69, 120
Rindt, Jochen, 243
Roberts, Floyd, 108, 120, 122, 123, 124, 126, 127, 140, 142, 148, 177
Roberts, Glenn (Fireball), 195
Robson, George, 140, 141
Rose, Mauri, 101, 103, 105, 115, 127, 128, 130, 131, 133, 134, 135, 139, 140, 142, 144, 145, 146, 148, 149, 151, 153, 155, 157, 158, 162, 175, 177, 179, 235, 250, 281
Ruby, Lloyd, 202, 207, 212, 222, 228, 236, 239, 241, 243, 244, 254, 264, 265
Rupp, Mickey, 227
Russo, Joe, 105
Russo, Paul, 135, 152, 158, 177, 185, 186, 187, 188, 190, 199, 206
Rutherford, Betty (Mrs. Johnny), 267, 281
Rutherford, Johnny (Gentleman Johnny), 216c, 216e, 216f, 244, 256, 261, 263, 264, 265, 266, 267, 268, 270, 271, 274, 275, 276, 278, 279, 280, 281: quoted, 266
Ruttman, Troy, 155, 164, 166, 169, 170, 177

Sachs, Eddie, 104b, 192, 194, 198, 204, 206, 207, 212, 216, 218, 219, 221, 225: quoted, 198
Sailer, Max, 56
Salih, George, 188, 191, 192, 197, 203
Sarles, Roscoe, 46, 49, 164
Savage, David (Swede), 256, 258, 260

Scarborough, Carl, 170
Schneider, Louis, 87, 89, 90, 91, 95
Scott, Bob, 167
Sessions, Sam, 239, 254
Shafer, Phil, 56, 63, 67, 71, 87
Shattuc, W. E., 67
Shaw, Boots (Mrs. Wilbur), 130
Shaw, Wilbur, 72, 75, 76, 90, 92, 95, 101, 106, 108, 111, 112, 115, 116, 118, 120, 122, 124, 126, 127, 128, 130, 131, 132, 133, 134, 139, 142, 146, 148, 153, 157, 175, 177, 179, 203, 204, 235, 246, 250, 281: quoted, 127
Sheffler, Bill, 140
Shore, Dinah, 181, 183
Simon, Dick, 265, 268, 277
Sneva, Tom, 216e, 268, 270, 274, 276, 278, 280
Snider, George, 104b, 275
Snowberger, Russ, 87, 89, 90, 96, 101, 105
Snyder, Jimmy, 116, 120, 124, 127
Souders, George, 72, 74, 75, 78, 230: quoted, 75
Spangler, Les, 98, 100, 108
Sparks, Art, 120, 164
Spence, Bill, 81
Spence, Mike, 236
Stanwyck, Barbara, 157
Stapp, Egbert (Babe), 72, 75, 78, 109, 127, 157
Stevens, Myron, 90
Stevenson, Chuck, 207
Stewart, Jackie, 228, 230, 231
Stubblefield, H. W., 90, 101
Stutz, Harry C., 57
Sullivan, Lambert G., 42
Sutton, Len, 212, 213
Swanson, Bob, 124, 127, 131
Sweikert, Bob, 155, 157, 181, 182, 183, 187

Teague, Marshall, 190
Templeman, Shorty, 207
Tetzlaff, Teddy, 18, 20
Thomas, Joe, 45, 52
Thomas, Rene, 27, 29, 32, 38, 40, 45
Thompson, Mickey, 211, 215
Thomson, Johnny, 182, 187, 197, 198, 199, 201, 202
Thorne, Joel, 120, 122, 127, 128, 131
Thurman, Arthur, 38
Thurman, Mrs. Arthur, 39
Tierney, Gene, 126
Tingelstad, Bud, 202, 222, 227, 251
Tolan, Johnny, 194
Tomei, Louis, 118
Towers, Edward, 16, 37: quoted, 16, 37
Triplett, Ernie, 90, 98
Turner, Jack, 204, 206
Turner, W. H. (Wild Bill), 16, 17, 37

285

Index

Unser, Al, 104g, 227, 234, 236, 242, 244, 245, 246, 247, 249, 250, 251, 254, 255, 256, 258, 263, 268, 271, 280: quoted, 247, 250
Unser, Bobby, 104g, 104h, 214, 216a, 231, 234, 236, 238, 239, 241, 242, 243, 244, 248, 250, 253, 256, 263, 264, 265, 268, 271, 274, 275, 279, 280: quoted, 238, 274, 280
Unser, Jerry, Jr., 192, 197
Unser, Jerry, Sr. (Pop), 104g
Unser, Mary (Mom), 104g
Unversaw, Earl, 91, 104, 105: quoted, 91, 104

Vail, Ira, 41, 48, 49, 52, 61, 70: quoted, 48, 70
Vandewater, W. H., 170
Van Raalte, Noel, 32
Veith, Bob, 104a, 187, 190, 192, 202, 230
Vidan, Pat, 170, 263, 270, 271
Villoresi, Luigi (Gigi), 140
Vollstedt, Rolla, 277
Vukovich, Bill (the Mad Russian), 155, 157, 161, 164, 166, 170, 172, 175, 176, 177, 179, 181, 182, 183, 185, 190, 192, 211, 250, 258: quoted, 177
Vukovich, Billy, 172, 216h, 239, 251, 258, 261, 265, 275: quoted, 258
Vukovich, Esther (Mrs. Bill, Sr.), 172, 179, 181: quoted, 172

Wagner, Fred, 104
Wallard, Lee, 149, 158, 161, 162, 163, 166
Walther, David (Salt), 256, 280
Ward, Rodger, 162, 179, 187, 197, 198, 199, 201, 203, 207, 211, 212, 213, 215, 217, 218, 222, 223: quoted, 213
Watson, A. J., 185, 186, 192, 194, 197, 198, 201, 204, 208, 211, 213, 218
Wearne, Frank, 122, 127, 131, 135, 140
Weatherly, Clay, 106
Weiler, Wayne, 203
Welch, Lew, 139, 148, 151, 155, 161, 162
Wente, Bob, 222
Weyant, Chuck, 197
Wheeler, Frank, 8
White, Johnny, 222
Wilcox, Howdy, 20, 25, 31, 32, 37, 38, 40, 41, 54, 76: quoted, 40
Wilcox, Howdy, II, 92, 96, 97, 101
Wilke, Bob, 213
Williams, Carl, 234, 247
Williams, S. J., 69
Winn, Billy, 96
Winnai, Fred, 82, 96
Wishart, Spencer, 12, 14, 17, 24, 25
Wonderlich, Jerry, 52
Wood, Gar, 100
Wood, Glen, 225
Wood, Leonard, 225
Woodbury, Cliff, 71, 80

Yarborough, Cale, 253, 254
Young, Loretta, 162

Zengel, Len, 20
Zimmerman, Denny, 251
Zink, John, 185, 186, 211